U.S. Foreign Policy:
Perspectives and
Proposals for the 1970s

U.S. Foreign Policy:
Perspectives and
Proposals for the 1970s

edited by
Paul Seabury and Aaron Wildavsky
University of California, Berkeley

McGraw-Hill Book Company
New York, St. Louis, San Francisco, London, Sydney, Toronto, Mexico, Panama

E
840
.U47

U.S. Foreign Policy:
Perspectives and Proposals for the 1970s

Library of Congress Catalog Card Number 70-82137

1234567890vʙvʙ7654321069

Preface

This book of essays by nine Berkeley political-science faculty members, plus Max Singer of the Hudson Institute, brings together under one cover several perspectives for an agenda on America's foreign policies in the 1970s.

It reflects an awareness of the striking changes in our nation's mood and its current relationship to the world. Our combining to offer these essays signifies a belief that colleagues can and should display a diversity of judgment on crucial questions of public policy.

The essays touch upon basic long-range policy areas within which American policy now must act: The credibility and risks entailed in our current commitments; our stance toward new regimes and states; our future posture in Asia and Europe; our strategic relationship with allies and with the Soviet Union and China; our force commitments in Asia, especially Southeast Asia; our position on the Middle East crisis; and the character of our response to political change in the "third world."

In the past several years, as the Vietnam-inspired great debate has gone on, two extremely abstract public positions have developed on the question of America's interests and responsibilities. One, labeled "neo-isolationism" by some, has made Vietnam an occasion to argue for drastic curtailment of America's commitments and involvements everywhere. Another, called "neo-imperialism" by others, has argued for steadfast commitment to a proclaimed national role for the United States as principal guardian of international peace and security. Each side has chanted its slogans at the other, and each has served the other as its easy strawman.

The editors feel that this collection of essays gives an indication of the range and complexity of problems confronting the United States, which such extreme and simplistic prescriptions overlook. Obvious points of disagreement divide the contributors—especially with respect to America's future role and strategies in Asia—but the common mood of these papers suggests a more sober and less melodramatic approach to foreign policy than has been the case in the recent past. If a credibility gap existed during the Johnson administration, it reflected not only a sharp contrast between repeated official optimistic forecasts and grim, persistent reality, but also a gulf between inflated official rhetoric and less melodramatic purposes—however correctly such purposes were chosen. Though the new administration has inherited the problems and dilemmas of the previous one, it can selectively dispose of the bequeathed rhetoric. All of these essays accept a view which, ten years ago, seemed either absurd, premature, or unrealistic: The world within which policy operates is not a simple either/or world of global confrontation between two and only two systems. The identification of conflict situations is no less, and no more, important than the identification of situations of cooperation—tacit or explicit—between adversaries as well as among friends and allies.

Shrewd readers quickly will discover that our book is not a complete, symmetrical panorama of foreign-policy agenda items. For example, the question of Soviet-American relations is nowhere treated as a unit. Rather the theme is woven into all the essays. We do recognize that the subject is of central importance to all the problems with which we deal. So also, certain critical questions of America's role in overseas economic development are not directly taken up.

In several senses this book is an experiment. It combines observation and advocacy, analysis and prescription. It also contains much disagreement, which it does not seek to reconcile. The reader himself should judge among our varied perspectives. These perspectives reflect the diversity and, we would like to think, the vigor of a department which includes and encourages diversity.

Paul Seabury
Aaron Wildavsky

Contents

1

The Revolt
Against Obligation

Paul Seabury

A new American presidency is always the occasion for national stocktaking. It is a time for Americans to pause and ask themselves: Where were we last time? Where are we now? Where should we go?

The situation now faced by America's foreign-policy makers differs fundamentally from that faced by the Kennedy administration in 1961. The problems encountered in the transition from Presidents Truman to Eisenhower today seem light years away.

What now exists is a condition of great friction between United States domestic and foreign priorities; moreover there exists a new psychological climate within which the problems of world politics are perceived.

For the past four years, America's mood has been basically introverted. Our obsessions have come to center on the inner cities and inner moral crises, such that even the Vietnam war sometimes seems chiefly to be an American family quarrel. But much more is involved in this turn toward introspection than the phenomena on which it focuses. A savage crisis of civic style is underway—sharpest in the cities and universities but clearly present in many other configurations of American cultural life. It is a crisis chiefly characterized by the old conflict between civic obligation and individual conscience (a conscience which can embrace both selfishness and selflessness). This crisis of style bears directly upon the consensual basis of American foreign policy. The revolt against obligation is widespread, but is nowhere more conspicuous than in its severe questioning and frequent rejection of classic "cold war commitments" and the old judgmental assumptions of United States foreign policy.

NEW CLIMATE, NEW ATTITUDES

In January, 1961 it was still possible for an incoming President to remark plausibly in his inaugural address: "Let every nation know, whether it wishes us well or ill, that we shall pay any price, bear any burden, meet any hardship, support any friend, oppose any foe to assure the survival and success of liberty." Such remarks now seem out of order. For a variety of reasons, the phase of American history when this nation was the world's prime specialist in the architectonics of world order is now past. Military bipolarity still exists, and the power equilibrium between the Soviet Union and the United States remains the principal equation determining our survival. But the 1960s brought an end to *political* bipolarity. The world of new states with independent tendencies and revolutionary waves as it now exists may be no safer than it was eight years ago; but it is certainly politically multipolar. In these new circumstances, it will no longer be appropriate for the United States to formulate sermons or doctrines on how other nations should conduct their affairs. (One can recall, for example, the remarks of John Foster Dulles during the Budapest revolt of 1956: "Let me add a word about future relations with the peoples who compose the Union of Soviet Socialist Republics. They, too, can have hope.")

One reason for this shift in American attitudes is that effective parts of the American public have lost their zest for international institution-building. The halcyon Marshall Plan days of new, universal alliance-building are at an end. The McCarthyism of 1968 suggests further that many Americans, however wisely, now have little concern for what we might call "international system-maintenance," i.e., the employment of United States resources and influence to sustain the fragile order which we and others have been able to contrive.

Furthermore, the popular consensual basis for foreign policy now seems less viable than at any time since the late 1940s. It will be interesting to see whether and how the new administration succeeds in reestablishing a viable consensus.

SHIFT TO INTROVERSION?

There are some who argue (like Professor Samuel Huntington of Harvard) that the United States recently may have reentered a cyclic phase of introversion in its relationship to its world environment. Drawing upon some old assumptions, Huntington speculates that a time cycle—alternating periods of introversion and extroversion in roughly 25-year intervals—governs the manner in which America reacts to the rest of the world. The last extrovert phase (1941-1966) followed a previous era of introversion (1918-1941); now another era of introversion has set in. But this cyclic theory (or is it simply a series of coincidences?) is not altogether persuasive. It seems no more credible as a predictive tool than another strange historical "law" of American politics, which says that presidents who die in office are the ones unfortunate enough to get themselves elected in years divisible by the number 20, i.e., Harrison, Lincoln, Garfield, McKinley, Harding, Franklin D. Roosevelt, and Kennedy. Exceptions to this "law"—Adams and Monroe (1800, 1820)—give grounds for doubt. And certainly our new President has no rational excuse to disband the Secret Service or dispense with the White House physician—any more than the cyclic introversion-extroversion law would allow him to disband the State Department and the armed services.

The experience which now dominates our foreign policy thinking is Vietnam. Measured in the length of time that United States combat forces have been involved, this war already is longer than any previous one in American history except the American Revolution. We can almost call it epochal. It dominates our current perspectives about our dealings with the rest of the world. It is like the word "Calais," said to have been found engraved on Queen Mary's heart when she died, so great was her obsession in losing it. Also, like the depression of 1929 (which lasted even longer), Vietnam already has become a commanding phenomenon around which the judgmental furniture of our political minds is arranged. Whatever it can tell us about what not to do in the future (and probably its transferable lessons are not very many), it has—more than anything else in a very long time—prompted many Americans to rethink the broader issues of our role in world politics more carefully.

Perhaps the experience of the Vietnam war has most affected what might be called the "central assumptions" that have underlain almost three decades of American foreign policy. For it is safe to say that, from Roosevelt's time, the dominant leadership in America assumed that an identity of perspective existed between the goals of American foreign policy and the larger, more comprehensive objectives of the entire system of world politics. To paraphrase the Bible, one might say that whenever a nation fell, its fall did not go unnoticed by Uncle Sam. The proper perspective within which American strategic policies were to be judged was that of the entire globe. The task was either that of defending the free world against the spread of Soviet or Communist power or, more simply, that of fashioning a comprehensive and stable world system within which the United States might safely exist.

SHOULDERING RESPONSIBILITIES

It seems clear that this conception of America's international responsibilities emerged out of the experiential cauldron of the late 1930s and 1940s. The special (and rather astonishing) circumstances of those times were that the United States had somehow managed to be the only large civic society which escaped the twin horrors of internal political collapse and vast wartime destruction—and then, by virtue of this fortune, had become the fulcrum around which the new postwar political order would reform. To describe this extraordinary historical phenomenon in such abstract language does not, of course, do full justice to its importance. For the fact that the United States, not some other power, played this unique role had an absolutely decisive effect upon the general character of the postwar world. In those areas of the world where American influence was strong, the stamp of constitutional democracy was placed upon the newly emerging postwar societies. (We have only to remember, by contrast, the situation of 1940-1941, when it briefly seemed that the principal architects of a postwar world would be the totalitarian states: Germany, Russia, Italy, and Japan.)

It is also important to note that the political judgments of the new internationalists both during and shortly after World War II were decisively shaped by the events which had led to the war. The doctrine of

American "responsibility" within the international system replaced the doctrine of American isolation, which had rejected such responsibility. American isolationism between 1919 and 1939 had permitted events abroad to deteriorate progressively, so that only a huge and costly American eleventh-hour response had proved sufficient to restore civilization. What thus chiefly distinguished the new internationalism from the previous isolationism was the idea that any such process of deterioration of the international system should not be permitted to occur again. The new internationalism expressed a ubiquitous concern for new crisis situations and America's responsibilities toward them. Admittedly, in practise, America's global strategies at no time made claims to be able to do everything everywhere; there were at all times clear strategic priorities for United States action (the stress upon European priorities as against Asian, for instance). The vast majority of political upheavals which came in the wake of World War II proved to be ones in which American power and influence played marginal roles, or no role at all.

Even as recently as May, 1966 Secretary McNamara could note in a Montreal speech that in the 164 outbreaks of significant violence within nations since 1958, only 15 were military conflicts involving two or more states. In only seven of the 164 was America directly involved—Cuba, the Dominican Republic, and Vietnam being the most prominent. If the United States has been the world's policeman, as some critics of American policy allege, it has been cautiously shirking most of its beat.

Yet, by the mid-1960s, it certainly was clear that the United States had become the only real world power—i.e., a power with concerns spanning each ocean and encompassing both the mature industrial societies of Europe and the newly independent nations of Asia and Africa. The expression used by President Kennedy in his 1960 Inaugural speech reminds us of the intensity of this global concern: America was "the watchman on the wall of freedom."

With the benefit of hindsight, it now seems clear that the early postwar architects of American international security policy miscalculated. They assumed that the reemergence of a pluralistic state system, more or less along the lines of the traditional prewar system, would result in or make possible a progressive reduction in America's role of maintaining world order. Commencing with the Truman Doctrine and NATO, American commitments to collective security arrangements outside the UN ranged from self-liquidating temporary expedients to permanent institutional guarantees. Yet, what our policy-makers did not adequately foresee was that the temporary scaffolding of transitional security systems, furnished by American strength and promises, might in fact become the permanent architectural framework itself—organic, central components of the postwar system. The Acheson notion, in the late 1940s and early 1950s, was that outstanding differences between America and Russia could be negotiated in comprehensive settlements at such time as America and the West obtained a comfortable and decisive superiority of power. But this notion did not take into account the possibility that extensive power, manifested in a variety of institutional frameworks, might become a permanent and even necessary fixture in a world where no solution of outstanding issues (Central Europe, for instance) was forthcoming. Our commitments thus became imbedded in reality.

GOING IT ALONE

Among the various structural shifts in world politics since Acheson's time, one special change, which transpired gradually, is of interest. Even in the late 1940s, after all the terrible damage of the war, there were several friendly nations (Britain and France especially) still accustomed, along with America, to thinking and acting "globally." It had in fact been a central assumption of Franklin D. Roosevelt's international thinking that *at least* five nations would share the police functions of the postwar international order—a notion still incongruously imbedded in the UN Security Council. But the grounds for such thinking gradually disappeared; today only Russia and America have such perspectives and pretensions.

It is important to note, in this connection, that the American system of global alliances was and is structurally a unique one: regional systems were individually linked to Washington, and were not necessarily connected with one another. Whether American force might be actively used or passively employed as a deterrent, it would be in conjunction with indigenous regional forces; but only the American ingredient was common to all (NATO, SEATO, the Inter-American system, the Japanese-American alliance, etc.). The only occasion when United States force was applied on a large scale in concert with multiregional forces was during the Korean war; but that occasion came before the demise of the other global powers. By contrast, in the conduct of the Vietnam war, the United States received at most some sympathy from its allies in other areas; its sole effective support came from indigenous forces. (One might note, moreover, that despite the much-touted fact of Communist polycentrism, all significant Communist states and parties lend active support to Hanoi.)

It is fair to say that this unique circumstance of United States centrality in its various alliance systems now represents the crux of America's political security dilemma. As Dean Rusk has tirelessly repeated, the willingness of the United States to honor its commitments has become a central issue in the preservation of peace; a bank which chooses to dishonor some creditors' claims is not because of this more highly respected by others. Yet the intent to honor such claims (and still others which might not have been put on paper) does subject the American nation to the prospect of an unusually high incidence of special occasions when it will be called upon to sanction and contribute to the employment of force in a wide variety of geographical and political circumstances.

The logic of this system of interlocked commitments, then, appears to be that America, *through time*, would be called upon to engage in active peacekeeping in more circumstances than any other nation in the world. By contrast, the situation faced by the Soviet Union is instructive. For the Soviets (whose security problems have surely been considerable) have not actually engaged their own military forces in direct hostile engagements with other powers since World War II. Assuming that the Sino-Soviet alliance is now inoperative, Russia's only contractual obligations are to its Warsaw pact allies. Its participation in other conflicts thus far has been by proxy; it may make trouble, and has—but at times and places of its own choosing, thus without the credibility problems which America itself has faced.

RESPONSIBILITIES VERSUS OVEREXTENSION

The so-called "great debate" on foreign policy over the past two years has focused on two contradictory themes arising from this situation. One of them, best represented perhaps by the views of General Maxwell Taylor, George Liska, and a few others, has it that America's broad range of commitments is justified by the enormous sweep of American influence and interests. The other holds that in recognition of global multipolarity and current stresses emerging from America's domestic crisis, the range of existing United States influence and interest should be scaled down. A key point in the latter thesis has been that, in a multipolar world, "gains and losses" in most regional conflicts need not necessarily affect directly the strategic balance between America and the Soviet Union, since a Communist "camp" in the monolithic sense no longer exists.

However true this generalization might be, it is still possible that the spread of Communist-led or Communist-infiltrated revolutionary movements might easily tilt the political-cultural balance of the world in the direction of those closed societies abhorrent to classic liberal values; the success of such movements could also have important feedback effects upon the more moderate Socialist states, prompting them to greater militancy.

Whichever theme one finds more congenial—America's imperial responsibilities or American overextension—one still must return to the world of facts within which realistic policy has to operate. Beneath the firmament of large generalizations, there is the world of concrete problems. Highly generalized policy, or policy criticism, is either deceptive or useless if it does not relate directly to specific international problems.

One such problem, which I have mentioned earlier, is the special long-range effect on national morale occasioned by the recurrent and protracted use of American force in a wide variety of circumstances. As John Roche has recently suggested, Vietnam has cast considerable doubt on America's future capacity to engage in a series of limited and localized military enterprises: a circumstance which has open-ended implications. It could, for instance, encourage the view in some military quarters that quick, decisive measures should be taken when trouble occurs—*no more Vietnams!* Or it could encourage the view that no localized conflicts are really worth the risk of American resources and lives—*no more Vietnams!*

AMERICA'S INTERNAL CONTRADICTIONS

At some later date, historians may point out the paradox of American political culture as it existed in the 1960s—namely, the bewildering contradiction between an astonishing degree of internal liberalization and the coercive requirements entailed in America's fulfillment of its international commitments. A civic culture which, in its dominant media and opinion groups, sanctions dissent and individual freedom as cardinal virtues is not likely at the same time to place a high premium upon civic obligation. Yet the need for civic obligation, as far as foreign policy is concerned, lies at the heart of a system of international collective security; at home, it has in the past accounted for the steadiness of American domestic consensus about foreign policy commitments.

One aspect of this problem is evident, for example, in the controversy surrounding the military draft system. It may be that universal conscription best works in nations under extreme international duress (when everyone realizes how serious the situation is) or in nations like Switzerland, where the purposes for which force might be employed are clearly and precisely defined as the preservation of national, territorial integrity. It certainly does not work well in instances like Vietnam, where goals are deliberately limited so as to exclude the possible psychic satisfactions of "victory," where the perception of vital threats is not very widespread, and where chiefly the maintenance of a distant regional equilibrium is sought. It is hard to encourage a civic obligation among young men to risk their lives for the dear old balance of power.

In these and other obvious sets of problems, it seems clear that the new administration cannot commence its career with the customary flourishes, proclamations, and grand designs—signals to a waiting world of a new epoch of American-inspired collective activity. For some time it has been very clear that Europe's own movement toward greater self-sufficiency and political-economic integration cannot be orchestrated from Washington, D.C. Similarly, the vitality of other regional groupings (in Southeast Asia, for example) cannot be provided by American architects.

It would now seem that if there is a common set of concerns shared by most nations, great and small, it is an acute absorption with urgent domestic problems—including ones like the crisis of youth and the universities—which lie spread-eagled across national boundaries. Aside from the Middle East and Southeast Asia, it seems likely that the major source of political tension in the immediate future will be domestic turmoil, revolution, and change, *not* the kinds of overt aggression and sponsored expansion with which American stategic doctrines, shaped in the cold war, were designed to cope in the past.

The fact is that America now shares with its major friends and adversaries some common perplexities about the character and the satisfactions of its own culture. In America and elsewhere a new ethic of freedom is developing which is no longer "civic"; in some respects it is increasingly uninterested in, or even angry about, the requirements of "system maintenance" or reform. Structural designs (e.g., alliances, foreign aid programs) are frequently regarded as domination systems, not civic-order systems.

Clearly, this development is not simply an American phenomenon; it is common to all the advanced countries. And it is very recent in its appearance. In the Kennedy period, barely five years ago, it could still be said that American confidence in a pragmatic approach to problems was at a very high peak. Things which Americans do to solve their own problems could also apply in the solution of problems faced by others. Included among these things were the legendary American skills and know-how which could be employed in the processes of nation-building, economic development, and political integration in the new nations.

There are obvious limitations on the ability of this or any other administration to reconcile the necessities of America's international environment with its current cultural foibles and domestic discontents. In a very generalized way one might admonish President Nixon to regulate incipient international crises (in concert with others of course) so as to lessen the risk that American force would have to be employed. But this kind of advice is cheap; for a very long time a principal object of American policy has been to prevent "something unfortunate" from happening, although it is usually hard after the fact to prove that the reason something unfortunate did not happen was because one succeeded in making it not happen. As Henry Kissinger has recently remarked, "deterrence is tested negatively by things which did *not* happen." Still, with regard to Vietnam, it is hardly consoling to be given such advice when one is digging out of an instance where deterrence failed.

FRIENDS AND ENEMIES

Another set of concrete problems which the Nixon administration faces relates to America's relations with its chief allies and its dealings with the nations of the Communist world. The most important of the questions posed in these practical relationships have only marginal bearing upon the American domestic crisis and upon the Vietnam war. With respect to them all, it is clear that no solutions or expedients can be achieved by unilateral American decisions. The grave dangers of a renewed Middle Eastern war—far more perilous than anything we have faced in Southeast Asia— require parallel Soviet and American actions to restrain their respective friends and clients. The new problems posed by a Soviet naval-military presence in the Mediterranean and North Africa suggest the need for renewed synchronization of European and American military planning.

The Czechoslovakian crisis suggests also the need for both America and its Western allies to reconcile their hopes for "bridge-building," on the one hand, with some realism about its essential limitations, on the other. The dangers of a renewed arms race require careful, perhaps parallel, American and Soviet measures to cope with further nuclear proliferation. And the current paralysis of United States aid programs suggests, finally, the need for synchronized policies among the developed countries to avert the dangers of widespread famine and economic collapse in the third world.

A TIME OF DISENCHANTMENT

Yet, undoubtedly, things have changed. The physician is now in the business of healing himself—and not doing very well at it, at that. Both here in America and in the advanced nations of Western Europe, the dominant cultural preoccupation is less with technique, building, and work than with a curious harangue about and experimentation in life-styles. Both here and there, the mood oscillates between being ashamed of power and expecting too much of power at the same time. A utopian perfectionism which demands too much of power can make the responsible exercise of power very difficult. For policy makers, including foreign policy makers, might easily fall under the spell of such moods and resign themselves to quick gestures and symbolic acts—more useful for show purposes than for rationality and known or probable consequences.

The new administration, however, must regard these qualities of mood, disenchantment, and introspection as given conditions. Probably, in common with other major powers, it should realize that in such a period of turning inward, where questions of domestic order not international peace are paramount, its foreign policy priorities should set a higher premium on steadiness and control than on dramatic experimentation.

Yet, at the same time, since one does not derive policy guidelines from moods, it would seem essential for opinion-makers to guide American attitudes out of their parochial obsessions. The fundamental issues of foreign policy still pertain to the structural problems of world politics, just as they did twenty years ago; and these extremely complex problems cannot be resolved by any simplistic generalizations. The United States still remains (as it has for a very long time) the largest and most dynamic power—the giant, as George F. Kennan once said, whose every movement in a small room affects all the other inhabitants. The giant cannot imitate Alice in

Wonderland by eating an "Eat Me" pill which causes one to become smaller, thus less envied and disliked than giants always are.

AMERICA'S HISTORIC IMAGE

It is nonetheless worth asking, with respect to America's international image, whether there have not been some important psychological constraints arising from American attitudes in recent years that limit the ways in which our national power can be exercised in the world.

It is probably true that most Americans—frequently with too much vigor—have tended to identify our most important international ventures with overriding "universal" principles or goals. Perhaps, as some have argued, this penchant for moralism can be a vice: What does one make, for instance, of Dean Rusk's remark on a recent occasion to the effect that "other nations have interests, but the United States has responsibilities"?

Whatever one makes of such examples of American idealism, it is doubtful whether our "imperial" qualities go very deep—i.e., whether American capacities for sustained (and often lonely) action on behalf of "order maintenance" are very great. Our historic image of ourselves does not fit well when our international role is preponderant and singular. In our own internal development our greatest national achievements have been accomplished with very little (acknowledged) outside help, but our proudest accomplishments in world politics invariably have been those in which we acted in concert with many others. The positive nature of our influence has depended in considerable measure on obtaining a reputation as a member of a concert, even when this membership was clearly *primus inter pares*. Perhaps this verifies the old truth that our principal international enterprises must, as in the past, be grounded upon broad coalitions and support.

2

A Third-World
Averaging Strategy

Max Singer
and Aaron Wildavsky

WASHINGTON (AP)—U.S. policymakers privately voiced unhappiness Thursday over the coup in Peru, but they expect the new military leadership to be pro-West and anti-Communist. And eventual recognition of the new regime seems likely. [Later dispatches reveal that the United States has suspended diplomatic relations and is reconsidering its foreign aid program in Peru.]

On the record, the State Department held to a strict no comment on judging the pre-dawn Army overthrow of President Fernando Belaunde Terry.

Press officer Robert J. McCloskey indicated the United States would consult with its hemisphere allies on what posture to adopt toward the new regime—but would like Latin Americans to make the first move.

Off the record, U.S. authorities acknowledged the military takeover came as a setback to the goal of U.S. policy and of the U.S.-supported Alliance for Progress hemisphere development program.

Covey T. Oliver, assistant secretary of state for inter-American affairs, had been citing the absence of a coup in Latin America since the June 1966 Argentine military takeover as a sign of growing democratic stability in the area.

Just what Washington will do next depends on developments.

After the latest previous coup in Peru, in 1962, the Kennedy administration tried to show U.S. disapproval by breaking off U.S. relations and aid. *Berkeley Daily Gazette*, Friday, October 4, 1968.

This routine press dispatch epitomizes everything that is wrong with American foreign policy toward developing nations. Why should American foreign policy makers be unhappy about a coup in Peru? Why should a normal, regular and all too predictable event be interpreted by American officials as a setback in foreign policy? Why should the success of American policy be predicated upon stability in areas characterized by turmoil? Why should the United States consult with anyone on what posture to take when there is no apparent reason for being anything other than correct in its behavior toward Peru? Why should the United States government be going through the old routine of considering whether or not to maintain diplomatic relations and foreign-aid programs in a nation that has done nothing to it? Why should the democratic character of a weak and strife-torn country be of greater concern to State Department officials than apparently it is to many of its citizens?

Our purpose is to suggest new ways of thinking about and implementing American foreign policy toward developing nations. These nations can do little either to help or to hinder the United States; yet for several decades the United States has been involved in frantic efforts to obtain their support and blunt their hostility. The resulting policies have been both unsuccessful and unnecessary, and still no one knows how to devise adequate policies toward these chaotic countries. We recommend abandoning the attempt to devise specific policies for each developing nation; instead the United States should adopt an averaging strategy by which the same policy of friendly benevolence and minimum political involvement is applied to all of them. We begin with consideration of how the international system has been perceived by those who make and debate American foreign policy. This discussion is essential because we believe that the supporters and the opponents of American foreign policy base their positions on images of international instability that are inappropriate for developing countries. Bad policies are the result of bad models. The frantic reflex action of intervention adopted toward nations like Peru is understandable only if one holds an image of a world perched on the brink of disaster unless America acts.

THE INTERNATIONAL SYSTEM

At a low level of analysis the nature of the controversies over American foreign policy seems to be reasonably clear. The "hawks" and the "doves," the unilateral disarmers and the proponents of preventive war, appear to be urging diametrically opposed policies. And so they are, up to a point.

At a middle level of analysis it is possible to discern two opposing models of international conflict. On the one hand, those who espouse the spiral model of nuclear war believe that nations get caught up in a cycle of events in which their responses become involuntary and extreme as they mistakenly believe they have enemies who are out to get them. Each side expects the other to do the worst and, by its very precautions, justifies its initial predictions. The conflict escalates as each party responds to the presumed provocations of the other until the spiral of events gets completely out of hand. The adherents of the rival appeasement model, on the other hand, see a world bully as the ultimate danger. As the great aggressor is appeased, its appetite grows until it becomes so inordinate as to threaten the complete destruction of others. The result is the same as with the spiral model—a final confrontation in a nuclear holocaust. Whether the disputants conceive of armaments and aggressive postures (spiral model) or lack of sufficient armaments and weak postures (appeasement model) as the major cause of world destruction, they agree that if their remedies are not followed cataclysmic events will take place. Although there are more subtle and complex versions of these positions, public debate and official action have been guided essentially by the more blatant models.

At a higher level of abstraction, beliefs about the nature of the international system are powerful determinants of a nation's foreign policy. In a "stable" system, small causes have small effects that generate countervailing influences which return the system to its former equilibrium. In an unstable system, small causes have large effects that throw the system into ever greater disequilibrium as (appropriately) in a nuclear chain reaction. It is evident that since the end of World War II most American decision-makers have considered the international system to be unstable. Hence the United States has been concerned to halt the advance of Communism everywhere lest a small cause such as a Communist victory in the Dominican Republic, Guatemala, or the Congo build up such large effects as to threaten American security. In a world it believed to be stable, the United States could view the apparent rise of some Communist regimes as small events whose consequences would soon be counteracted.

Perceptions about the stability of the international system are not the only perceptions about the system that influence foreign policy. In a "tightly coupled" system the component elements are so closely related that a disturbance of one link can transmit effects to many and distant links. In a "loosely coupled" system, however, most effects are localized in a particular subsystem and do not shake the entire edifice. If the international system is thought to be loosely coupled, then the occasional rise of Communist regimes can be seen as having essentially local impact. The ascendancy of Communists in Ghana or Guinea would be of primary interest and concern to the immediately surrounding countries (or at most to the entire subcontinent) but not to the United States.

Perceptions of the polarization of nations also affect America's foreign policy. Government officials in the United States feel they are operating in a primarily bipolar (or if China is included, a tripolar) world. Events, therefore, are interpreted not only for their intrinsic significance but also for their impact on the contest between America and the great Communist powers. The world is not only unstable and tightly coupled, it is also divided into two or three great camps. The importance of local events is magnified if they are viewed as part of a larger contest that the United States cannot afford to lose. A retreat here or a failure there is amplified because of its purported significance for whichever camp is ahead or behind in the cold war. In a multipolar world, however, there may be many contests only distantly related to one another: The Dominican Republic might be part of a Carribbean power struggle but it would not automatically be considered a part of the cold war.

Now the time has come to question the assumptions about the international system—instability, tight coupling, and bipolarity—that have guided the debate about American foreign policy. As a rough operational guide we can say that the international system has gone beyond the bounds of stability if there is a major cost to the United States (like World War II) or a comparable defeat to the Soviet Union. The international system appears in the past two decades to have operated within the limits of stability. Although violence between nations has occurred, it has been contained without spreading very far or involving a direct confrontation of the superpowers. While potential sources of instability exist, they have not yet manifested themselves. Unfortunately, the world may appear stable only to those who lack the wit to sense the disruptive forces building up behind the facade of seemingly insignificant events.

The trouble is that it is either too easy or too hard to confirm the existence of systemic instability. If a moderate level of violence is the major measure of instability, almost any continent where there is some open conflict appears unstable. The absence of revolutionary violence then becomes the only sign of stability. On the other hand, when the analyst must identify the faintly emerging causes of instability its presence is too difficult to verify. (For example, can it be said that the United States is unstable because of its race riots?)

Fortunately, we do not have to confront this dilemma directly. For if the world system is loosely coupled, causes in the developing areas are unlikely to have effects around the globe. Whether or not parts of the world are unstable, Communist victories or other ominous events in Latin America or Africa are unlikely to have continuously amplifying bad effects elsewhere. Instead, evident forces such as nationalism and disorganization are likely to interfere with trends in directions bad for America as well as with efforts in directions good for it.

The question of whether the world is bipolar or multipolar is one of power: Who controls international decisions? Or, differently expressed, it is a question of causal relations: What nations cause events to happen in the international arena? If only two or three nations control international decisions, then the world system may be described as bipolar or tripolar. If many nations exercise power, then the world is multipolar. Stated in this way, however, the test assumes that those who have power have all of it and those who lack it are totally devoid of it. Here it is crucial to specify the areas of policy over which power is being exercised. Actors may be powerful in some areas and lack influence in others. While the Soviet Union and the United States come close to monopolizing control of intercontinental delivery systems for atomic weapons, their ability to control the future of NATO or the international Communist movement is in grave doubt. It seems likely, therefore, that the international system is unipolar or bipolar in some respects, tripolar in others, and multipolar so far as different areas of policy are concerned.

In the unstable, tightly coupled, and polarized international system perceived by many Americans every change is continuously amplified —thereby causing ever greater instability. Forces restoring the system to a more stable position are absent. The United States must provide countervailing power in every instance, therefore, in order to prevent disaster. Those who wish to change American foreign policy must argue, as we do, that a policy of permanent intervention is not necessary, because events in the developing areas are unlikely to blow up the rest of the world.

We believe that developing nations exist in a state of dynamic stability in which there is much action but little overall result. The combi-

nation of large populations and high volatility produces internal turbulence but not external force. The image of dynamic stability suggests that
the great danger the developing nations pose for the United States lies not
in their intrinsic importance but in the temptation to intervene in their
affairs. Permanent chaos for them is mistaken for overwhelming danger for
us. It would make better sense for the United States to loosen the connec-
tions between its national interests and events in developing countries.
Instead of rushing to intervene, the United States should be reluctant to
get involved. Outside of nonpartisan grants of foreign aid allocated on an
objective basis, the American posture should be one of friendly concern
but not of direct intervention. We shall attempt to justify these policy recommendations by showing, first, that developing nations cannot affect
America's national interests and, second, that America cannot, in any
event, devise effective policies toward these nations.

ARE DEVELOPING NATIONS A THREAT TO ANYONE OUTSIDE THEIR AREA OF THE WORLD?

The question of national survival today is dominated by high-yield nuclear
weapons, superpowers, and the possibility of central war. Since the concept
of central war, in turn, is dominated by intercontinental missiles, submarines, satellites, and aircraft capable of delivering nuclear weapons over
long distances, strategic points on the earth's surface are becoming much
less significant than they have been. The developing areas lack the capability to engage in or interfere with central war. They are, therefore, increasingly less important in regard to ultimate problems of American survival.

It is not beyond human ingenuity, of course, to perceive overwhelming importance in these developing nations. By insisting that the
world is unstable, tightly coupled, and bipolar the United States can interpret the most minor event as crucial to its well-being. A central war that
vastly reduced the strength of the superpowers would obviously enhance
the importance of those nations left relatively intact. By then, of course,
few Americans would be left to care who was taking their place in the
pantheon of nations.

It is still worth considering, however, whether there are less catastrophic but still real dangers emanating from developing nations. Access to
their markets, we are told, is essential to the prosperity of the United

States. Perhaps America will suffer if these nations ally themselves with hostile superpowers. In the background there is the vision of continents on fire—and the implication that the United States must put out these fires or eventually be consumed in the conflagration. Each of these arguments is worth examination.

Before a nation can be a threat to anyone it must be able to organize itself. Because the developing nations cannot solve the problem of providing adequate government, we believe they threaten no one but themselves.

Adequate government is a supreme human triumph and it has only rarely been achieved. By adequate government we mean one able to assure internal peace and order, to provide for orderly succession of power, to defend itself against outside forces, and to reasonably satisfy most of its citizens. It seems unlikely that many of the underdeveloped countries will move rapidly toward adequate government. We can learn about the prospects for adequate government from the South American countries; they have not generally achieved it, although their task probably was not as difficult as that which now faces the African countries. We are not, therefore, in a position where with effort, skill, and luck we could bring about a fairly smooth and happy transitional period for the underdeveloped areas. Although we may have the resources to moderate the fate of these countries, many of them are destined for turbulence and misfortune regardless of what we do.

Most of us take government for granted. For us the words "country" or "nation" represent a group of people occupying a fairly well-defined area and having institutions reasonably capable of performing the usual functions of the state. Similarly we assume that power to control the state passes from one group to another in accordance with accepted practices. At least, we feel, control can pass; that is, the country can be taken over, and one can say who is in control. But even this is not always true. There may be no "control" which can make effective use of the resources of a country—which can be taken over, combined, or otherwise figured in the political calculus in the same way as the more familiar integers.

The factors that look so formidable to us as we consider the possibilities for peace, order, and growth in the underdeveloped countries also limit the danger to us from these countries, even if they "go Communist." The developing nations have highly volatile national systems and few national institutions or regularized patterns of action. Their expectations from the past have been disrupted without being replaced by new ones to regularize their social and political behavior. Internal groups exhibit hostility toward one another and do not evidence a strong sense of national identity. Desperate efforts are made to find instruments of nationhood through the army, party, bureaucracy, or some form of secularized religion; communications are poor; talent is woefully scarce. Though terribly small elites can cause large degrees of disruption and coups and counter-coups take place with some regularity, nothing much really changes.

Unable to order their national life, developing nations are tempted to look for solutions outside of their territory. But, as they can hardly secure a minimum level of agreement at home, they are quite unable to maintain effective supranational arrangements abroad. Hostile to former colonial rulers, they are no more favorably disposed to neighboring countries in view of traditional enmities or tribal differences. Should a foreign nation (or its ideology) establish a visible presence in or near these developing countries, a counterreaction is likely. "What are these (white, red, yellow) foreigners doing? No doubt they want to enslave us again." It may not be possible to know exactly what the new nations want, but it is obvious that what they do not want is outside interference.

It is difficult for the developing nations to follow any consistent course: They have trouble allying with other nations; their rulers are practically unable to predict the directions in which they are likely to move. It is most unlikely, therefore, that any force will move whole regions and continents in a single direction. These nations are too upset, too conflicted, too inconsistent, too suspicious, and too weak to be a large cause of anything much beyond their borders.

CONDITIONS OF INSTABILITY APPLIED TO DEVELOPING NATIONS

Our argument has been that the chronic weakness of developing nations means that they are unlikely to threaten American interests. Other observers have argued that it is precisely the pervasive disorder of these nations that compels the United States to take defensive measures before the chaos spreads to its shores. This brings us back to the tricky concept of international instability. Perhaps we can move the discussion forward by briefly examining the conditions of instability in the most important case since 1945—Soviet expansion into Europe.

After the end of World War II, Soviet armies had extended their dominion in Eastern Europe, Czechoslovakia had been toppled by a combination of external threat and internal subversion, and attempts were underway to repeat the process in France and Italy. These attempts were large causes, threatening to have large effects, and the United States responded appropriately in a massive way. The Soviet thrust was contained through active intervention in Greece, threats of force elsewhere, and large injections of economic aid in Western Europe. Had the Communist advance continued, Soviet control of the productive capacity and manpower of Western Europe might have directly threatened the security of the United States. This instability occurred under the following conditions: (1) the presence of a superpower with large ground forces and (2) economic capacity that (3) had already subjugated a series of contiguous nations. (4) These nations were near other threatened nations (5) which possessed trained manpower and great industrial capacity and (6) which had strong local organizations tied to the superpower. Under these conditions, processes with the potential for radically changing the system were clearly at work. These processes were checked by another superpower, which possessed equal or greater resources and was willing to use or threaten limited force, cooperating with local talented economic and political groups opposed to the aggressive superpower.

This set of conditions does not obtain, however, in those areas of the world in which most of the developing nations are located. None of the six potential destabilizing conditions of the European case exist in Africa. There is no superpower in physical possession of territory on the African land mass. No nation has "gone Communist" in the usual sense, though a few countries seem to lean toward one or another superpower. No African nation can be described as a great source of trained manpower with great industrial capacity, like France, Germany, or Italy. Nor are there substantial local Communist parties to invite speculations about whether they are closely allied with Moscow or Peking. Indeed there is doubt whether some of these peoples have the capacity to support "real" Communist parties. Moreover, such immediate success as the Soviets and Chinese appeared to have achieved has been rapidly reversed. Having been kicked in the teeth numerous times the superpowers have temporarily retreated from major participation in the area's internal disputes.

If there is any superpower dominating Latin America it is the United States rather than the Soviet Union. However, an American thrust through

Mexico down the isthmus into Central America seems unlikely, to say the least. If the United States does have the equivalent of satellites, it does not seem to be running them very well. The Soviets do not appear to have made anything like a satellite out of Cuba and the Castroites have been remarkably unsuccessful in spreading their brand of revolution. There are Soviet, Chinese, and Castroite groups here and there but these do not seem to be strong. Competition between them, as in Bolivia, limits the chances that any of them will succeed. There is certainly no immediate prospect that numbers of Latin American countries will choose some version of the Communist path. Except for Argentina, Brazil, and Venezuela (in different ways), Latin America possesses only limited economic resources and does not have the trained manpower and organization to exploit fully the resources it does have. From the partial viewpoint of defense of American interests, none of the conditions of international instability in Western Europe in the late 1940s exist in Latin America today. [1]

THE ECONOMIC IMPORTANCE OF THE DEVELOPING AREAS TO THE UNITED STATES

If events in developing nations do not seriously threaten America's political interests, what about the long-standing belief that America's economic welfare depends on cheap supplies of raw materials and privileged trading relationships? We can largely discard the assumption that the United States needs the developing areas as a market (or as an outlet for investments) in order to maintain roughly the standard of living it now has. Only a very small part of the goods and services produced by Western nations are sold in the developing areas. Trade with industrial Japan will soon be worth more to America than the rest of Asia combined. Although a good portion of the raw material used by the West is obtained from the underdeveloped areas, technological developments have reduced the importance of this raw material contribution. The increasing substitutability of resources (resulting in part from the ability to synthesize new materials and in part from the generally increased sophistication of modern technology) reduces the monopoly power of any single raw material. Raw materials, moreover, are becoming a less important part of total goods and ser-

---

[1] We are saving Vietnam and Southeast Asia for later in order to test the relevance of our policy recommendations in the toughest case.

vices. Therefore, the West can afford to pay a substantially higher price for raw materials—or their alternatives—without a major effect on its total economy. For these reasons, hostile control of the underdeveloped areas cannot produce a critical, long-term effect on the American economy.

This analysis is greatly strengthened if it is looked at from the other side. The goods and services which the underdeveloped areas receive from the West are a decisive part of their economies, particularly if they are to raise their standard of living. These countries are far more dependent on selling than America is on buying, as the abortive Arab oil boycott recently demonstrated. We cannot imagine that anyone can organize and control the underdeveloped areas in the next generation to such a degree that they can all be cut off from the West.

CALCULATING GOOD POLICIES

A decision to act should be based not only on a determination that one's interest are involved but also upon a corresponding judgment that one is capable of taking effective action. Having argued that American interests need not be seriously involved in the lives of developing countries, we should like to complete our case with the claim that the United States (like other nations) lacks the knowledge to make wise decisions about individual policies toward developing countries.

In order to exercise political influence in the developing countries we must be able to make the hardest kinds of judgment about their affairs— predictions of the political effects of proposed actions and possible counter-actions. Politics in America are stable and familiar compared to the politics of developing countries. Change takes place in small steps so that the political environment possesses a fundamental continuity. Yet it is exceedingly difficult to predict the outcomes of major elections or to discover long-term trends. If picking a winner or judging the extent of racial animosities is a dubious exercise in America, how can we expect to pick winners and judge the extent of racial animosities in West Africa? We can surely fall into evil ways, but we have little reason to believe we can do good except by ac-cident. Merely trying to do good is not enough. We are sophisticated enough to understand that "good can come from evil and evil from good." If we want to play chess with history, we have to be able to think at least one or two moves ahead. Yet we can hardly figure out what went wrong with our past moves, let alone estimate the consequences of future actions.

The formulation of foreign policy is a complicated process. The difficulties for an individual to try to understand the political situation in any one of the developing countries are magnified when all those in our country who participate in determining foreign policy come to grips with the intricate problems of all 75 or so developing countries.

Let us suppose that a shift in the situation in Tanzania requires a change in American policy. The first problem would be for those dealing with Tanzania to recognize that the situation is changing, to determine the direction of change, and to predict the impact upon U.S. goals and policies. (It is not easy to make these judgments: Though there were plenty of reports from Germany during the thirties about the profound changes taking place and the powerful forces at work, no generally accepted understanding of even the basic elements of the situation was arrived at in England or America until very late.) Reports from officials concerned with Tanzania will then have to be considered by the State Department people responsible for making policy in wider areas. It is unlikely that all of the diagnoses will agree.

Since the hypothetical change in the Tanzanian situation requires a shift in American policy, the ideas of Assistant Secretaries of State, policy planners, and numerous other officials will have to be changed. Since there probably was some controversy when the existing policy was adopted, and there is certainly controversy about related situations in other countries, the decision-makers will be reluctant to throw out an agreed-upon attitude and will be suspicious of the advice that it is necessary to do so, because of the relation of this advice to other controversies.

The efforts to change the ideas of the policy-makers about Tanzania must compete with their concern for 75 other underdeveloped countries and the other half of the world. They must also compete for their attention against efforts to carry out the old policy.

If a policy change is to be made and supported, it probably will have to face—sooner or later—opposition in Congress, the press, and small interested publics. Those people who have not learned about the changing facts in Tanzania, or who do not believe them, will oppose the new policy because it is in conflict with their understanding of the facts. In some cases it will not be possible for the State Department to reveal the new facts or the theory which produced the new policy. Thus special interests built up around the old policy will resist change. The change in Tanzanian policy may become involved in irrelevant disputes in Congress or elsewhere.

If two groups in the administration, the Congress, and the public have different approaches to problems of the underdeveloped areas or foreign policy in general, they are likely to differ on many specific policy questions. These differences will be mediated by our political process, and neither side will win all the time. Therefore, people from all schools of thought must expect that they will consider some of the decisions to be wrong. There is an inherent tendency toward inconsistency in this process of give and take. For the country to "understand" what is happening in the underdeveloped countries necessarily involves a great deal more than the intellectual difficulties confronting any individual.

To some it may appear that the United States is uniquely ill suited to carry out large numbers of discriminating policies for developing nations. The fragmentation of power in the political system militates against fast action and consistent policies. The taking of incremental steps and the use of feedback to judge the next small move—procedures that work reasonably well in a stable, democratic country—may be irrelevant to problems of developing nations. The impatience of the population and the desire for clear-cut outcomes may prevent the careful handling of intractable problems. Yet there is no need to carry analysis further. While the American system has defects, so do the Soviet and Chinese systems, and these nations handle such problems as badly as the United States, if not worse. Indeed, it does not appear that any great power is able to handle these problems. If, as we suggest, the difficulties reside both in the characteristics of the developing nations and the inherent weaknesses of complex organizations like the United States government, the proper course is to devise a policy orientation that takes these sources of difficulty into account.

AVERAGING STRATEGIES

The United States government can adopt three general decision-making postures toward the developing nations. The first is to call for the adoption of policies appropriate to the special circumstances of each country under varying conditions. American policy before, during, and after bloody racial warfare in the Sudan would fit in this category. The second posture is to recommend devising individual policies only for a few nations chosen for their special interest or critical position. Whenever a crisis occurred in or near these nations, new policies would be devised; the rest of the developing nations would be covered by general policy guidelines. The preferential treatment once afforded Nigeria, when it was regarded as the hope of the African heartland, belongs in this category. The third posture of decision-making specifically rejects creating special policies for each developing country. Nor does it single out a few nations for unusual attention. Instead, this alternative maintains the same policy for all such nations. The rationale for adopting the same policy for an entire class of nations is that the results would, on the average, be better than trying to work out specific policies for all or a few of them.

Averaging strategies originate as a response to conditions that make it prohibitively expensive to calculate new policies for each new situation. As an example, consider the problem that every corporation faces of making sure executives retire before they are too old. We can assume that when people exhibit a certain degree of senility, they should be required to retire; however, people reach this degree of incompetence at different ages. (There is, after all, the "young fogy" problem.) The organization loses out if people are forced to retire either too early or too late. In order to do justice to each employee and to retain the best people, new organizations often begin by considering each case on its merits. Determining "the merits," however, turns out to be much more difficult than it had originally appeared. Not everyone agrees on criteria of excellence in work—on the trade-off, for instance, between experience and vigor. A great deal of time must now be spent working out detailed criteria. The alternative is to act intuitively toward each individual—this one looks good and that one should go—but the absence of formal criteria leads to charges of favoritism. If the man forced into retirement merely feels aggrieved, the cost is only personal unhappiness. But if he happens to be highly placed, or if the decision regarding him is taken as symbolic of a factional conflict, the costs are likely to be much higher. A relatively small matter has now been invested with much larger significance. A campaign for support is initiated; a *cause célèbre* is in the making. Feelings run high almost in inverse proportion, it seems, to the intrinsic importance of the case.

After a number of traumatic episodes, an organization will usually adopt an averaging strategy called an automatic retirement rule. Top executives know that it may be possible to specify the age at which any individual should be retired with more accuracy than the automatic rule provides, but rather than saying to those involuntarily retired, "You are senile," most organizations would rather take the small losses due to early and delayed retirements by making the much less invidious statement, "You are 65." The averaging strategy results in small losses due to people being retired when they might be productive for another few years. On the other hand, considering each retirement on its merits leads to substantial costs of search (investigating each case), decision (time, energy, negotiation), and organizational strain (because fighting over the outcome is regarded as a loss or gain for various factions). An averaging strategy is desirable when the inherent significance of the problem is minor, because the possible gains from correct individual decisions are much smaller than the likely losses from wrong ones. Conversely the high cost of individual bad decisions may be avoided by accepting the low cost of having an automatic policy.

The case for adopting averaging strategies toward developing countries is much stronger than suggested by the problem of executive retirement. No one could doubt the ability of intelligent men to make basically sound decisions about who should retire early and who should be kept on a job. There is no reason to believe, however, that capable men know enough to devise good policies for developing nations. The risk of disaster is always there. And the costs incurred by making these many individual choices must also be measured by opportunities lost to devise better policies in more critical areas.

Suppose that the United States faced a choice of active intervention in 100 developing nations. Direct action might be justified in fifteen cases. But there is no theory or observation to decide which of the hundred deserve the investment. In order not to overlook most nations deserving of intervention, at least double that number must be tried. Yet some nations requiring direct action must be left out and others in no great need are included. Multiple interventions increase foreign policy difficulties enormously. Instead of seeming active and in control, the United States paradoxically appears insecure and on the defensive, because it is always trying to extricate itself from an unfortunate involvement. It is difficult to know when success has come because it was never clear whether the threatened danger was real or whether it would have been mitigated by local conditions. What is clear is that the stakes of intervention in some cases have dramatically increased because of the importance the United States has ascribed to the case. Yet American ability to control events does not escalate along with its deeper involvement. We need an averaging strategy to bring investments and risks in line with potential gains and losses.

A SPECIAL PROPOSAL

Consider the following major components of the proposed averaging policy:

1. A policy of abstaining from the internal politics of the underdeveloped countries, dealing with each on the basis of tolerance and generous correctness. What is proposed here is *not* a withdrawal of the United States from these areas, but a change in its mode of participation in their affairs.
2. A large-scale economic aid program in which a regular part of our national income (or national growth) is committed to helping any of the underdeveloped countries that wish such aid.
3. An ability and willingness to fight overt military aggression. The United States should be prepared to nullify the effect of Russian or Chinese military power by its readiness to come to the aid of victims of that power. But America should be cautious about committing itself to providing immediate assistance to nations that do not really need the help and use American participation as a weapon against their neighbors.

Each case would be decided on its own merits: the ability of the United States to successfully defend the threatened nation, its willingness to help defend itself, its importance to vital American interests, the presence or absence of democratic processes, all these should play a part in the American decision.

Abstaining from the politics of the underdeveloped countries would mean:

1. Not trying to maintain particular governments in power.
2. Not making alliances, or encouraging countries to commit themselves between the East and the West.
3. Not having particular "friends" or "enemies" among the countries of the underdeveloped areas. The United States should treat all of these nations with equal respect and propriety regardless of their policies and personnel. (This does not mean that the government should allow countries to abuse it by provocative acts, e.g., requiring the United States to reduce its diplomatic staff to 14 people on 48 hours notice.)

4. Finally, abstention would mean not trying directly, except by advice and persuasion, to end any internal political policy such as feudalism or repression. The United States would not, for example, use its aid in order to keep a "good relationship" with anti-Communist governments. The United States would not associate itself in special relationships with particular governments or countries to try to prevent them from "going Communist." The United States would not allocate aid among underdeveloped countries on the basis of which are in the greatest danger of "going Communist."

If the United States approves of some governments and disapproves of others it will be hard for it to avoid having to pass judgment on all governments, and people will read approval or disapproval into everything it says or does. If the United States becomes tied to the success of particular governments by making them, in effect, its protégés, at the same time, if it builds policies that depend on the success of particular governments, it takes on possibilities of defeat in situations which it cannot control, without gaining in return a reasonable likelihood of benefit. This way America loses its freedom of action. It is forced to adjust policies out of loyalty to these governments or for fear of weakening them, regardless of principles or long-run interest. The United States cannot always force reform on governments it depends on, but often, if they do not reform, they fall and the United States suffers. Furthermore, when it becomes associated with a particular government, the United States is tempted to use short-term efforts to save it. When these actions fail the government never knows whether more intervention will save the day or whether the situation is hopeless.

Of course it would be foolish to treat these prescriptions as absolute rules; rather they should be treated as general rules which the government should be extremely reluctant to violate. In the nature of things there will always be temptations to intervene. There will be a constant series of situations where political action by the United States seems necessary to prevent some terrible thing from happening (or to seize some lovely but fleeting opportunity). But these situations will be misleading. If the value of abstention could be seen in such immediate situations there would be no need for a general rule. The general rule of abstention is proposed precisely because it would be unwise on the whole to do what seems wise in each particular case. The way to stay thin is to abstain from eating too much. Even though each piece of cake tastes good and has no immediately visible bad effect, most pieces of cake must be rejected. The fact that temptation is tempting makes it hard to resist and that is why one must make a resolution to resist.

America's proper attitude towards the underdeveloped countries should be friendly politeness or correctness to all. It should have a large economic aid program whose explicit motivation is benevolence or altruism. The President should decide whether benevolence is a sufficient justification for a large nonmilitary development assistance program (say 0.5 percent of gross national product per year). If he does, he should present the case for a decision to recognize this obligation of benevolence.

The position should be that the program is justified even if it involves no advantage to the national interest; that the American people can hope in the long run a policy of generosity and benevolence will turn out to be of some value in ways that cannot be predicted. This should be more a matter of faith than of explicit reasoning (like "honesty is the best policy"). Furthermore, there is only a modest chance that more explicit calculations of the national interest would lead to a more effective program, and there are advantages to not trying to make such a calculation.

Selling the program to Congress and the public should stress the argument of benevolence and duty. The case is very simple: They are very poor and we are very rich; therefore we should help them.

It would be consistent with the American character to undertake regular foreign aid as an obligation of generosity. Even today many people think of it in these terms. The altruistic case for foreign aid is a good case. We believe that the American people can be convinced of the merits of a regular foreign aid program on this basis, although a decision of this scope takes a long time to make. There must be widespread public discussion, articles in magazines, resolutions by national organizations and their local chapters. There must be long congressional struggle, hearings, bills, amendments, compromises, debate, delay. But when a decision is evolved out of this kind of struggle and debate, it survives; it is not challenged every year. Social security and medical care for the aged are good examples of accepted policies. Although it would be the target of regular peripheral sniping, such a major decision on foreign aid probably would become an automatic part of everybody's platform like past reforms enacted amid much controversy.

Once the decision is made that simple humanity requires our giving a small part of our income to the underdeveloped nations each year, there will be no good basis for the annual argument about the need for and value of foreign aid, because every year the situation will be the same: They will be poor and we will be rich. If foreign aid is not considered a way to stop the spread of communism, to induce countries to become our allies, or to assure peace and democracy in the underdeveloped areas, then there cannot be annual debates about whether it is working or not. If there are no short-term objectives there can be no short-term failures. If the aid is to be allocated on the basis of standards which, compared with a crusade against the Reds, seem prosaic, objective, and technical, then Congress will not be so concerned about having a major share in the decision-making; the allocation of foreign aid will become a settled policy.

If over a number of years we do not use our aid as a political device, if we give without bias or favor, the nature of our program will come to be understood, and people will learn that our aid is not support for particular governments. All factions in recipient countries will know that if they gain power the aid will continue to come on the same basis as before. To this end, our aid should be allocated and administered on principles designed to minimize as much as possible the relationship of the aid to the particular governments in power in the recipient countries.

A vast bureaucracy is now employed to see that foreign aid is spent for the purposes the United States regards as most desirable. The result is that America courts hostility from the recipient nation in order to achieve an indifferent level of success in securing worthwhile expenditures. The bureaucratic and decision-making costs of foreign aid may be virtually eliminated by simply providing grants to whatever government exists on an objective basis.[2] No doubt a fair amount of money might be squandered, but that is the case today. And the United States might avoid the difficulties of trying to maintain control through large foreign-aid establishments abroad. Each recipient nation would have to justify to its own population the use

---

[2] Our objective is to set up a foreign aid system that will (1) commit the United States to substantial yearly expenditure, (2) remove the political costs of supervising aid, and (3) provide incentives to encourage recipient nations to oversee each other. Our immediate purpose is to show how a new foreign-aid program would fit in with our averaging strategy. Considerations of specific criteria—population, birth rates, spending by other growing nations, stability of currency, and measures of effort for development—must wait for a separate paper.

of these funds. Despite evident difficulties, this policy would center responsibility where it belongs—on the nation receiving the funds. If our foreign-aid proposal is regarded as too radical, its essence might be assured by channeling all funds through international organizations, regional associations, and multination consortiums whose major personnel are not American. The amount of aid would still be geared to objective criteria and the amount determined by the United States; how and for what the aid was spent would be determined by others.

The existence of India, with a huge population, and nations like Pakistan, Indonesia, and Brazil, with large populations, raises the question of whether they should be treated as special political cases. Under our proposal they would be treated differently in one crucial respect: since the amount of aid would be determined by such criteria as population size, these countries would naturally get more than others. We could not go beyond this point without endangering the policy of nonintervention. After a while, the cutoff point for special consideration would be difficult to determine. Population is not the only factor that might serve as a basis for special treatment. Interest in oil or uranium might bring in other countries. The United States would then be in the same situation from which it was trying to extricate itself. The past American enthusiasm for India is a case in point. The Chinese Communists disrupted the Pakistani-American alliance simply by invading India. Immediate American overreaction led to large arms shipments to India. The result was that Pakistan was alienated even though we did not have strong reason to believe that India was really in danger of conquest. The maintenance of special relationships is similarly fraught with danger throughout the world.

CAN THE UNITED STATES MOVE TOWARD AN AVERAGING STRATEGY FOR SOUTHEAST ASIA?

While an averaging strategy might have made sense before the United States became deeply involved in the developing nations, it may appear that its time has passed. Too many commitments have been made. Too many acts of intervention have taken place to permit a policy of self-imposed restraint. Has the original sin become the everlasting flaw? Having once eaten the fatal fruit, must the United States forever choose a steady diet of intervention? The toughest test of our averaging strategy is Southeast Asia.

In the 1950s the United States could have afforded the absorption of South Vietnam by North Vietnam. South Vietnam was not intrinsically important, but the huge American intervention made that nation a symbol of American ability to protect small nations. This action made the possibility of victory for North Vietnam much more costly to the United States than it would have been had we not intervened. One of the benefits that is sought by a policy of very limited intervention is a reduction of the risk of such artificially created costs.

The question before us now, however, is not whether the United States should enter Vietnam but whether it can extricate itself. A policy of helpful and respectful distance will not be applicable to South Vietnam for a long time. But the United States could, over a four- or five-year period, gradually withdraw its troops. This policy requires no coalition government or agreement with the Vietcong or the North Vietnamese. Should the South Vietnamese government collapse, that would end the immediate problem. Should that government survive, the United States would continue to provide military and economic assistance for a decade. The objective of American policy would be to disengage from South Vietnam sufficiently to permit an averaging strategy to be applied in the surrounding area.

There are ample opportunities to move toward an averaging strategy elsewhere in Southeast Asia. If Japan, for example, were in danger of overthrow through internal subversion or external aggression, the United States would have to consider armed intervention. Japan is a potential superpower, and its dependence is of critical importance to the United States. But the Japanese refuse to believe that they are in serious danger. And so long as South Korea remains independent, it will be difficult to convince the Japanese to do more for their own defense. America should not be more interested in the defense of a country than its own people are. Running after a reluctant ally creates a false position, which is bad for American self-respect and Japanese capacity to assess its own interests. Americans may ask whether they really gain anything from a maintenance of military bases in Japan. In order to keep these bases, America now makes disadvantageous economic agreements. (For example, the Japanese sell us their excellent cameras, but we may not sell our superior color film in Japan.) A new policy should be adopted. Having arranged for commercial ship repair facilities and transit rights for airplanes, the United States could move its military bases to Okinawa. Legal sovereignty over

Okinawa would be returned to Japan as the United States withdrew its obsolete atomic weapons from the island. Even this limited arrangement should not be made without public acknowledgment by the Japanese government of its own interest in keeping the American bases.

Indonesia is the kind of troubled developing nation with whom the United States should avoid special relationships: The "low posture" policy currently being followed by the American embassy is excellent, except that it is threatened by the large number of administrators required to do the paper work on foreign aid. Malaysia, which has never received American aid because it manages its affairs too well, should at least get some economic assistance. Nascent nationalism and economic piracy in the Philippines should be met by a marked reduction in America's military and civilian personnel. The historic relationship between the United States and the Philippines might justify continued subsidies in the form of a special sugar quota, but history does not justify vast military bases and a swollen civilian bureaucracy. As rising nationalism leads the Philippines to look for scapegoats for its poverty and injustices, the United States should be making itself scarce. American troops should remain in Korea, however, where a strong and vigorous government is determined to defend its people against the real threat of armed attack. Should the unexpected occur—a full-scale North Korean invasion of South Korea backed by Communist China—the United States might again find itself at war, but one far better adapted to its moral and military strength than Vietnam. The provocation would be obvious, as would the capacity of the Koreans to assist in their own defense. There would then be no need to urge the Japanese to rearm; they would figure out where their safety lay without our help. Over a period of time, therefore, the United States (while still capable of direct action under special conditions) could move toward limited engagement in Southeast Asia.

CONCLUSION

The United States is a great world power and, as such, cannot escape being a prime actor in world affairs. Thus it must inevitably appear to some to be "throwing its weight around." Though history has decreed against escapism, playing a major, often unpopular role in world affairs need not mean total involvement everywhere all the time. A sense of proportion should be introduced into American foreign policy: Distinctions need to be made between major events and minor annoyances. The present overload on foreign policy-making machinery, introduced by constant concern about developments in dozens of developing nations, should be reduced. A sense of calm and restraint should replace the frenetic atmosphere that induces intervention as a reflex action. We hope that it will prove helpful to replace the old view of the international system as highly unstable, tightly coupled, and bipolar with a fresh view of it as stable, loosely coupled, and multipolar particularly as regards the developing nations.

We believe that an averaging policy toward developing nations, based on genuine friendship, aid, and respectful distance, will enhance the quality of American foreign policy. Such a stance will facilitate greater attention to more important matters. Armed intervention, if and when it occurs, will take place under more clearcut circumstances—more likely to enhance support from the threatened nation and from the American people. The self-image of Americans as decent, responsible, and effective citizens will be improved, and fateful days of decision will not be clouded by endless petty squabbles about trivial issues in unimportant places. No doubt developments that might have been headed off by direct action when they were small will grow larger. But such action is as likely to fail as to succeed and to it must be added numerous difficulties resulting from unwanted or unskillful intervention. There will still be failures. But on the average the United States should do better and feel better about what it is doing.

3

Vietnam, Western Europe, Latin America . . . : Where Do Our Vital Interests Lie?

Leslie Lipson

American foreign policy today is verging on bankruptcy. The time has come to rethink it and restore its solvency. Any policy, domestic or external, becomes insolvent when its declared aims and formal commitments considerably outweigh the means available. Although not the sole instance, Vietnam provides the crowning proof that many of the leading ideas pursued for sixteen years by Secretaries Dulles and Rusk have resulted in a tragedy of errors. In that land of unlimited impossibilities, the Johnson policy failed—not through the poor execution of good ideas, but because the ideas themselves were at fault. No methods, techniques, or gadgetry could accomplish goals which had been wrongly conceived. Too many of the recent programs in Southeast Asia were constructed in a world of self-deluding myth, which hard facts have repeatedly exposed as false. That is why we have had a phenomenon politely called "the credibility gap."

To prevent the repetition of such blunders—a conviction popularly summarized in the phrase "no more Vietnams"—Americans must now reexamine our international position in the light of our vital interests, resources and capabilities. And no time is more appropriate for raising basic questions than the year when a new administration takes office in Washington. The principal errors in our external policy have been these: (1) We reversed the order of priority in our foreign relations; (2) we affirmed a broad commitment to objectives which, as a people, we could not fulfill; and (3) we exceeded the limits of our power. The foreign policy of the United States will become solvent and, for that reason, realistic only when we have correctly reassessed our various external relationships in terms of the degrees of their importance to us, when we undertake only those responsibilities which lie within our means, and when we recognize that beyond certain limits even the vast power of this great country ceases to be effective. This national effort at reappraisal need not be agonizing. It would, however, be agonizing, as well as intolerable, to continue along the course of recent mistakes and persist in attempts to justify them as a Grand Design.

To begin, we require a candid inventory of our strengths and limitations. It is a fact that the United States, measured by any international scale, ranks as a superpower—a category only one other state occupies at present. As such, we have worldwide interests and a continuing concern that the balance of world power should either be tilted in our favor or at least not be tilted against us. The latter alternative implies another fundamental fact: Our strength, although very great, is not infinite. We are potent, but not omnipotent. There are certain things which even we cannot do; some goals which we might wish to attain, but cannot. An insolvent policy fails to recognize what these are. Realism, on the other hand, requires the wisdom of self-restraint; distinguishing not only between the desirable and the undesirable, but also between the practical and the impractical. Realism also calls for scaling our external relations in order of priority—an order which we must determine according to our conception of where our greater interests lie.

The first priority, of course, is always to maintain those interests which are vital to the United States. Vital means whatever is essential for safeguarding American security by political or military power. Since there are limits to our power, a vital need is always to cooperate closely with governments that most nearly share our basic values and ideals—on the reasonable assumption that it is these whom we can most safely trust and these who would harm us least. Although our interests extend globally (and even nowadays extraterrestrially), they are not all of equal importance. In the protection of vital interests, we should be ready to commit American military forces when necessary. But to uphold interests which, however important, are not vital, our assistance to other governments should always be restricted to the supply of dollars and equipment. Hence we should assess what our priorities are, with the corollary that we should never sacrifice a vital interest to a lesser. All this leads to the concluding query: where should we, as a people, draw the line?

We are living in a world where no one state is so mighty that its government can persist with impunity in flouting the opinions of others, and none so self-sufficient that it can withdraw into a fortress of its own isolation. Therefore one needs allies, among whom, hopefully, one may even find some friends. The pattern of alliances is influenced partly by physical considerations—e.g., the given facts of geography, the potentialities of resources and technology, military apparatus, and so on—but also in part by subjective and political factors—ideologies, attitudes, and opinions. The latter have relevance to the clustering of governments within the framework of alliances because of their effects on mutual understandings and on the willingness or refusal of peoples and governments to pull together.

Hence we should take note of a basic paradox of the American image abroad. Most of the world sees us, at one and the same time, as revolutionaries and conservatives. In our external contacts, we attack the foundations of the established social order while we support the power of its traditional custodians. We plaster the ceiling even as we undermine the floor. To other peoples, we fly in as social revolutionaries—along with our gadgets, know-how, consumer goods, and the fluid individualism of our quicksilver society. Wittingly or not, we travel around the world as restless innovators—disturbing conventional modes of conduct, uprooting ancient relationships, exposing accepted inadequacies, imparting new techniques. Others feel stimulated to adopt us for their teachers and to study us as a model to imitate. Yet when it comes to political cooperation or maintaining diplomatic ties, the stance that comes naturally to us is conservative. Where we have a choice between rival groups to support in a foreign country, almost without hesitation we side with those on the right less disposed to basic social change which could threaten their ascendancy. In several recent cases where we have intervened militarily to join in ousting or propping up a regime, our efforts generally have been directed against those initiating change from the left. Thus while we automatically oppose the extreme left (whose hostility to us is a foregone conclusion), we succeed in repulsing and converting into our foes the moderate left who crave for much of the social innovation which we represent. Hence many of our efforts abroad, many of our aid programs, have a quality of Sisyphus—tremendous effort expended in futility.

Such contradictions in our external posture bear directly on the solidarity, and thereby the efficacy, of the alliances we have entered. For, although an alliance stands as a contractual agreement between governments, to implement it in a given instance is a political act; its provisions must be interpreted and then applied (if indeed they are) by regimes which may fear to act positively when they encounter a sharp division in their public opinion. In this context, let us analyze the network of alliances to which the United States has become a party since 1945. The historic decision of the years 1944-1949 to abandon the traditional policy of isolationism was itself a realistic recognition of the altered power structure of the mid-1940s. It was endorsed nationally by clear bipartisan majorities in the Senate and executed by Presidents of both parties. At some stage, however, the evolution of our postwar policy went astray. We forsook realism for unreality, fact for fiction, interest for illusion. Where was it that we went wrong? Can the mistakes be rectified?

The method of our policy has been to construct a system of alliances which would enlarge the security of ourselves and others by collective means. In virtually every instance, because of the relative power of the countries involved, the United States has emerged as the producer of security among allies who are its consumers. Largely, these alliances result from the work of the last two decades. Some are bilateral, others multilateral. They extend to certain areas of the world which are of permanent and proximate interest to the United States—such as Western Europe and Latin America—or to regions more remote which are weak and unstable and could use some strengthening from outside. Geographically, these alliances are mostly located near, or round the rim of, the countries ruled by Communist governments. An evident aim in their strategy has been to resist the appeals of communism and contain the expansion of such regimes.

Because of their varied memberships, our alliances differ vastly in character. There is only one, NATO, that has developed any significant cohesion or produced a working organization. NATO is unique in that it provides for integrated training and planning in peacetime as well as for an integrated command in wartime. The other alliances are loose or even tenuous. They have practically no structure and generate scarcely any reciprocal support.

Now let us take a comprehensive view of the formal commitments into which our government has entered since World War II. Under the Charter of the United Nations we share in the general obligation of all members to help in enforcing peace as authorized by the Security Council, where, if we choose, we can exercise a veto. Also we have entered into regional security arrangements under NATO, OAS, SEATO and ANZUS, and we are committed to assist our various partners (e.g., Japan, South Korea) by a string of bilateral agreements. Under the regional pacts, an attack on any one member is automatically construed as an attack on all and involves an obligation to assist the victim. But, as I shall explain later, there is nothing automatic in either the nature or the degree of that assistance. When you add up all those agreements, together they amount to this: We are committed to help defend Western Europe, the Americas, parts of Southeast Asia, South Korea, and various island states in the Pacific. Count the countries and governments—their total reaches forty-four![1]

Some critics have concluded that our government has been the victim of "pactomania." What is clear in my judgment is that we overextended ourselves, so that what started with some misbegotten pacts has ended in some disastrous acts. One is entitled to inquire whether the net result for the United States is collective security or an insecurity policy. We replaced the excessive isolationism of the years before 1941 with a chain of postwar commitments. But in practice, these commitments have led us, because of unsound doctrines and plain errors of calculation in Washington, into an excess of interventionism. Hence it is imperative for us at last to strike a balance between the earlier harmful excess of isolation and the recent harmful excess of intervention. This need is now both pertinent and urgent because of our military overcommitment in one place—South Vietnam. Our government intervened with large-scale warfare in an area which

---

[1] This includes the other fourteen parties to the North Atlantic Treaty, the other nineteen members of the Organization of American States and the Rio Pact—excluding Cuba—the three Asian members of the Southeast Asia Treaty, plus the three states named in the connected Protocol, Australia and New Zealand, as well as Japan, Taiwan, and South Korea.

many Americans do not consider a primary interest, and we have appeared, to many of our own statesmen as well as to numerous leaders in other countries, to be acting the role of world policeman. Is this really what our vital interests require?

In essentials, my argument is this: Outside of North America, the vital interests of the United States are linked to three regions which together constitute our primary, permanent, and fundamental concern. These are the North Atlantic (which includes Western Europe), Latin America, and the Pacific Ocean. Other parts of the world—Africa, Eastern Europe, the Middle East, South Asia, and the mainland portion of Southeast Asia—are all important. But none of these is vital to the United States in the sense defined above. I shall begin this review of our relations with other areas of the world by a critique of Vietnam, which is the classic example of what not to do and where not to do it. Since the implications of that involvement will be with us for a long time, they should be analyzed with care if we are to avoid the future repetition of similar mistakes. Then I shall turn to the positive discussion of what we should be doing instead.

The great aberration of the sixties, enlarging on earlier errors of judgment of the mid-fifties, was the notion that the mainland portion of Southeast Asia constitutes an interest so vital to the United States that it must be embraced within the boundaries of the *pax Americana.* Already we have paid dearly for that mistake, at home as well as abroad. Our involvement in that area was officially expressed in the Southeast Asia Collective Defense Treaty of 1954 and its Protocol. This was one of Mr. Dulles' dreams which became our nightmare. It was he who seized on the conceptions of the pacts for the North Atlantic and the South Pacific (ANZUS) and reproduced them in Southeast Asia. But his assumptions were invalid because Asian conditions are so different. Many of our blunders in this region have resulted from the error of reasoning by false analogy—of applying lessons from another region (e.g., the North Atlantic) or another time (e.g., the 1930s) where they did not fit. The Vietnam story is a striking confrontation of fact and fiction. Not until March 1968 did President Johnson finally realize that he could not attain his objectives, so that belatedly he started the movement in reverse—from escalation to extrication. I shall discuss the problem by raising three questions: What is the true nature of the conflict? What brought us there? What are our real interests in that area?

Let me begin with some basic facts. We have been involved in the affairs of South Vietnam ever since the mid-fifties. It all started with economic and military assistance under President Eisenhower. Next, President Kennedy sent military personnel, called "advisors," numbering some 17,000 at the time of his assassination. Then early in 1965, a few months after being elected, President Johnson launched his policy of escalation, including systematic bombing of targets in North Vietnam. By the spring of 1969, some half-million Americans were stationed in South Vietnam. More than 30,000 young Americans are already dead. For over four years military operations have been conducted on a large scale by land, sea, and air. The cost, in the single year of 1968, has been placed at $30 billion. Our newspapers report that a greater tonnage of bombs was dropped on the adversary than on Germany in World War II. No contrast could be greater than that between the opponents, a traditional Asian society possessing for the most part a primitive technology and little modern industry, and ourselves who form the greatest concentration of power in the world. Nevertheless, despite such an effort, we have been unable thus far to bring these operations to a military conclusion. One naturally asks: why?

The answer, in my judgment, cannot be military. Purely in military terms, we should have won long ago. There has to be another explanation, which leaves only one possibility. It is political. Fundamentally, this is a conflict between several rival segments of Vietnamese. It consists, first, in a struggle for independence and unification and, second, in a civil war within a society which contains deep internal divisions and where the stakes are the form of government and social system to prevail in the future. These are the central aspects of the situation in Vietnam: nationalism and civil war. Into the depths of that swamp, our unwise government plunged gratuitously, dragging with it the American people.

When a government chooses to intervene, militarily and politically, in the affairs of another people who differ in civilization, race, and religion, as much as Asians do from Americans, there is one essential requirement for success. The intervention must be on the side of an indigenous regime whose authority is solidly based on adequate popular support. When that condition is absent, no outsider can attain his objectives. Unless he is prepared to resort to direct colonial rule, he cannot run the show himself. Nor can his fiat create those who will govern for him. What we did in Vietnam was to Americanize the war because of the incompetence of the South Vietnamese and the absence, after Diem's overthrow, of any government worthy of the name. As Westerners, we doomed ourselves to fight in the teeth of an Asian nationalism compounded by civil war. Thereby, we intensified the enmity of those we opposed, without really gaining the good will of those whom we backed. Too often, among their compatriots, the latter are branded as our puppets, which vitiates much of what they try to do.

Hence, due to a basic political miscalculation, all our programs, military and civil, have foundered on the same dilemma. Our avowed political aims—those of a limited war—restricted our military means, particularly because we dared not extend the arena or level of conflict to the point of directly challenging the Soviet Union or China; at the same time our military means have stultified our political ends. A staff officer of an allied army, himself friendly to the United States, said to me a year ago: "You cannot use tactical methods to rectify a strategic error." I agree, and would amplify his remark thus: you cannot use military means to rectify a political blunder. War is always a political act; when the politics are wrongly conceived, military victory is unattainable.

Now the second question: Why are we there? The short answer is that, as a people, we are the prisoners of the faulty ideas of a dead man, Mr. Dulles. He originally built this trap into which successive administrations fell ever deeper. Our intervention in the Vietnamese war has been justified by five principal arguments, which may be called the Five Fictions. Among these, two lines of reasoning stand out: one legal, the other political.

The legal case, or Fiction Number One, was regularly reiterated by Mr. Rusk. As he saw it, the government of State A, North Vietnam, committed aggression against the government of State B, South Vietnam, by sending men and supplies across an international frontier to overthrow its neighbor. "It is," we have all heard him say, "as simple as that." He asserted that we are committed to protect South Vietnam under the Southeast Asia Treaty and its connected Protocol and that this government honors its signature and fulfills its obligations. How simple it would be if that were always true! How deeply one wishes that were the case! Others, however, reading both the Geneva Agreement of 1954 and the Southeast Asia Treaty can draw quite opposite conclusions.

In the first place, the Geneva Agreement refers only to Vietnam. Nowhere does it name, or provide for, two separate states of North and South Vietnam divided by an international frontier. It does speak of two zones on each side of the truce line which marked the end of hostilities against the French, and it provided for free elections to be held in July, 1956, in both zones to establish a single government for the whole country. The Agreement was silent about how free elections could be held in the North. But the test of that point never came, because Diem, with our support, took measures to prevent elections in the South. This is no war between two states, but a civil war among a people who are emerging from a long period of colonial control by Chinese, French, and Japanese; who are not yet a nation; who have yet to organize a state; and who have been incapable in the South of establishing a competent government on a broad popular base.

Nor is our legal position stronger under the terms of the Southeast Asia Treaty. The true character of that "Alliance" is revealed in its membership. The parties were the United States, the United Kingdom, France, Australia, New Zealand, Pakistan, the Philippines, and Thailand. Of those eight, five were not Asian. Excluding China, of the other major countries of Asia (namely India, Pakistan, Japan and Indonesia) only Pakistan signed. In fact, the Treaty was plainly conceived to bolster up Western influence in Southeast Asia, and two of the three Asian countries which it did include, namely Pakistan and the Philippines, retain strong Western links. Politically therefore, SEATO was bound to run afoul of Asian nationalism and anticolonialism. Laos, Cambodia, and Vietnam are not parties to the Treaty, but its protection was extended in a separate Protocol to embrace their area. [2] Thus our Department of State has argued that by intervening in the war we are honoring our commitment.

What actually does the Treaty require? The document describes two situations when the parties are bound to render help to one another or to a protected government. One such situation arises in the event of "aggression by means of armed attack in the treaty area," in which case each member is obliged "to meet the common danger in accordance with its constitutional processes." What happened in South Vietnam was that successive Saigon "governments" were collapsing in 1964 under the blows of the Vietcong, and President Johnson after winning his election proceeded early in 1965 to Americanize the war. Only after he put our military forces into action in the South and began bombing in the North did North

---

[2] The Protocol, like the Geneva Agreement, does not recognize two separate Vietnamese states. What it mentions by name is "the free territory under the jurisdiction of the State of Vietnam."

Vietnam send its regular army units into the South. And so far from conforming to our "constitutional processes," our government never observed
that requirement. We have conducted a large-scale war which the President never requested the Congress to declare. What about the solemn
commitment of our elected officials to honor the Constitution? That pro-
vision was written by the founding fathers so as to prevent just such an
eventuality as that of a chief executive taking the country into war by his
unilateral decision and then confronting the Congress and the country
with the *fait accompli*.[3]

The other situation that can invoke the operation of the Treaty exists
whenever the integrity of a member is threatened by other means than
armed attack (internal subversion, for example). In that event, the only
obligation specified in the text is for the parties "to consult immediately in
order to agree on what measures to take." But when the Johnson administration decided to intervene in the war in January, 1965, no such consultation occurred. That was a strictly unilateral decision for which subsequent endorsement was sought—a way of behaving that was similar to the
Dominican intervention a few months later. The response of the other
Treaty members has shown what they thought of our action. Of the European countries, neither Britain nor France took any part whatsoever.
Australia and New Zealand have both contributed small forces—understandably, because they are paying the premium on their insurance policy
with the United States, which is the ANZUS Treaty. Where this country
leads, whether wisely or unwisely, they must follow. Of the three Asian
members, only Thailand and the Philippines are participating militarily
and, of course, both of their governments are heavily dependent on us.
Significantly, the lone major Asian signatory, Pakistan, refuses to involve
itself. President Ayub Khan, a professional soldier, has declared that if it is
the aim of the United States to prevent South Vietnam from becoming

---

[3] Those who take the Gulf of Tonkin resolution of August 7, 1964, as legal authority for President Johnson's military actions after January, 1965, should note these words of Senator Fulbright: "Many Senators who accepted the Gulf of Tonkin resolution without question might
well not have done so had they foreseen that it would subsequently be interpreted as a sweeping
Congressional endorsement for the conduct of a large-scale war in Asia. Literally, it can be so
interpreted, but it must be remembered that the resolution was adopted during an election campaign in which the President was telling the American people that it would be a mistake for the
United States to become involved in a major war in Asia while criticizing his opponent for
proposing just that." *The Arrogance of Power*, Random House, Vintage Book, New York, 1966,
p. 52.

Communist, the struggle could last for forty or fifty years. In short, SEATO is a farce. It is a flimsy device which our government has sought to adapt to our ends—not an organization with substance or an alliance with significance. The architects of an unwise policy cloaked their misconceptions of America's interests in the inappropriate language of honor and contract.

So, let us turn to considerations of interest and power, i.e. the political reasons advanced in favor of land warfare in Southeast Asia. A favorite argument in this category—it is Fiction Number Two on the list—is the "domino theory." The theory's major premise is that Southeast Asia is of vital interest to the United States; its minor premise is that the whole region stands or falls together. Whence the conclusion: we must shore up each piece, or all will come tumbling down and America's security will be imperiled. At their best, these are unproven and unprovable hypotheses. At the worst, they are pure fantasy. They are authoritatively asserted as if they were the truth, so that the onus of disproof is shifted to those who doubt them; whereas properly the burden of proof belongs with those who have proposed a doctrine so speculative and novel.

The belief that this entire region is a vital American interest, sufficient to have justified our large-scale intervention in land warfare, has been emphatically rejected by responsible authorities—political, diplomatic, and military.[4] Vital is no term to be used lightly. It should signify that if the balance of forces within an area is tilted adversely to the United States, our security is in danger. Certainly we have no material stake in Southeast Asia—property, investments, and so on—comparable to those which the British, Dutch, and French attempted in vain to defend. As for the assertion that Americans have to fight in South Vietnam in order not to fight at some future time in Hawaii or California, it is political rhetoric and particularly reprehensible when employed to order the needless deaths of young men. I shall argue later that the United States does have a permanent interest in maintaining preponderant power in the Pacific Ocean, which means, of course, that our links with island states are vital. But the logic of this reasoning stops just where the water ends and the land begins. The mainland portion of Southeast Asia is not vital to us in any directly meaningful sense. Indeed, I would state the contrary, that to have allowed

---

[4] To name a few: Senators Fulbright and Aiken, Ambassador Kennan, Mr. Lippmann, Generals Gavin and Shoup.

ourselves to be sucked into land warfare against Asians in Asia is harmful to our vital interests, since we weaken ourselves by an endless hemorrhage without gaining a commensurate benefit.

Similarly, for the thesis that all the pieces are interconnected and that as goes one so go all, the sensible answer is from *Porgy and Bess:* "It ain't necessarily so." In one instance, that of Indonesia, our officials tried to argue that its change of regime and the consequent swing from left to right were prompted and made possible by our stand in South Vietnam. But that is only one more myth out of the Washington wonderland. It was in fact vigorously repudiated by the Indonesian government and press, which insisted that their liquidation of local Communists was a domestic operation uninfluenced by our military stance.

Fiction Number Three derives from the contention that we must stop world communism and affirms that in Vietnam we have met and are blunting its spearhead. This is partly oversimplification and partly delusion. If true, it would presuppose a global conspiracy directed from one central source—something which had a foundation in fact during Stalin's lifetime and then survived in the dreamworld of Dulles.[5] The reality of the fifteen years from 1953 to 1968 was a widening of the split between the Communist states. If anything, however, has served in some limited degree to unite them, it has been our military intervention in South Vietnam which in this respect was counterproductive as in so many others. In any case, to the extent that what we are opposing is communism and to the extent that part of communism is its ideology, we cannot hope to combat it by military means. However, since what we have faced in Vietnam is as much a phenomenon of nationalism as of class conflict, it is doubly unfortunate for us that a Communist, Ho Chi Minh, has also been so effective a nationalist. We chose earlier to put our money on the French, who failed; then on Diem, who failed; and latterly on the Kys and Thieus, who would not be where they are without our tanks and dollars.

Fourth comes the fiction that our objective in South Vietnam is to contain China. The logic of this argument I have never grasped because I do not see how the means we employ will lead to that end. There is no

---

[5] Dulles phrased his dreams thus: liberate the oppressed peoples of Eastern Europe, unleash Chiang Kai-shek, massive retaliation, go up to the brink of war, conduct an agonizing reappraisal (of our relations with France). All this was empty rhetoric. In practice, he did nothing of the sort. One reappraisal was conducted, not by us but by de Gaulle—and we were the ones to be agonized.

disputing the fact that the present regime in China is abhorrent and repulsive to us. Mao's successors at some future date could menace our security. But even so, how in fact would they attack us? The Chinese can only reach the United States across the sea, by air, or through space. I fail to comprehend how our control of the area of South Vietnam would deny, or even discourage, their use of any of those three routes. Conversely, if we should ever need to defend ourselves by counterattack, it is not from sites in so vulnerable an area as South Vietnam that we would launch our missiles against China's industrial centers. In any future war with China, the one military use we could make of South Vietnam would be as a base for dispatching land forces into southern China. Whoever thinks that the way for us to defeat the Chinese would be by land warfare in Asia has lost touch with reality. It is political folly and strategically unsound to challenge an opponent on a terrain and under conditions where he possesses the maximum human and geographical advantages and where all the techniques and assets in our arsenal are deployed at their greatest disadvantage.

Finally, the Fifth Fiction is in the official mythology, which asserts that our action will prevent World War III, that we are doing in Southeast Asia what should have been done in Europe before 1938. Really, this is a classic example of the abuse of analogy. It consists in pretending to discover a parallel in another situation, whose accompanying conditions differ substantially, and then seeking to draw similar lessons from both. South Vietnam in the 1960s is not the Rhineland or Austria or Czechoslovakia of the thirties. Mao is not Hitler. The appeals and aims of Chinese communism are not those of nazism. The culture and technology of China are not those of Germany. Nor can South Vietnam be sensibly compared to Greece and Turkey in 1947, where again the circumstances differed. Those two countries had been long established and were viable entities. At least they had governments able to govern. Their national feelings drew the majority to our side and they share many of our values. Far from preventing the outbreak of World War III, our deepening involvement actually increased, instead of lessening, that danger.

The last point could be expanded at considerable length. So far from bringing any solid, measurable gain, the policy pursued in Vietnam since 1955, and particularly since 1965, has brought heavy and measurable loss. It is we, both at home and abroad, who are the losers. More than any foreign policy of recent times, that of President Johnson tore this country apart. Conscientious opposition has been voiced to a war which never commended itself to the good sense of a large section of the American people. To say and feel "my country, right or wrong" is not synonymous with "my government, right or wrong"—not in a democracy at any rate. Thus loyal and dedicated citizens have criticized a war in which they were never convinced that the United States had a vital interest. Nor for that matter was the public opinion of our friends on other continents persuaded of the merits of the Johnson-Rusk theses. Increasingly during the last four years, many who wish us well and who have willingly gone along with our leadership in the past, have been dismayed at our unwisdom. The reaction of some was ethical. They saw us as a giant trying to smash a dwarf into a pulp, none too successfully, and sympathy has gone to the dwarf. Others have had a political reaction. In their eyes, we just acted stupidly, since few were ever persuaded by the sophistries of the Five Fictions. The erosion of our prestige has been frighteningly rapid, especially in Europe where we most need respect and good will. In recent years I have heard repeatedly from responsible European leaders—persons who want and work for close ties with the United States—such remarks as: "Why don't you Americans learn from our mistakes in colonial policy? Why do you repeat them yourselves?"

That brings me to the question: What are our real interests in the area of Southeast Asia? I shall start from two axioms. First, we must never again allow ourselves to become overcommitted and pinned down in an area where our vital interests do not lie. Since 1965, because of the deep involvement in Vietnam, we have lacked adequate forces in immediate readiness to cope with emergencies elsewhere. What could we have done effectively during that time in Europe? Or the Middle East? Or in Latin America? Second, it makes absolutely no sense for Americans to collect and seek to salvage the wrecks of fallen empires—be they British, Dutch, French, or Japanese. When the political trends of this century were working against them—as Washington used continuously to preach in the nineteen-forties and fifties to the sinful imperialists of Western Europe—why should our officials now suppose that they would work for us? My point is that we, being what we are, cannot enter on a large scale such countries as those of Southeast Asia, being what they are, without recreating the essential relationship of an imperial power to a colony. Mask the reality by what disguises you will; the fact remains.

For a case history, look at the current situation in South Korea, where in 1968 violence continued to erupt along the frontier with the North. Korea is sometimes compared with Vietnam, and those who approved our decision to defend South Korea in the early fifties are asked to see South Vietnam in the same light. But again, the circumstances are different. In Korea there was a clear and unmistakable attack launched by regular forces from the North. This happened at a time when we were already stationed in the South because our forces had occupied that area when the Japanese surrendered. Hence we had no choice but to respond, and that response received the sanction and authority of the United Nations. Even so, take a glance at the present Korean situation, a decade and a half since hostilities ended. According to published figures, the South Koreans now have an army of 500,000 while we keep as many as 50,000 Americans alongside them. The North Korean army reportedly numbers 350,000 without any stiffening by Chinese or Russian troops. Why should the South Koreans, with such a numerical ratio in their favor, not yet be able to defend themselves without the presence of American personnel? How long do client relationships of this kind have to continue?[6] Do we have any real need to expose our personnel to incidents such as the capture of the *Pueblo?*

And *a fortiori*, what does anyone think will be the position in South Vietnam some five or fifteen years from now? In Paris since January, 1969, a delegation from the United States, the world's most powerful country, has been seated at a conference table with no less than three squabbling, mutually discordant groups of Vietnamese—and it was our government which unnecessarily involved the American people in their chaotic politics. What sort of sense does this make? That is not America's interest. For how long do we doom ourselves to pay for and prop up a regime in Saigon? Are we not retreading the old familiar tracks of bygone empires?

There is a logic in such questions which implies its own answer. The policy we pursued for the last fifteen years is now bankrupt. We should devise one which will work more to our interest by drawing a line where the political and strategic factors operate to our advantage. The question is: where?

[6] Equally unwise is our involvement in Thailand, where according to press reports another 50,000 Americans are now stationed. The Thai government is much resented in northern areas where another Vietnam may be brewing. Let the Thais defend themselves, with U.S. equipment.

It should be self-evident that our government was mistaken in trying to control positions on the Asian mainland. We have no business being there. On the mainland, we have no stake, no vital interest to ensure. But there is somebody else who does. It is the Soviet Union which has real stakes on the Asian continent and faces direct danger from Chinese territorial expansion. The Soviet Union has the need, which the United States does not, to establish a continental balance of power. One of the cruelest features of the blundering policy in Vietnam is that our government sent young Americans to fight and die for what are essentially Russian interests. That is a privilege we should have left to the Russians.

Now, what are America's interests? Our security is vitally concerned with the Pacific. We do need to retain a preponderant position throughout the ocean up to the edges of the Asian coastline, and technically this is more manageable for us than to control a slice of the continent. Even in this age of air and space power, seapower continues to make a difference, and its advantages are decidedly ours. If possible, we should retain alliances—and, hopefully, active friendships—with all the island states. However, this does not mean that every single island state must always remain in alliance with us and may never withdraw. It would be politically counterproductive for us to restage in the Pacific Ocean an American version of Russia's occupation of Czechoslovakia. It is preponderance we need, not monopoly.

Having drawn such a line, we should seek to exploit the division between the two great states with Communist governments. As a clue to the making of an intelligent policy, let me quote from that master of *realpolitik*, Bismarck. When the French in the 1880s were embarking on colonial expansion in North Africa, Bismarck, rather than opposing, encouraged them. A friend, reminding the Chancellor that the French were burning for revenge against Germany, inquired why he did so. The reply was a piece of classic statecraft: "I have sent the fiery steed of French ambition galloping into the sands of North Africa. They will find it heavy going." His prediction, seventy years later, proved to be correct. If we had more sagacity at the top of our State Department, this is what we would have tried to encourage, since it is always in one's diplomatic interest to help a competitor into situations which will only cause him trouble. The unwise are those who gratuitously grab the trouble for themselves, which has been our government's policy. Our aim should be to entice the Russians into the region where we have adventured. The jungles, swamps, and mountains of

Vietnam belong to the Bear, not to the Eagle. After all, there is a genuine Russian interest in securing positions in the rear of the Chinese so as to challenge them from both sides.

I would therefore hope that, as the negotiations in Paris lead to a planned withdrawal of American forces from Vietnam, we would welcome the introduction of a multinational peace-keeping force. This should include not only Asian units from countries which have not been engaged in the war, but also contingents from the Soviet Union and Eastern Europe. It is America's interest ·to help the Russian Bear encircle the Chinese Dragon. Meanwhile on the mainland, our policy should be to assist selected governments with dollars and equipment only. The principal recipient of such help, of course, has to be India. For the rest, among the island states we must recognize the reality of the resurgence of Japan. At present, like West Germany, Japan has strength without power. But its power will come, and it will be felt in the seventies when the Japanese economy will have developed into the third strongest in the world. At that point, a new era will open in Japan's relations with the United States. It is the mutual interest of both that these be cooperative and friendly.

American concern with the Pacific and Soviet concern with the Asian mainland suggest, for that hemisphere, a possible division of spheres of interest appropriate to the vital needs of the two superpowers. But any arrangement for coexistence on that side of the world requires a parallel understanding in Europe where both are also involved. So let us now consider what American policy has been, and should be, in the Atlantic region.

There is no question in my mind that of the three areas with which the vital interests of the United States are linked externally—the North Atlantic, Latin America, and the Pacific—the first of these is first in priority. Now and in the future, the prime objective of our statecraft should be to develop the closest practicable relationship with the peoples and governments of Canada and Western Europe. Indeed, I would assert this axiom for the foreign policy of the United States: Any American policy which reinforces our links with Western Europe is justified in terms of American interests. Conversely, no American policy elsewhere in the world can be justified if it tends to weaken those links. The reasons for this can be simply stated. Foremost of all is the fact that the peoples of Western Europe and Canada belong to the same civilization as ourselves. When we associate with them, and they with us, it is in order to preserve jointly the values that make us what we are. Hence it must always be our top external priority to cooperate with them as intimately as possible. In the future, the destinies of Western Europe and North America will continue to be linked in a special relationship just as they have been in the past. This is not only the consequence of history, culture, and geography; even if we wished, we could not ignore the current realities of world politics and economics. We and the Canadians need an association with Western Europe because that area constitutes in its own right a tremendous center of actual and future power—industrial, scientific, technological, and political. Together, Western Europe and North America can reinforce one another in a world where long-term population trends are decidedly disadvantageous to us.

The truth that the security of the United States is connected, mutually, with that of Western Europe has received formal recognition in the North Atlantic Treaty. Since the United States had twice within a quarter of a century become a participant in World Wars originating in whole or in part in Europe, it was understandable that U.S. public opinion and political parties after 1945 should accept the notion of organizing collectively to prevent a future recurrence of the same. Had Great Britain and the United States given clear, public warning before 1914 that they would oppose any act of military aggression in Western Europe, it is virtually certain that the German government would not have gambled on invading Belgium and Northern France. Had the United States made it unequivocally clear to Hitler prior to 1938 that if he sent his panzer divisions across European frontiers the United States would definitely intervene to oppose him, World War II in Europe would most probably have been averted. This reasoning underlay the provisions of the North Atlantic Treaty signed in April 1949, when Western Europe once again confronted a clear and present danger. That danger was present after the coup by the Communist Party in Czechoslovakia in 1948, an event whose stage managing was quite reminiscent of Hitler, and to anybody who had eyes to see, the danger was clear again in June 1950, after North Korea attacked South Korea. All that it then required was one signal from Stalin to launch a similar movement from East Germany westward. Hence the North Atlantic Treaty rapidly evolved into an Organization—the "O" in NATO, which the French like to emphasize—and the NATO shield was constructed.

Now, twenty years after, we are in a position to appraise its results and thence to make some guesses about the future. Assuredly in terms of its initial objective—to deter an armed attack on Western Europe and

North America—NATO has been a success. At any rate, no such attack was attempted, and it is reasonable to hold that this has been due in no small part to the existence of both the Treaty and its Organization. Indeed, so strongly has the sense of security grown latterly in Western Europe that various groups[7] within some of NATO's member states have been increasing their opposition to the Treaty. Moreover, in the case of France, a government withdrew from military participation in the Organization and peremptorily ordered NATO's military headquarters off French soil.[8] A few years ago, it was not uncommon in Western Europe to hear NATO dismissed as "an alliance in search of an enemy."

But the events of 1967-1968 have done much to modify this attitude. The two new realities are the continued presence of a significant Soviet fleet in the Mediterranean and the occupation of Czechoslovakia in August 1968 by Warsaw Pact forces, including—blunder of blunders!—troops from East Germany. The Soviet fleet, sailing the waters of the Romans' *mare nostrum*, has reawakened concern in Italy and Greece for NATO ties, while the military suppression of a liberalizing Czech regime has sent a shock wave pulsating throughout the West. For the immediately foreseeable future the argument is irrefutable that the military defenses of the North Atlantic region will have to be maintained until a general plan for disarmament can be negotiated and mutually enforced. Since national defenses are no defense, a single integrated supranational system is required; and this, to be effective, should be organized for purposes of insurance in advance against the events which it is designed to prevent. The Gaullist contention that one can safely defend oneself by an independent national force fails for this reason: Such a force cannot be a credible deterrent to a would-be aggressor because to build it nowadays to a level of credibility would overstrain the means of any state except a superpower. What happened in France in May-June and November of 1968 supplies some evidence on this point. Had the French government devoted less of its re-

[7] The reference here is to non-Communist groups. The opposition of Communist groups is, of course, taken for granted.

[8] General de Gaulle did not withdraw, however, from the Treaty, which legally he could not do before April, 1970 at the earliest. Contrary to what one often hears or reads, the North Atlantic Treaty does not expire in 1969. All that happens in this year is that Article 13 comes into force, permitting any member to give notice of its intention to leave the alliance. The departure would then come into effect twelve months after such notice has been given. For those who do not take this step, however, the Treaty continues in force indefinitely.

sources to nuclear nationalism and the pursuit of prestige, it might have alleviated much of the pent-up discontent whose explosion so weakened France internationally and then compelled cuts in the atomic program itself. And *a fortiori*, what is true of a medium-rank power is truer still of one yet smaller. Even if the Czechs in 1968 had had some rockets and nuclear bombs of their own, surely no one supposes in view of their geography that their allies would have been deterred from invading them.

But saying that national systems of defense in Europe can scarcely be credible does not solve the genuine difficulty to which these are addressed. Granted that the contemporary technology of military security requires ever broader integration of peoples, areas, and resources, one comes back to the stubborn facts inherent in the North Atlantic alliance: namely, that it is constituted as an alliance of the governments of separate nation-states, some of which are understandably reluctant to surrender to another the decisions on which their survival may depend. Such considerations are a blend of the political and psychological. NATO remains the cornerstone on which the external military and political relationships of the United States are built, and within it we are the leader. But, thus far, we have not succeeded in solving the political problems generated by the dynamics of this essential alliance.

The crux of the matter is the inequality of the allies. This grouping of fifteen is strangely composed in that the military strength of one exceeds the combined strength of fourteen, and owing to this disproportion the Organization functions under evident strain. Thus diplomatic formulae which proclaim equality of status, or which announce the right of all to participate jointly in decisions, do not square with basic realities. The United States, of course, can lead unilaterally, in which case the only certainty is that criticisms will be forthcoming. For their part, our allies can debate—which they do. But they can decide nothing unless at least Great Britain, France, and Germany agree, and even if they should agree, they lack at present the wherewithal to lead or act effectively without us. The result, almost inevitably, has been a tendency for several members of the alliance to go their own ways in pursuit of what they conceive (or misconceive) to be their vital interests—as did Britain and France at Suez, France in Algeria, Belgium in the Congo, the United States in Cuba and the Dominican Republic and Vietnam—and then to be pained when allies have expressed displeasure.

When seeking escape from these dilemmas, many take refuge in the idea of consultation as the magic formula whereby the needs of all can be incorporated into the process of decision. But since a right to be consulted is not the same as a capacity to act, the faith in that formula, though it will work in some instances, is bound to give disappointment in others. For at the core of the issue is the very character of NATO—a defensive regional alliance organized with much more structure than any previous grouping in modern peacetime history. [9] Politically it represents a stage in the journey from separate nation-states to a possible supranational entity, along which road no halfway house is ever an endurable resting-place.

From this point, the path to the future could fork off in any of four directions. One of these is the road back whence we came. It takes us to the revival of nationalism, the reassertion of "sovereign" independence, the refusal to organize collectively for preventing disaster before it arrives. This is the Gaullist road. In the first half of this century, it led two generations into two World Wars. Why then retrace it?

A second route is to follow the leader, to accept the power of the strongest, to go wherever Washington beckons. Substantially that was what happened in the fifties when Western Europe and Canada acquiesced in American initiatives and leadership, albeit with muttering and grumbling at times. But we are now about to enter the decade of the seventies. This emergent Europe—thanks to the efforts both of Europeans and of North Americans—is no longer that Europe. And in any case, after witnessing our policy in Vietnam, Western Europeans will certainly sign no blank checks to join us in global adventurism. They have grown too skeptical of the wisdom of Washington.

A third route avoids detours and brings us directly by a quick shortcut to a supranational authority, the region-state of the Atlantic peoples. This would eventually mean transferring the power to provide for the common defense to an agency common to North America and Western Europe. For the institutions to bring this about, we have no lack of models at hand. They already exist in the principles of federal union whose practice this country invented. Is the majority of the American people yet ready for such a step? Specifically, would the Congress agree to relinquish unilateral

[9] An ancient parallel is the Confederacy of Delos, organized and led by the Athenians in 477 B.C. after the repulse of the Persian invasion. But that came to a sticky end.

control over America's nuclear arsenal? We cannot expect others to take this step if we are not prepared to take it ourselves.

The fourth route is that of partnership. Its goal is a United States of Western Europe linked to North America with enough of a structure to execute policies formulated in common. The principal argument in its favor for Europeans is that this alone ensures equality with the United States. Since states of medium size—such as Great Britain, France, Italy, and West Germany—cannot separately attain equality with a superpower, they could do so if they were united with one another and with their smaller neighbors. The obstacle to this does not come from the United States, which ever since the inception of the Marshall Plan has steadily encouraged all programs leading to the integration of Western Europe. It comes, of course, from President de Gaulle who employs the language of Europe as a symbol to cloak what he intends as a French hegemony. Although he urges independence of American power, he resists that consolidation of Western Europe through which alone the power of the United States can be equalled.

Of the four routes, I rule out the first as potentially destructive for all, and the second as unrealistic because it is no longer acceptable to our allies. That leaves open either the third route or the fourth. The former will require that we too abandon some nationalism of our own in the interests of a wider interdependence. The fourth must obviously await the departure of de Gaulle from active political life.

The choice between the two latter routes makes overt an ambiguity which has been latent in American policy towards Europe ever since 1947. For two decades we have given our blessing both to Western European integration and to Atlantic union. Evidently we assumed that the twain are compatible. One could be in favor of uniting Western Europe and also for uniting it with North America, without either foreclosing the other. Gaullism has at least accomplished this much: it shattered the facile belief that these aims were necessarily harmonious. Had the General been less of a French nationalist, he could conceivably have been the leader of a European movement functioning separately from, and in opposition to, North America. Nor is it impossible that some other statesman of Western Europe might seek this role.

For the United States, as well as Canada, the weightiest issues revolve around the answer to the question posed in recent years on the other side of the ocean: Can you be both European and Atlantic, or must you choose to be one or the other? The difference goes deep to the roots of Western culture. "Either. . .or" expresses the Cartesian logic of the French; "both. . .and" is the pragmatic empiricism of the English speaking. American diplomacy, as should be evident, has to argue "both. . .and." We must contend for the Atlantic association because our security and prosperity are so vitally connected with those of Western Europe—and theirs, as we believe, with ours. At the same time, precisely because we admire the traditions and cultures of the peoples of Europe and because we respect their sense of pride and dignity, we should prefer a partnership with equals to a hegemony over dependents. It is thus that we can understand the message which Servan-Schreiber conveys in his book, *The American Challenge.* His advice to fellow Europeans is to reorganize their economies, as well as their social and political structures, so as to utilize the potentialities of the new technology. For the fact that American corporations have exploited some of these possibilities in Western Europe more speedily than Europeans have done, he blames not the Americans but the Europeans. His argument, in essentials, is not hostile to the United States, but rather a tribute to this country's effective pioneering. To Europeans he is saying: "Learn enough from America to be equal and to do the same."

The concept, however, of a Western Europe united within an Atlantic union contains another implication for American policy of which we should be explicitly aware. De Gaulle has dreamed of a Europe extending from the Atlantic to the Urals. This appealed to many Europeans who resented that manifestation of the cold war—a political line bisecting the continent from north to south. To reknit the severed limbs of Europe, thus permitting easy circulation east and west, was indeed a design grand enough to compete with the alternatives of the superblocs. For several years, the General made some mileage with that diplomacy. But, like Napoleon's *Grande Armée,* it died in Moscow.[10] The invasion of Czechoslovakia in August 1968 by the Soviet Union and its allies in the Warsaw Pact, plus the continued military occupation since that date, have shattered the Gaullist offensive. From 1964 to 1968 there was considerable progress towards an east-west *détente,* and these moves were initiated independently by the French, Germans, and Italians at a time when the United States, hopelessly bogged down in Vietnam, was incapacitated, morally and diplomatically, from effective action in the area where our most vital interests lie.

---

[10] Did he ever seriously expect the Russians to relinquish what they hold east of the Urals?

The Russian action in Czechoslovakia was thus a significant turning-point. What it has done is both to alter the perspective and redefine the context of future east-west relations. The Russian position in the center and east of Europe is stronger in the short run, although it may have been weakened over the long. The present Kremlin leaders have put everybody on notice that they will not tolerate a significant degree of internal liberal-ization—political, economic, or cultural—in any country within their sphere of influence. There will be no more Yugoslavias if they can prevent it. Thereby they indicate their determination to sit on the lid, even at the expense of holding down some resentful fellow-Slavs and national Commu-nists. Ultimately, this decision is more a sign of weakness than of strength because it reveals an awareness among Soviet ruling circles of how brittle is the structure of their own domestic power. But for the time being, irre-spective of the folly or wisdom of their policy, they possess the definite means to make it stick.

In the light of these events and their political aftermath, the questions for American policy-makers are these: What deductions should we draw from their action and how can we turn it to our benefit? The truly signifi-cant point for us to grasp is the meticulous emphasis of the Russians that Eastern Europe was their sphere of influence, that they were confining their intervention to their side of the line, and that we should stick to our side. In other words, the Russians were behaving aggressively within their own alliance, but defensively from the standpoint of ours. Let us take it from there, because in this situation is a possible advantage for us which we should be astute enough to seize. It is our interest, as I have argued earlier, to encourage the Soviet Union to cope effectively with Chinese expansionism on the Asian mainland, as it is equally our interest to see the two major exponents of Communist power devoting their energies to one another. But the Soviet Union, spreading from Eastern Europe all across Asia, must always think of its two fronts. It cannot deploy sufficient force, political or military, against China if it feels insecure in the rear. And this is where we come in. It is in our interest to offer the Soviet Union assur-ances that if they focus their activity on their Asian problem we shall see to it that their defenses in Europe will be undisturbed. We shall stick to our side of the line in central Europe while they deal with the Chinese, whether in the northeast of the Asian mainland or the southeast.

That brings the argument straight back to the future relevance of NATO and our role therein. Again, this is where we differ radically, and must differ, from de Gaulle. He has propounded the idea of a series of bilateral arrangements between individual countries, west and east, including the Soviet Union itself. The disadvantage here is that it opens the way to all manner of separate relationships where every single country, whether small or medium, is going to be played off against every other—a return, in point of fact, to the inadequate system of the eighteenth and nineteenth centuries. The one reliable way to arrange an agreement between east and west is to organize it collectively. We need a revitalized NATO as the appropriate instrument for negotiating and enforcing a system of mutual security and *détente* with the countries of the Warsaw Pact. Then we can say to Moscow: "Go east, and good luck!"

Whether NATO, besides it military and diplomatic roles, can be developed in the future to meet our other vital needs in the Atlantic region is an open question. Because its immediate task was to defend the west in the period of intense cold war, NATO early received an imprint which was heavily military. It has ringed the North Atlantic region with a protective shield, but has not set out to organize an (or, is it "the"?) Atlantic Community. The social and cultural ideals expressed in the Treaty's preamble and in Article 2 have not been vigorously pursued. Neither in spirit nor letter do the present governments of Greece and Portugal conform to the professed values of the alliance; and Turkey, although westernized, belongs to the Islamic civilization. The economic goals of the Treaty were left to OEEC, the organization for the Marshall Plan. Since then, the notion of transatlantic economic cooperation has been the responsibility of OECD whose membership has been broadened to include the neutrals of Western Europe and also Japan, while economic union within Europe belongs to EEC and EFTA.

Undoubtedly, America's vital interests require a close continuing association, both economic and cultural, with our partners in Western Europe, an association which cannot be truly effective unless it be institutionalized. This is why for the United States the country with the key role to play in the Atlantic region is Great Britain. The British are both European and Atlantic. They form the natural bridge between the two continents. This is exactly why de Gaulle has banned them from the Common Market, whose future significance the British government of the mid-fifties was too myopic to foresee. Hence the United States and Great Britain are in fact linked in a special relationship where their vital interests mutually coincide.

As for the eastern perimeter of Western Europe, the German situation has to be faced—and faced realistically. During the fifties and the early sixties, the attitude of Germany's major allies—our own government included—was one of double-talk. Officially they were on record in favor of reunification. In practice, they did nothing to bring it about, and could do nothing in the teeth of Soviet opposition. The plain truth was that public opinion outside Germany did not wish to see the two parts rejoined, and the official postures of western governments were often at variance with what they privately felt. In Eastern Europe, for obvious reasons, these feelings were as strong as in the west, if not stronger. Indeed, one can argue that the United States and the Soviet Union acted in this matter on parallel lines from a sense of common need to maintain the division. Were the two segments of Germany to be reunited, the power thus formed would be too great to be neutralized or bound permanently by treaties of limitation which some future German government could, if it chose, repudiate. A reunited Germany would once again determine the balance of the European continent. If it swung to our side, Russian security would be gravely threatened. If it swung east, our vital interests would suffer. This was a risk which neither Washington nor Moscow could contemplate. Hence for identical reasons, we have sought to link West Germany to ourselves, as Russia has done with the East. By now, even in West Germany, opinion is divided over the merits of being reunited. There are many, particularly among the post-Nazi generation, who shrink from the prospect of reabsorbing East Germany as it has developed under the odious Ulbricht regime, although understandably they desire the freer movement of persons east and west. It is America's interest, therefore, to foster the closest connection with West Germany inside a system flexible enough to be both Atlantic and European.

In addition to the North Atlantic and the Pacific Ocean, the third region of vital concern to the United States is Latin America. This is the unavoidable result of the fact of geographical proximity. Viewed in geopolitical terms, Latin America is "the soft underbelly"[11] of the United States. Latin and English-speaking Americans are neighbors in the same hemisphere. Because the former lag behind in social, economic, and political

[11] The phrase is Churchill's. He referred to Italy in World War II as "the soft underbelly of the Axis."

development, the United States is, or ought to be, concerned with this area for reasons both of altruism and self-interest. The great majority of the countries in Central and South America have never yet passed through the kind of revolution which makes the difference between a modern people and a traditional one. Evidence of modernization, of course, abounds throughout Latin America. But generally these are isolated oases—or, to change the metaphor, a thinly spread veneer—in whose benefits the mass of the population share too little. The social structure and, with it, the economic system and prevailing political order are pyramids rising to a sharply tapered apex. Naturally, therefore, Latin America is explosive. The entire area seethes with the forces of change, while in one country after another repressive authoritarian regimes (many of them military) attempt to maintain control.

The United States is linked to Latin America by commerce and a considerable body of investment. A cultural connection also exists, but this is not as close as with Europe for the simple reason that most of the North American culture does not derive from the Iberian peninsula. Contractually, our bonds with our neighbors to the south are written into the Rio Treaty of Reciprocal Assistance (1947) and the Charter of the Organization of American States (1948). The inter-American system has developed a political arm, which has a skeleton but little muscle. The military arrangements do not even begin to compare with NATO. In this case, the contrast between the overwhelming superiority of one country and the inferiority of the rest is too glaring to make alliance or reciprocity meaningful. The political interest of the United States in what takes place in the Caribbean and south of the Rio Grande can be expressed in minimal terms, thus: We would never want to see the overall balance of forces in Latin America tilted adversely to ourselves.

Granted that the Americas are permanently joined in an inescapable nexus, it is indeed surprising that Latin America has not held a higher position in the external priorities of the United States. Instead of placing this connection where it should be—second only to Western Europe—we have generally neglected it, and in my judgment we neglect it at our peril. Indeed we only begin paying it attention when something unusual happens which we do not understand and, instinctively, do not like—the revolution in Cuba, for example. Moreover, of the aid which has been given to this region too much continues to be military and too much has been given to governments which persistently disregard the legitimate needs of their poor and underprivileged. More than one military *coup d'état* has been conducted there with equipment which we supplied. The Batistas we are able to swallow, and habitually we do business with them. A Castro, however, we cannot stomach, and similarly we draw the line at a "Papa Doc."

In our relations with Latin America during the last decade we have been obsessed with the fear that Castro's style of revolution might spread. Consequently, our government has opposed any drift to the left in which it thought it detected the possibility of another Cuba. This, I suppose, explains, although I would deny that the circumstances justified, the military intervention by President Johnson in the internal affairs of the Dominican Republic in April, 1965. Where much still remains obscure[12] about that operation, one aspect is abundantly clear. That intervention was in direct violation of the treaties we had signed. Our government did not honor its commitments in the Dominican case. It broke them.

The announced pretext for intervening was the need to protect American lives and property during a tense internal struggle for power. The real reason appears to have been—as resulted in point of fact—to prevent Juan Bosch from regaining power and to ensure the installation of a group oriented more towards the right.[13] But irrespective of motive, our government's action was in any case prohibited by Articles 15 and 17 of the Charter of the Organization of American States. Nor can it be upheld under the Rio Treaty. Article 6 of the latter agreement allows for collective assistance to any state whose political independence is threatened by other means than those of armed aggression. In these cases, however, the parties are required to consult immediately with one another in order to agree on what measures to take. No such prior consultation was initiated or requested by the United States. Instead, President Johnson ordered this mil-

---

[12] For instance, no convincing evidence has yet been made public to support the belief that the government was likely to fall into Communist hands.

[13] On this topic, Senator Fulbright has written: "Four months later, after an exhaustive review of the Dominican crisis by the Senate Foreign Relations Committee meeting in closed sessions, it was clear beyond reasonable doubt that although saving American lives may have been a factor in the decision to intervene on April 28, the major reason was a determination on the part of the United States government to defeat the rebel, or constitutionalist, forces whose victory at that time was imminent. Had I known in April what I knew in August, I most certainly would have objected to the American intervention in the Dominican Republic." *The Arrogance of Power*, Random House, Vintage Book, New York, 1966, pp. 49-50.

itary intervention unilaterally. Only afterwards was the OAS consulted—so as to approve the *fait accompli.* Some units were then dispatched to the Dominican Republic from other American Republics at the expense of the United States, and a Brazilian[14] was eventually designated as commander to lend the whole operation a pan-American camouflage.

This episode is of interest for many reasons. It was conducted by an Administration which, seeking simultaneously to justify its military operations in Vietnam, proclaimed repeatedly that the United States was honoring its commitments to Saigon. Even if the latter point were true, a contention I have sought to refute, the Dominican intervention flagrantly belies the argument. Moreover, in August 1968 our government condemned the invasion of Czechoslovakia, which plainly violated both the Preamble and Article 8 of the Warsaw Pact. Washington did in fact apply a double standard during the years from 1965 to 1968. It broke its commitments to Latin America while it professed to be honoring its commitments in Southeast Asia. It condemned the Soviet Union for occupying Czechoslovakia and molding the politics of that government, but asserted its own right to occupy the Dominican Republic and mold their government to our liking. One cannot have it both ways. If one approves what Mr. Johnson did in the latter case, one should condone what Messrs. Brezhnev and Kosygin did in the former. But if one condemns the Soviet action, one should be consistent and condemn the action of the United States. For in essentials, the two were alike. The latter judgment, incidentally, is widely held in Latin America, where in the long run our return to the interventionism so freely practised before 1933 will probably prove counterproductive to our interests.[15]

In the framework which has been sketched out here, I have concentrated on what appears essential. Various topics were therefore omitted because, although important, they are not vital. The essentials are to draw the line of our security within the limits of our needs and power, and then arrange our priorities according to our interests. Neither the Middle East nor Africa has figured in the discussion because, important though they

[14] Brazil was governed at that time by a military junta to which we were supplying financial and other assistance.

[15] Instances in the nineteen-fifties and sixties have been Guatemala, Cuba, and the Dominican Republic.

are, neither is vital to American security. In the former region, we certainly have a moral obligation to see that Israel survives; in helping the Israelis defend themselves, we have the cogent political reason that the Arabs side actively with the Russians. Now that Soviet fleets are sailing the Indian Ocean and the Mediterranean, we should be in no hurry to see the Suez Canal reopened. Israel manifestly needs no manpower from the United States. Our assistance there should be confined to equipment. With this in their hands, the Israelis are quite capable of looking after themselves.

In Africa, the case is different. There, the crying need is for economic and social development—in which so much has to be done that whatever aid one supplies can never suffice. Of recent years, our international aid programs, in the form of economic and technical assistance, have declined except in Southeast Asia. The decline has been both absolute, as represented in the amounts appropriated annually, and relative, expressed as a percentage of our gross national product. Among the international comparisons, we continue to be the world's largest donor to less developed countries. But in relative terms, the French ranked first in 1968 and we were tenth. At present, our aid has fallen below the 1 percent of gross national product which UNCTAD has suggested as a target. For the future, our total contribution should be increased and should be distributed as far as possible through UN or regional agencies and less through bilateral programs.

Public opinion in the United States has reacted unfavorably in recent years to the aid program in general, and congressional cuts have reflected this reaction. The reasons are not unfounded. Too much of this aid has been abused by the corrupt or wasted by the incompetent. Moverover, in some situations, aid has initiated a tangle of involvements eventually ending up with a Vietnam. This national mood to lessen the volume of external aid is linked with the realization by the American people that much is wrong with our society at home and that our urgent priority is to set our own house in order. Such feelings have been deepened by the sheer vexations of de Gaulle and utter frustration at the futility of the Vietnamese morass. The danger is that these understandable reactions could run to excess and result in a neo-isolationism. If this should be the immediate first consequence of reversing the recent spate of interventionism, one would not be altogether surprised. But it can never be too strongly emphasized that a neo-isolationism is no solution to our present problems. It is neither viable nor desirable. For a superpower no such escape route is open. The whole theme of this essay is a plea for a balanced view of our interests, for active involvement and creative leadership where they are vital, but for restraining ourselves elsewhere.

At a ceremony in Rome more than twenty-one centuries ago, when Cato was ending his term as censor, the public clerk read aloud the traditional prayer, beseeching the gods to grant that the Roman Republic would continue to grow. Cato stopped him, and prayed instead that Rome be allowed to stay within the limits it had reached. May we in the American Republic likewise understand our interests, priorities, and limits. Thus may our foreign policy become successful and solvent.

4

A New

Recognition Policy

for the United States

Ernst B. Haas

I. RECOGNITION IN INTERNATIONAL RELATIONS

A. What is "Recognition"?

Recognition is the formal act whereby an established government makes known its intention of maintaining normal diplomatic relations with a new state or a new government. Recognition implies that treaties can be concluded between the established and the new entities; that travel can take place freely among them; that trade can be undertaken by private and public agencies; that the nationals of the two countries can freely sue and be sued in the courts of both; that judgments will be executed; and that contracts are binding. Recognition, in short, is the preliminary formal step making possible the initiation (or continuation) of normal and peaceful relations among the nationals and public agencies of both countries.

Diplomatic practice considers the accreditation of ambassadors, or the expressed intention of doing so, as the final formal act whereby recognition is granted. Other expressions of the desire to recognize may precede it, such as a diplomatic note, an official statement, or an assurance expressed in the United Nations. Whether the presence of consuls and other lesser diplomatic agents, the maintaining of "unofficial" contacts, or the tacit continuation in force of earlier treaties also constitute acts of recognition is a moot question. Recognition is a political, not a legal, act. But it undoubtedly brings with it very important legal consequences.

An established state has three choices when confronted with the presence of a new entity—state or government. It may extend recognition without special negotiations or assurances from the new entity ("automatic recognition"); it may extend recognition after conducting special negotiations and seeking special assurances ("conditional recognition"); or it may, after failing to receive the assurances sought or after deciding that the new entity is wholly unpalatable, refuse to extend recognition ("nonrecognition").

What is it that makes recognition and national recognition policy such a bone of contention? Very often, recognition shades easily into intervention, or at least it is perceived by the parties as amounting to an act of intervention. In the case of civil war, for instance, the recognition of the insurgent regime by third countries is always considered an act of intervention by the established government. Hence the U.S. government exerted itself mightily, between 1861 and 1865, to forestall the recognition of the Confederacy by the European powers and threatened Great Britain with various measures if that nation carried its friendly relations with the Confederacy to the point of recognition. Conversely, the continued recognition of the former government after the insurgents have won military victory and have succeeded in establishing themselves is invariably regarded as intervention by them. The case of China at the moment illustrates this condition. It appears that whether we recognize or fail to do so, somebody is bound to consider action and inaction as constituting intervention.

The reasons are both legal and political. International law contains rules involving the rights of "insurgents" which are triggered when a third country "recognizes" the rebels. Further, at a certain stage the insurgent group may begin to enjoy "belligerent rights" triggering the international law of neutrality and limiting the freedom of maneuver of the established government in conducting military operations against the rebels. "Insurgency" and "belligerency," while legal categories, are called into being in a concrete situation by acts of external recognition. These acts are, or may be, political judgments on the part of third countries. They may be designed to aid the rebels or to hinder them. They are bound to be perceived as political or military intervention by somebody.

One historical case, among many similar ones, illustrates the difficulty. In 1926, there occured a disputed election in Nicaragua. The Conservative Party's candidate, Adolfo Díaz, appeared as the successor to a staunch friend of the United States, outgoing President Emiliano Chamorro. The opposition Liberal Party's candidate, Juan Sacasa, had close ties with the Mexican Government. His victory was interpreted by everybody as a victory for Mexican influence and interests in Central America over those of the United States. The disputed election led to civil strife, with Mexico recognizing the Sacasa forces as "the government" and the United States recognizing Díaz. In order to forestall a military victory by the Liberals, U.S. Marines were landed and fought to cement the power of the Díaz "government." The intervention, of course, lasted until 1933.

B. When is Recognition an Issue?

In a slowly changing situation, nationally and internationally, the issue of criteria regarding when and how to recognize does not often arise. Recognition policy becomes a vital issue only when there are rapid internal changes in many countries, posing uncomfortable problems of adjustment for the older and established nations. The burning issue for the United States today is China: Should we abandon the recognition of the defeated regime (and perhaps recognize it as the new state of Taiwan)? Should we admit that the Peking regime effectively rules China and swallow our distaste for the policies it follows and the values it professes?

My point is that this issue is as old as the industrial revolution and the surge of national self-consciousness. It helps us understand the China issue if we remember that this is merely the burning current example of a problem which has a continuous history dating back to the beginning of the nineteenth century. Following the Congress of Vienna (1815), the major powers of Europe faced the constant problem of whether to recognize new states and governments which arose contrary to the ideological and territorial dispositions made at Vienna. Revolutions in Greece and Belgium posed the issue of new states claiming recognition: if Greece were to be recognized, the "legitimate" rights of Turkey would be infringed; if Belgium were to be accorded recognition, what about the rights of the king of the Netherlands? Civil war in Spain and unrest in Germany created problems of recognizing insurgent regimes. By 1830, the earlier agreement not to recognize such challenges to the system established in 1815 had given way to conditional recognition.

Latin America illustrates the same issue. The successful revolutions against Spain in the early decades of the nineteenth century posed the problem of recognition for the United States and for the European powers. The United States bid first with a policy of automatic recognition; Britain followed; the remaining European countries felt unable to accept the affront to Spain implied in their recognizing the new Latin American states and delayed their eventual acts of recognition by several years. Finally, the continuing unrest in the Balkans during most of the nineteenth century highlighted the problems of national self-determination and recognition. The Ottoman Empire was recognized as the legitimate ruler over what came to be Bulgaria, Rumania, Serbia, and Albania. When revolts occurred, which party was to be accorded recognition? No clear policy was followed by any major power at that time and conditional recognition competed with nonrecognition, depending on whether the powers favored Turkey, Russia, or Austria-Hungary in the politics of the Balkans.

For the United States the continuing issue came to be Central America and the Caribbean, where no government seemed to enjoy popular support for any length of time and where civil strife seemed endemic. "To recognize" came to imply "to support"; to withhold recognition, to punish. Crises in Haiti, Cuba, Santo Domingo, Honduras, Guatemala, and Nicaragua involved these choices from 1898 until 1932. Mexican-American relations from 1910 to 1923 epitomize the issue. A nationalist, reformist, and xenophobic revolt engulfed Mexico in 1910. American-owned mining property was threatened with expropriation and American investment with discriminatory legislation. American nationals were in personal danger. Some thought that American military and diplomatic predominance in the Caribbean was threatened by a stridently anti-American Mexican revolutionary movement. Should Washington recognize the successive governments of Madero, Carranza, Huerta, and Obregón? None reached power by "normal democratic" means. American policy hesitated between conditional recognition and nonrecognition and resulted in armed intervention in 1915 and 1916. Only the agreement of the Obregón government in 1923 to submit outstanding issues to arbitration resulted in a final act of full recognition, made conditional on the willingness of Mexico to accept arbitration.

In 1917, the most persistent recognition problem arose—before China came to plague us. The success of the Communist revolution in Russia added the issue of the acceptability of communism and Communist foreign policy goals to the earlier problem of national self-determination. The response of the United States was sixteen years of nonrecognition and the unsuccessful intervention of 1918, with its occupation of Vladivostok. To recognize a Communist regime, it was argued, implied approving of a violent, international revolutionary ideology and its associated foreign policy. Nonrecognition implied punishing the Soviets for refusing to honor the international financial obligations of the czars and for expropriating American-owned property in Russia. So consistent was the American policy that the three Baltic states—Latvia, Estonia, and Lithuania—which had seceded from Russia in 1918 were not accorded recognition until 1922 in order not to "approve" of the new situation created by the Bolsheviks.

Again, however, the recognition problem is by no means a purely American one. Today's young African states face exactly the same issue when they must decide whether to recognize a new military regime in Ghana, a new state in Mauritania (whose right to exist was challenged by Morocco), or a new president in Togo, who came to power when mutinous soldiers assassinated his predecessor. Rapid change breeds political instability; the heady new doctrines of national self-determination, African socialism, proletarian solidarity, etc., beget movements which inevitably challenge the international legal and political order accepted by the older nations. Whenever these forces are felt, states crumble and new ones arise on their ruins. Whenever this kind of unrest is a fact of politics, regimes are toppled, insurgents roam the countryside, and rival claimants to the mantle of legitimacy are clamoring for international acceptance. And the older countries are given the choice between automatic recognition, conditional recognition, nonrecognition—or intervention.

C. Where Will Recognition Remain an Issue?

The obvious candidates for creating the need for unpleasant choices are Africa and Latin America. Since 1964, successful coups against "recognized" governments have taken place in a dozen African nations; there is no reason for thinking that the epidemic has passed its peak. For the

United States the choice has been easy because some of these coups have involved the toppling of pro-Chinese regimes by moderates, often pro-Western; others have simply not posed issues relevant to the major lines of American foreign policy. But what guarantee do we have that the next round of coups will not involve a swing of the pendulum back toward the East? Do we then play the same game which we played in the Caribbean until 1933 and again in the Dominican Republic in 1965?

In Latin America the next cycle of coups will almost certainly be in a pro-Eastern or, at least, neutralist direction. They need not be of the traumatic quality of Castro's Cuba. The Bosch movement in the Dominican Republic was far from being a carbon copy of Castro's. But it is most unlikely that there will be many more conservative-military upsets of the kind which took place in Brazil in 1964. Hence the United States will face, for the foreseeable future, repetitions of the kind of confrontation which is illustrated by the Dominican Republic—pitting a reasonably popular, nationalist, reformist "socialist," and anti-American insurgent movement against an unpopular, slow-moving, moderately conservative, and pro-American government (whether military or not). The issue of "democracy" is a false one in any event. Neither the government nor the challenger is likely to conform to our notions of democracy. The unpleasant choice, therefore, is bound to arise in Latin America, particularly since the insurgent movement is certain to have Cuban and Communist support even when it is not Communist-controlled.

D. A Radical Solution: The Estrada Doctrine

In 1930, the Mexican Government announced that henceforth it would no longer have any recognition policy at all. The new policy took the form of the "Estrada Doctrine," designed to sidestep once and for all the issue of "constitutional legitimacy" of new governments. The Mexican statement held that:

> . . . the Government of Mexico has transmitted instructions to its Ministers or Chargés d'Affaires in the countries affected by the recent political crises, informing them that the Mexican Government is issuing no declarations in the sense of grants of recognition, since that nation considers that such a course is an insulting practice and one which, in addition to the fact that it offends the sovereignty of other nations, implies that judgment of some sort may be passed upon the internal affairs of those nations by other governments, inasmuch as the latter assume, in effect, an

attitude of criticism, when they decide, favorably or unfavorably, as to the legal qualifications of foreign regimes. Therefore, the Government of Mexico confines itself to the maintenance or withdrawal, as it may deem advisable, of its diplomatic agents, and to the continued acceptance, also when it may deem advisable, of such similar accredited diplomatic agents as the respective nations may have in Mexico; and in so doing, it does not pronounce judgment, either precipitately or *a posteriori*, regarding the right of foreign nations to accept, maintain or replace their governments or authorities. [1]

The trouble with the Estrada Doctrine is that it is clear in principle and impossible in application. Wherever there are two claimants to the governmental title, third countries are still compelled to choose between them. Simply to continue to exercise normal diplomatic representation without bothering to recognize is possible only if it is clear to whom the ambassador is accredited. Granted, in the event of minor civil strife this poses no problem if the government remains in control of the bulk of the country. But what if this is not the case, as it was not in the Dominican Republic? In that case the Estrada Doctrine merely begs the question. It is not surprising, therefore, that no other nation has espoused or accepted it. Nor has Mexico practiced it consistently.

II. RECOGNITION IN INTERNATIONAL LAW

All commentators agree that the international law regarding recognition is very murky, to put it charitably. Many argue that the practice of states makes it evident that there is no law regarding recognition at all, that recognition is a purely political act which carries with it certain legal consequences. As a political act, however, it is not subject to any norms, whether based on treaty or custom. No general convention regarding recognition has ever been enacted. The best that can be said is that certain arguments and terms recur regularly in the debate concerning recognition. These arguments and terms demand examination in the current context as well, if only because any changes in national policy will be, in part, debated in such terms. The major distinction to be made is the "recognition of new states" as opposed to the "recognition of new governments." Since the case of China can be argued under either rubric (and undoubtedly will be

[1] Herbert W. Briggs (ed.), *The Law of Nations*, Appleton-Century-Crofts, New York, 1952, p. 123.

so argued once Washington moves off dead center), I shall use China as an illustration of the legal situation.

A. *Recognition and New States*

What do we mean when we say, "The United States recognizes the new state of Israel"? Do we mean that the state did not exist until we recognized it? That it existed but that we do not acknowledge this as a fact until we say so? That we acknowledge it as a fact but for other reasons do not choose to say so until certain conditions are met?

The main debate is between those who say that recognition is "constitutive," i.e., the new state does not legally exist until recognized, and those who say it is merely "declaratory," i.e., recognition merely confirms the older state's acknowledgment that the new entity exists. Another debate rages between those who say that a new entity can be recognized *de facto* (i.e., provisionally and subject to the confirmation of hopes, suspicions, or demands on the part of the recognizing state) or *de jure*. *De jure* recognition is final; except that, of course, states can interrupt the legal consequences of *de jure* recognition when they decide to break diplomatic relations. So where are we?

Few people today contend that the recognition of a new state is anything but declaratory. States clearly do exist even when they are not formally recognized. Under this doctrine, recognition grants the new state no rights because the state enjoyed the rights all along merely by virtue of existing. It merely "declares" the recognizing state's knowledge of the fact of existence and the associated rights. The basic document of the Organization of American States, the Bogotá Charter (1948), makes this point unmistakably clear:

Article 9. The political existence of the State is independent of recognition by other States. Even before being recognized, the State has the right to defend its integrity and independence, to provide for its preservation and prosperity, and consequently to organize itself as it sees fit, to legislate concerning its interests, to administer its services, and to determine the jurisdiction and competence of its courts. The exercise of these rights is limited only by the exercise of the rights of other States in accordance with international law.

Article 10. Recognition implies that the State granting it accepts the personality of the new State, with all the rights and duties that international law prescribes for the two States. [2]

[2] *Ibid.*, p. 101.

The United States is, of course, a party to this treaty and therefore bound by it in relation to the other members. The only support for the constitutive doctrine which can be marshaled is the practice of the victorious powers in 1919 when they "recognized" the new states of Poland and Czechoslovakia by virtue of the Treaty of Versailles. Other examples might be cited from nineteenth-century history in relation to the emergence of the Balkan states and of Belgium. Since 1919, no similar instances of constitutive acts have occurred.

This is not to suggest that reliance on the declaratory doctrine is calculated to standardize and civilize recognition procedures. Quite the opposite is the case. The United States in 1903 supported an insurgent movement in Colombia and, when this movement succeeded in carving out a piece of territory for itself, recognized this territory three days after the secession was militarily accomplished. Thus the new state of Panama was born. Former UN Secretary-General Trygve Lie, in addressing himself to the issue of Chinese membership in the UN, wrote:

> The recognition of a new State, or of a new government of an existing State, is a unilateral act which the recognizing government can grant or withhold. It is true that some legal writers have argued forcibly that when a new government, which comes into power through revolutionary means, enjoys a reasonable prospect of permanency, the habitual obedience of the bulk of the population, other States are under a legal duty to recognize it. However, while States may regard it as desirable to follow certain legal principles in according or withholding recognition, the practice of States shows that the act of recognition is still regarded as essentially a political decision, which each State decides in accordance with its own free appreciation of the situation. [3]

What about the *de facto* as against the *de jure* recognition of a new state? Clearly, governments do differentiate in the methods of recognition they use. The United States appeared to give *de facto* recognition to the Baltic states in 1918 by maintaining "commissioners" there, but this was transformed into *de jure* status only when ministers were exchanged in 1922. Again, however, the gesture is a political one. *De facto* recognition of a new state is designed to leave the recognizing state some opportunity for reviewing its policy. The legal consequences of *de facto* and *de jure* recognition of new states appear to be identical. Some international lawyers

---

[3] Quoted in Oscar Svarlien, *An Introduction to the Law of Nations*, McGraw-Hill Book Company, New York, 1955, p. 99.

even maintain that *de facto* recognition can occur as a result of acts "implying" the acknowledgment of the new state's existence, such as the maintenance of unofficial trade relations, the holding of ambassadorial talks on the soil of a third country, or joint participation in international conferences where negotiations do, in fact, go on. Under this criterion, the United States has already recognized, *de facto,* the Peking regime. Whether this implied recognition concerns the government or the state of China, however, is another question.

B. The China Problem: Which China is a "New State"?

The Peking and the Taiwan regimes stoutly maintain that each is the legitimate government of "China"; both vehemently deny any possibility of there being "two Chinas." Indeed, the Taiwan government applauded the Peking regime's conquest of Tibet because the historical boundaries of China where thereby being reaffirmed. The rest of the world, however, takes a less consistent position because several countries maintain diplomatic relations with both Chinas.

It would be difficult to argue that mainland China is a new state. Following a series of court decisions in the years immediately following the Bolshevik revolution in Russia, we ought to say that even the most radical change of government in a historical entity does not abolish the former state; it merely gives it a new regime. It seems to me that this argument would have to prevail in the case of mainland China. Taiwan, however, may well be treated as an instance of a new state by third countries. If the United States wishes to normalize its relations with mainland China without yielding to its demands for Formosa, it has no choice but to recognize Taiwan as a new state. In view of the passion aroused by this issue, it is well to bear in mind that history contains ample precedent for recognizing a part of a former entity as a new state; the most recent examples are the recognition of Kuwait over Iraqi protest and the recognition of Mauritania over Morocco's.

In a curiously backhanded way, the California courts have come close to finding that the United States has extended *de facto* recognition to the Peking government as a state. In a 1964 decision, *In re Eng* (39 Cal Rpts. 254), the District Court of Appeal, Second District, held that a Chinese national is unable to inherit property left in California because the 1946 Treaty of Friendship, Commerce, and Navigation between the United

States and the Republic of China does not confer rights on residents of mainland China. The court found this to be true even though the treaty continues to be in force and even though the United States "continues to regard the Republic of China, presently residing on the island of Formosa, as the government of China." The court, like the U.S. government, speaks of "China," not "China and Formosa."

However, the court also found that "notwithstanding its refusal to extend recognition to Communist China, our government has on occasion dealt with representatives of that regime. In 1955, representatives of the United States and representatives of Communist China conferred and entered into a written agreement concerning the return of civilians to their respective countries. Further: ". . . the declaration of the official spokesmen for American foreign policy have made it clear that the policy of nonrecognition is not based upon any doubts that the communist regime is in power, but is the result of the acts and attitudes of that regime." In short, these facts suggested to the court that "Communist China" appears to be a separate entity, not covered by the 1946 Treaty, and "recognized" as being separate by virtue of special executive and legislative acts directed against it and because of special contacts maintained with it.

C Recognition and New Governments

While the issue of the constitutive or declaratory character of recognition does not arise with respect to a new government, the problem of *de facto* as against *de jure* recognition does. When do states have to recognize a new government? Only when there has been a forceful or extraconstitutional displacement of the already recognized government by a new group of men. Obviously, this event occurs with almost predictable regularity in Latin America, Africa, and certain Asian countries.

The issue, therefore, has been on what criteria the act of recognition is to be based: factual control over the territory, the means whereby power was obtained, or the ability to discharge and meet international obligations? Almost all countries have been so inconsistent in their practice that there is no point in laboring the issue of the "law." At one time or another all three criteria have been cited as demanding fulfillment; at other times *de facto* control over the territory has been considered sufficient. I would hazard that if we were to count up the actual instances of acts of recognition in the last fifty years, the overwhelming majority would emerge as having been based solely on the criterion of effective control. Only when governments, for reasons of national policy, wish to influence the new regime in some way do they advance the other two criteria.

De facto recognition is often used in order to test the permanence of effective control. A new regime may be recognized *de facto,* and after it has demonstrated its ability to survive, the recognition *de jure* will take place. In other situtations, evidence of constitutional legitimacy may be demanded before *de jure* recognition is conferred. For instance, the United States in 1948 recognized *de jure* the *state* of Israel, while indicating that its recognition of the *government* remained *de facto,* pending the holding of elections and the choice of a president.

Lack of democratic legitimacy, then, has most often been invoked as a criterion for not conferring recognition on a regime which rose to power by insurgency, *coup d'état,* rigged elections, or massive revolution. However, this criterion has not prevented the recognition by all major states of the "illegitmate" governments of Ghana, Togo, Algeria, both Congos, Nigeria, Dahomey, Upper Volta, and Uganda—all of which came to power by force in the last few years. Yet the same argument was used concurrently by the United States in withholding recognition from the Bosch forces in the Dominican Republic, Cuba, East Germany, North Vietnam, and North Korea. It has not prevented the recognition of governments in the Soviet Union, Bulgaria, Rumania, Hungary (despite the events of 1956!), Poland, Czechoslovakia, Syria, Iraq, etc. Consistency may be the hobgoblin of little minds, but the bigger minds which scorn it do not seem to profit thereby.

D. The China Problem: Which China is the "New Government"?

There is clearly nothing in the law regarding the recognition of new governments which imposes on the United States the *duty* to recognize Peking. However, neither is there anything in the law which prevents the United States from recognizing Peking as the new government of an old state, if Washington chooses to do so. Peking is in effective control, a fact conceded by the United States. It lacks democratic legitimacy and it is demonstrably unwilling to live up to its international obligations. These facts are equally applicable to a long list of new governments which we have recognized nevertheless. I shall discuss the political utility of non-recognition below. Here I merely wish to establish that the law does not bar recognition of Peking.

What about Taiwan in the event of a change of policy in Washington? Recognition as a successor state to the former Chinese Republic, which I urged above, would have to be accompanied by recognition of whatever government prevails in Taipei at the time of "independence." Effective control would, once more, have to be the only criterion on which we should rely. Raising questions of democratic legitimacy and willingness to discharge international obligations would serve very little purpose, legal or political.

E. The Law of Recognition: What is the Minimal Consensus?

In order to make the act of recognition less capricious and dependent on the whims of foreign policy prevailing at any one time in any single country, many writers on international law have attempted to distill, from the practice and customs of governments, a minimum common denominator. Most of them agree with the famous British jurist J. L. Brierly in summing up the law thus: "The primary function of recognition is to acknowledge as a fact something which has hitherto been uncertain, namely, the independence of the body claiming to be a State, and to declare the recognizing State's readiness to accept the normal consequences of that fact. . . ."[4]

Nevertheless, acts of recognition *should* and usually *do* take place only if and when the recognizing government is assured that four conditions are met by the new entity, whether state or government. These conditions are: (1) the new entity must have people; (2) it must occupy a definite territory; (3) there must be a government effectively in control of both people and territory; and (4) the government must possess the capacity to enter into international relations, i.e., it must be "independent." The act of recognition summarized so tersely by Brierly is no more and no less than an acknowledgment by the recognizing state that these four conditions have been met. These conditions are the minimum held necessary to result in *de jure* recognition. If the recognizing state entertains some doubt on one or more grounds—usually on condition number three—the act of recognition ought to be *de facto*.

---

[4] J. L. Brierly, *The Law of Nations*, 4th ed., The Clarendon Press, Oxford, 1949, p. 124; quoted in Briggs, *op. cit.*, p. 116.

To make the act of recognition dependent on the satisfaction of *more* than these four conditions takes us into the realm of international politics, beyond the routine practice of states which is more or less legally sanctioned. Any insistence on special assurance beyond these four matters of fact takes us into conditional recognition or nonrecognition. And here the law is silent and politics supreme. It is only the practice of automatic recognition which is satisfied with the legal minimum.

III. INTERNATIONAL ORGANIZATIONS AND RECOGNITION

A. Does Membership in an International Organization Imply Recognition?

Trygve Lie, in the memorandum quoted above, also noted that "the primary difficulty in the current question of the representation of Member States in the United Nations is that this question of representation has been linked up with the question of recognition by Member Governments. It will be shown here that this linkage is unfortunate from the practical standpoint, and wrong from the standpoint of legal theory."

However, there is some ground—historical and practical—for the confusion. In popular parlance, the seating of a new state or government in an organ of the United Nations is often equated with the recognition of that entity by the member states acting in their individual capacities. The superficial identification of the two practices is given some credence by the fact that certain states, notably the Soviet Union and its allies, have argued that since they do not maintain diplomatic relations with the applicant for membership (in that instance, Jordan and Nepal) they were unable to vote for admission to the UN. However, the states in question were admitted anyway, irrespective of national Soviet recognition practices and no further difficulty arose. Further, the practice of the League of Nations was somewhat different, at least initially. There, Luxembourg and Yugoslavia did imply that the admission to the League of Estonia, with which the two did not maintain diplomatic relations, constituted national recognition as well. On the other hand, Great Britain had not recognized Lithuania, Belgium and Switzerland withheld recognition from the Soviet Union, and Colombia steadfastly refused to recognize Panama; yet all agreed that the admission of the three new states (or governments) was different from national recognition and implied nothing with respect to it. Many Latin American countries continued not to recognize the Soviet government even after the admission of the Soviet Union to the League in 1935.

The International Court of Justice pronounced itself quite clearly on this question in its Advisory Opinion on the Admission of New Members (1948), holding that national recognition of an applicant was not a condition to be imposed in considering the applicant for membership. In fact, the practice of the United Nations has been almost uniform in *not* challenging the credentials of delegates on the basis of the presence or absence of recognition on the part of the other members. The obvious exceptions to this practice are China (where the annual argument over the "admission of Communist China" is really a debate over the seating of the delegation from Taiwan) and Hungary in the years immediately following 1956.

In short, the practice of the United Nations, except in these two cases (and the Hungarian case was resolved eventually as were all others involving the "legitimacy" of revolutionary regimes, i.e., with national recognition and seating in the UN), is uniform in establishing that: (1) a vote for the admission of a new state or the seating of a disputed delegation implies nothing with respect to national recognition, and (2) a member could therefore so vote without having to change its national policy at all. National recognition of a state or government is one thing; voting to admit it to the United Nations or to seat its delegation (in preference to a rival delegation) is quite another.

B. Is There Collective or Simultaneous Recognition?

The discussion of UN admissions procedure suggests that there can be, strictly speaking, no such thing as collective recognition of a new state or government. The instances in which the recognition of new states took place in a setting of decisions made in international conferences provide no consistent pattern. At Versailles in 1919, at Potsdam in 1945, and at Geneva in 1954, the assembled powers did negotiate revisions in the territorial status quo, calling into being new states or new governments for old states. The presumption was that the powers agreeing to the new order would then recognize the resulting regimes and that these regimes would attain international legitimacy as a result of that recognition.

Versailles "created" Poland and Czechoslovakia. Potsdam fixed the boundaries of the post-1945 Polish state "provisionally" and "recognized" the Lublin government (over its rival residing in London). Geneva "created" the independence of Laos and Cambodia and made "provisional" arrangements for North and South Vietnam. Obviously, these statements are legal fictions. Other circumstances, in each case, were responsible for the independence of the states in question and the conferences merely ratified the facts. Not all participants in the conferences extended recognition afterward to all the new regimes and even when they did, recognition did not imply a uniform policy toward the new countries. The recognition, then, was not "collective" in any meaningful way. At best, it was "simultaneous recognition" extended by the conference powers. The same can be said about a variety of decisions of this type made by the inter-allied Conference of Ambassadors sitting in Paris immediately after World War I in its efforts to tidy up questions of this kind in Eastern Europe and the Balkans.

An already murky legal and political picture in the field of recognition is not likely to be cleared up by reliance on a doctrine of collective recognition by an international organization. Such a policy has often been advocated. The argument suggests that the seating of a new state and/or government *should* constitute collective recognition by the world community, thus obviating conditional recognition or nonrecognition by individual nations. All the argument about the uncertainty, capriciousness, and variability in recognition policy would thus be avoided.

There is no certainty that a policy of collective recognition through the United Nations would approximate the practice of automatic recognition. Conditions can be exacted in the United Nations as well as elsewhere, the opinion of the International Court of Justice to the contrary notwithstanding. Such conditions were, in fact, exacted in the case of the Hungarian delegation, though they were dropped later. A commitment to universality of membership, maximum and continuous communication among nations irrespective of their democratic legitimacy, and continuous dialogue argues against a doctrine of collective recognition. Such a doctrine could all too easily develop once more into a new Holy Alliance, thus undoing what automatic recognition might achieve.

C. Should There Be Collective Nonrecognition?

The same arguments which militate against a policy of collective recognition by the United Nations suggest the undesirability of collective nonrecognition as a sanction. This point requires further discussion. Collective recognition is merely a doctrine, not an established policy or a settled point of law. Collective nonrecognition, on the contrary, is a policy actually followed by both the League of Nations and the United Nations. A desire to return to a policy of automatic recognition suggests that this practice is undesirable.

The cases in point are as follows. In 1931, the League of Nations considered the Japanese invasion of Manchuria and its culmination in the creation of the "independent state of Manchukuo," set up in defiance of a League request for peaceful settlement of the Chinese-Japanese dispute. Secretary of State Henry L. Stimson then suggested that the world adopt a policy of nonrecognition of Manchukuo as an expression of its displeasure with and disapproval of the Japanese step though he, like the rest of the powers, was quite unwilling to resort to any stronger sanctions. The nonrecognition policy was then adopted by the League of Nations as well as by the U.S. It carried the usual legal consequences of such a step, consequences which seem not to have bothered Japan in the least.

Even though the Stimson Doctrine hardly demonstrated its utility in preventing aggression, the United Nations proceeded to follow in the League's footsteps. In 1946, nonrecognition was invoked as one of several sanctions against Spain, then considered the sole surviving Axis regime. Member states were asked to break off diplomatic relations by the General Assembly. While a few countries followed the recommendations, most did not. Again, the resilience of the Franco government—still going strong in 1969—suggests the futility of the device.

Rhodesia provides the current example of collective nonrecognition. Both the Security Council and the General Assembly, in 1965, adopted resolutions demanding that member states refrain from recognizing the government of Ian Smith or the "state of Rhodesia," which had just declared its independence unilaterally. All member states obeyed the UN's resolution this time and Britain did most emphatically. Whether the device will be effective in bringing about a change of policy in Rhodesia is far from clear. So far, collective nonrecognition here has been as ineffective as in all the other instances, even though it was linked with a complete embargo and trade boycott.

D. *Can International Organizations Neutralize the Recognition Issue?*

Clearly, international organizations cannot restrain member states successfully by practicing collective nonrecognition. The reasons are obvious. If the state so stigmatized is economically and militarily strong, the gesture of withholding recognition from one of its satellites will hardly cause any serious embarrassment. Japan's case is not the only illustration. It seems not to have bothered the Soviet Union particularly that its East German satellite has been stigmatized by nonrecognition for over twenty years by the bulk of the UN membership. The same was true of Outer Mongolia between 1921 and 1955. But if the nonrecognized state is merely a minor power a UN declaration is still not necessarily effective. If the government is well established it can dispense with international recognition for years. And the mere fact that it is established sooner or later causes the nonrecognizing countries a certain amount of difficulty because of the obstacles to trade, travel, and communications created. Then, one by one, they unobtrusively recognize the erstwhile outcaste.

The temptations, difficulties, and frustrations involved in using international organizations as instruments of approval or disapproval for states and governments are illustrated by the experience of three contemporary regional organizations—the Arab League, the Organization for African Unity (OAU), and the Organization of American States (OAS). I stress that each of these organizations is the most "legitimate" in its region because each includes *all* independent countries in its particular area among its members. At the same time, the experience of these organizations suggests a way of neutralizing the recognition issue by providing a tacit and collective means of automatic recognition based on the mere facts of existence and effective control.

Thus the Arab League includes five member states which have been characterized by considerable governmental instability, frequent coups, alternation between civilian and military cliques, and occasional civil war—Algeria, Sudan, Yemen, Iraq, and Syria. Yet the issue of which of several claimants to the title "government" to seat in meetings of the League has not often arisen. The case of Yemen has proved to be the only difficult one. The League has simply accepted whichever group survived long enough to be considered the government in effective control, even though some name-calling and even intervention may have preceded the silent acceptance of the survivors. When name-calling proves fruitless and intervention without success, the other governments simply accommodate themselves—in the spirit of "Arab brotherhood"—to the new status quo.

In the OAU this tradition is not yet firmly established, though practice since 1964 suggests that it soon will be. The slogan uniting the African states, like the symbol of Arab brotherhood to the north, is Pan Africanism and opposition to colonialism. It is the declared purpose of the

OAU to advance and protect both of these aspirations. Hence when President Sylvanus Olympio of Togo was assassinated, some member states refused to recognize his successor because he seemed tainted by colonialism. The same arguments were heard when Kwame Nkrumah was overthrown. On that occasion, four militant Pan African member states walked out of OAU meetings when the bulk of the members recognized the successor military regime. The lesson, however, is *not* that the legitimacy of the successor governments was impugned; rather it is the tacit recognition accorded to the successors once they proved to be in effective control. This is true even of Tshombé's Congolese government, which aroused the ire of many OAU members by using foreign mercenaries in fighting internal revolts and in approving of the joint United States-Belgian airdrop at Stanleyville in 1964. After calling Tshombé many unpleasant names and seeking to exclude him from OAU meetings, and despite assistance given to the rebels by some African governments, i.e., intervention, the Congolese prime minister was accepted in OAU councils anyway as long as he demonstrated that he was in effective control of the Congo. What is this but tacit automatic recognition by the international organization after the claimant demonstrates his resilience?

In the OAS this policy is anchored not only in practice but in legal doctrine as well. While the Estrada Doctrine has not been officially adopted by any member government, there is a strong feeling that conditional recognition and nonrecognition are acts of intervention. Since so many governments do owe their origin to extraconstitutional acts, they share an interest in making recognition as automatic as possible. Hence the charter of the OAS is replete with condemnations of intervention and assertions of absolute and untrammeled sovereignty and equality among the members. This includes, in the minds of most Latin American governments, the notion that any regime which survives is entitled to acceptance in OAS organs. In practice, revolutionary regimes are recognized once they demonstrate that they are exercising effective control. Credentials disputes in the OAS are very rare. Again, then, the willingness of the OAS to seat a delegation representing a government which has come to power by force or fraud illustrates an appreciation of simple facts of political life. Such a willingness does not take the place of national acts of recognition. But where such acts are withheld, the government in question gains quiet acceptance in the meantime by virtue of the fact that it is seated in OAS organs.

There are some exceptions in OAS practice. The Cuban case was unique and no accommodation has taken place. On the other hand, the effort at collective nonrecognition of Cuba made in 1961 has been only partly successful, with Mexico, Chile, Costa Rica, and Brazil refusing to heed OAS resolutions. Uruguay has often urged a policy of collective non-recognition for undemocratic regimes, though other member states have declined to follow this lead. But among OAS members it has been the United States which has most consistently practiced conditional recognition or nonrecognition in its bilateral relations with new Latin American governments. Yet only in the case of Cuba has Washington attempted to push that policy to include a multilateralization of nonrecognition.

These experiences suggest that international organizations provide the instrument for a certain amount of face-saving and tacit accommodation in the event of national nonrecognition, a measure of neutralization of the whole issue though not an escape from it. They make it possible for a national government to maintain a stance of stern disapproval if it insists. They enable statesmen to maintain their ideological purity in their home constituencies. However, they also make it possible to avoid the possible interruption of contact and communication attendant upon a policy of disapproval of a new state or government. When an international organization tacitly "recognizes" a new regime without exacting special conditions, by virtue of seating its delegates, the possibility for contact and communication among *all* members is intact. The international legitimacy of the regime appears unimpaired even though individual member governments have declined to accord it formal recognition. [5]

I suggest that the United Nations has moved to a position very similar to that of the OAS. On December 21, 1965, the General Assembly adopted a "Declaration on Non-Intervention" by vote of 109 to none. This declaration does not mention recognition expressly. However, it is so sweeping in its denunciation of all conceivable types of direct and indirect intervention as to imply that anything but automatic recognition *is* intervention. Any revision or reconsideration of current United States recog-

---

[5] In an effort to push this practice one step further, i.e., to facilitate the collective nonrecognition of governments that owe their advent to nondemocratic means, the Second Special Inter-American Conference (Rio, 1965) adopted a resolution under which OAS member-states would agree to consult with each other on whether or not the new regime was likely to hold elections and whether intervention had been involved in the overthrow of its predecessor. After consulting, however, each government could proceed as it wished.

nition policy ought to consider the impact and meaning of that declaration.[6]

IV. RECOGNITION IN UNITED STATES POLICY

A. Automatic Recognition: The "American Doctrine"

In 1815, the Western world seemed to be divided into republican and monarchical states. The monarchs had just defeated Napoleonic France (and the French Revolution, they thought) and proceeded to set up a "legitimate" monarchical order in Europe. Recognition policy came to be a vital tool in the maintenance of that order. Revolutionary challenges to the order were not to be recognized. Recognition of a state or government implied approval by the established states. The offical "legitimist" doctrine of recognition was that a new regime would be accepted only if it were monarchical. The recognition policy here propounded was, of course, a policy of conditional recognition or nonrecognition, linked with intervention to aid legitimacy.

At that time the United States stood for untrammeled automatic recognition. The aim was the defense of republican—"illegitimate"—institutions, notably in Latin America. And so close was the identification of this concern with the policy of automatic recognition that the doctrine became known as "the American doctrine." American statesmen deliberately ignored the distinction between *de facto* and *de jure* recognition.

Jefferson defined it as follows:

It accords with our principles to acknowledge any government to be rightful which is formed by the will of the nation substantially declared.

. . . We surely can not deny to any nation that right whereon our own Government is founded—that every one may govern itself according to whatever form it pleases, and change these forms at its own will; and that it may transact its busi-

---

[6] General Assembly Resolution 2131(XX). Subsequently, however, the General Assembly's Special Committee on Principles of International Law concerning Friendly Relations among States could make no progress in translating the declaration into a legal norm acceptable to a majority of the membership. Nevertheless, the Special Committee, over the dissent of the Western delegations, voted that Resolution 2131 "reflects a universal legal conviction which qualifies it to be regarded as an authentic and definite principle of international law" (UN Document A-6230, 27 June 1966).

ness with foreign nations through whatever organ it thinks proper, whether king, convention, assembly, committee, president, or anything else it may choose. [7]

The only qualification which Jefferson sometimes inserted was that the recognition of any regime should take place if it rested on "the popular will substantially declared." Daniel Webster and James Buchanan, both secretaries of state, however, inserted no such qualifications:

> From President Washington's time down to the present day it has been a principle, always acknowledged by the United States, that every nation possesses the right to govern itself according to its own will, to change institutions at discretion, and to transact its business through whatever agents it may think proper to employ. [8]

> In its intercourse with foreign nations the Government of United States has, from its origin, always recognized *de facto* governments: We recognize the right of all nations to create and reform their political institutions according to their own will and pleasure. We do not go beyond the existing government to involve ourselves in the question of legitimacy. It is sufficient for us to know that a government exists, capable of maintaining itself, and then its recognition inevitably follows. . . . [9]

Many years later, Dean Acheson repeated this doctrine, advising only that the United States postpone recognition in order to see whether the new regime was in effective control and able to carry out its international obligations:

> We maintain diplomatic relations with other countries primarily because we are all on the same planet and must do business with each other. We do not establish an embassy or legation in a foreign country to show approval of its government. We do so to have a channel through which to conduct essential governmental relations and to protect legitimate United States interests.
> When a freely elected government is overthrown and a new and perhaps militaristic government takes over, we do not need to recognize the new government automatically and immediately. We can wait to see if it really controls its territory and intends to live up to its international commitments. We can consult with other governments, as we have often done.
> But if and when we do recognize a government under these circumstances, our act of recognition need not be taken to imply approval of it or its policies. It is recognition of a set of facts, nothing more. We may have the gravest reservations as

[7] John Bassett Moore, *A Digest of International Law*, Government Printing Office, Washington, 1906, vol. 1, p. 120; quoted in Svarlien, *op. cit.*, p. 100.

[8] Moore, *op. cit.*, p. 126; quoted in Svarlien, *op. cit.*, p. 100.

[9] Moore, *op. cit.*, p. 124; quoted in Svarlien, *op. cit.*, p. 100.

to the manner in which it has come into power. We may deplore its attitude toward civil liberties. Yet our long-range objectives in the promotion of democratic institutions may, in fact, be best served by recognizing it and thus maintaining a channel of communication with the country involved. In this way we are also able to discharge our basic function of protecting the interests of our government and our citizens there. Since recognition is not synonymous with approval, however, our act of recognition need not necessarily be understood as the forerunner of a policy of intimate cooperation with the government concerned.[10]

B. Toward Conditional Recognition

With the adoption of an active military and commercial policy on the part of the United States in the Caribbean after 1898, this doctrine was abandoned. Two conditions were, henceforth, made part of the recognition of new governments (except, of course, in the case of Panamanian independence): (1) Governments were asked for assurances that they would respect the international obligations of their predecessors. This meant, in practice, they were put under pressure to respect the lives and property of American nationals and of American firms which had investments in the countries concerned. (2) Governments were put under pressure to demonstrate their constitutional legitimacy. However, this change in policy was at first confined to Latin America. China and Eastern Europe were included as a result of the revolutionary events of the first two decades of the twentieth century.

At first, the United States merely insisted that a new government *be able* to carry out its international obligations. In the first years of the twentieth century, however, a new government also had to demonstrate that it was *willing* to do so. Hence willingness to conclude arbitration agreements was sometimes stipulated as a condition of recognition, or even the willingness to pay specific claims. Woodrow Wilson was the first to add the dimension of democratic legitimacy, based on his express desire to push the southern neighbors of the United States toward democratic reforms. As he said in 1913:

> We hold, as I am sure all thoughtful leaders of republican government everywhere hold, that just government rests always upon the consent of the governed, and there can be no freedom without order based upon law and upon public

[10] *U.S. Department of State Bulletin,* XXI, No. 534, September 26, 1949, pp. 463-464; quoted in Briggs, *op. cit.,* p. 130.

conscience and approval. We shall look to make these principles the basis of mutual intercourse, respect and helpfulness between our sister republics and ourselves.[11]

When the advent of the Huerta regime in Mexico violated the condition of democratic and constitutional legitimacy, nonrecognition was linked to active American military intervention.

The case for conditional recognition was put in very clear terms by Secretary of State Charles E. Hughes for the three Republican administrations which followed Wilson:

> The fundamental question in the recognition of a government is whether it shows ability and a disposition to discharge international obligations. Stability, of course, is important; stability is essential. Some speak as though stability was all that was necessary. What, however, would avail mere stability if it were stability in the prosecution of a policy of repudiation and confiscation? In the case of Russia we have a very easy test in a matter of fundamental importance, and that is of good faith in the discharge of international obligations. I say that good faith is a matter of essential importance because words are easily spoken. Of what avail is it to speak of assurances, if valid obligations and rights are repudiated and property confiscated?[12]

During the 1920s, the position of the United States in the Western Hemisphere was sufficiently strong to block several efforts by inter-American legal bodies to arrive at a doctrine of reasonably automatic recognition based on objective criteria of effective control and the mere *capacity* to meet international obligations. At the same time, and for related reasons, the United States succeeded in blocking an inter-American declaration against intervention.

Not even the adoption of the Good Neighbor Policy by the Roosevelt administration in 1933 implied a return to automatic recognition. The problem of recognizing the Bolivian military junta which seized power in 1936 is typical of many cases which arose. That junta expressed a desire to nationalize certain foreign-owned properties in order to "strengthen the nation's economy within purely socialistic standards." The State Department recognized the regime nonetheless after certain general and perfunctory assurances had been given to respect international obligations. However, in the following year the Bolivian government expropriated the

---

[11] *Foreign Relations of the U.S.*, 1913, p. 71, quoted in C. Neale Ronning, *Law and Politics in Inter-American Diplomacy*, John Wiley & Sons, New York, 1963, p. 11.

[12] *American Journal of International Law*, XVII (1923), p. 296; quoted in Svarlien, *op. cit.*, p. 101.

Standard Oil Company's properties in Bolivia, whereupon the military junta resigned and turned the government over to civilians selected by it. That regime, in turn, was recognized by the United States only after it had given assurances that it "intends to respect Bolivia's International obligations and the legitimate rights of private property." The assurances also included an understanding that Standard Oil would be compensated.

The issue of democratic or constitutional legitimacy was not always raised; indeed, it was ignored in the Bolivian case discussed. However, it did become an issue when a junta suspected of Nazi ties seized power in Bolivia during World War II and when the government of Argentina was overthrown by the Perón forces in 1943. Sometimes both conditions were stipulated, sometimes only one, depending on the circumstances and the American interests considered involved.

In the years since 1945, recognition certainly has been far from automatic. Democratic legitimacy has been the predominant criterion for withholding recognition or exacting conditions; respect for American property, under the guise of the "willingness to accept international obligations" formula, has declined as an important theme, though it still figured heavily in our initial dealings with Castro. Further, the cold war and communism introduced a new theme into the democratic legitimacy formula: military juntas of the right as well as Communist insurgents on the left were often stigmatized with nonrecognition, depending on the emphasis of the moment.

C. How Effective is the Withholding of Automatic Recognition?

To say that United States recognition policy has been inconsistent is to understate reality. During World War II, conditional recognition and nonrecognition—unilaterally and collectively through the inter-American system—were used as blunt weapons to punish regimes suspected of siding with the Axis. After the onset of the cold war, this practice was intensified against regimes considered pro-Soviet. With the advent of the revolution of rising expectations in Latin America and Asia (and later in Africa), the United States faced the dilemma of satisfying *nobody* with its selective recognition policy and earning the catcalls of social reformers on the left as well as of military oligarchs on the right. The supreme irony of the situation is the fact that even when Secretary of State Byrnes, in 1946, announced a (temporary) return to the policy of automatic recognition, this solved nothing.

The reasons for this apparently insoluble dilemma require an explanation. The explanation takes us back to the close link between intervention and recognition policy. In a tight network of international relations between a very powerful state and a number of weak, unstable, and economically dependent states, intervention and nonintervention tend to be the same thing in terms of their political consequences. As Talleyrand put it in 1815, "Non-intervention is a phrase invented by diplomats to describe a situation in which intervention is taking place."

Many Latin American and Asian countries are perceived by the major powers as a battleground: each wishes to prevent the other from controlling the area. In order to achieve this, each may seek—at one time or another—to penetrate the area economically or militarily simply in order to prevent the other one from getting there first. (Examples: Congo-Kinshasa and Vietnam.) Superimposed on cold-war conflict is the locally rooted fight between the forces of social reform, economic development, and popular discontent arrayed against whatever the local "establishment" may be. The temptation always exists for the great powers to support one or the other local force in the context of the global struggle. Why then do intervention and nonintervention amount to the same thing?

For a weak and dependent government, international recognition is a desirable asset. Recognition may determine whether it will be seated in the councils of the world, receive economic aid, technical assistance, and military support. To grant recognition to such a government will be interpreted as intervention by its opponents, foreign and domestic. To withhold recognition will be scored as intervention by the new government and its supporters. And invariably, such a government will have foes and supporters as determined by the alignment of reformist as against conservative forces. Invariably, one or the other will then seek the support of the United States or the Soviet Union, and the civil war runs the risk of becoming an international confrontation.

A policy of automatic recognition, moreover, is no guaranty against the occurrence of this chain of events. In fact, the United States has been attacked by reformist forces in Latin America for using the automatic recognition policy as a tool of intervention! I cite only the example of the Trujillo regime in the Dominican Republic. True to the purity of nonintervention and automatic recognition, the United States did little to aid Cuba and Venezuela, in 1960, in seeking to stigmatize the Trujillo regime and bring about its downfall. To have done so would have been "to intervene."

However, the "correct" policy of the United States then earned Washington attacks from reformist forces in Latin America, who claimed that recognition and nonintervention were merely a guise for protecting a dictatorial government—which indeed was the consequence of the policy of self-restraint. The issue was "resolved" only with the first instance of *collective intervention* mounted by the OAS, after the Dominican assassination attempt on President Betancourt of Venezuela and Trujillo's own demise.

But a policy of conditional recognition is no help either. I cite two examples. In 1948, the United States withheld recognition from the revolutionary military regime of Perez Jiménez in Venezuela, which had just overthrown a reasonably democratic government. The grounds for waiting to recognize were the questionable constitutional legitimacy of the new regime and the desire to extract conditions for its reform. The efforts failed and the government was fully recognized two months later. Yet in the eyes of conservative forces in Latin America, conditional recognition was used by the United States for purposes for intervention. In 1960, the government of El Salvador was overthrown by a military junta which professed strong social reformist objectives and appeared influenced by Castro. Again, the United States withheld recognition in an effort to discover the extent of Cuban influence and, if possible, to check it. Whatever the results of its inquiries, the new government was fully recognized some weeks later. This time, the elements of the left denounced the American policy as covert intervention. Clearly, the United States is damned if it recognizes and damned if it waits.

After recognizing the inevitable character of this dilemma, then, let us return to the question of the effectiveness of conditional recognition and nonrecognition as arms of American foreign policy. After all, the fact that we earn foreign opposition for whichever policy we follow still leaves unsettled the effectiveness of the policy.

I consider it established beyond the shadow of a doubt that a policy of nonrecognition of new states is completely ineffective. The new state is not prevented from living a life of its own, from receiving support from its allies, from trading and developing, even though it is denied international legitimacy by us. The classic examples are Manchukuo, North Vietnam, North Korea, and East Germany. None of these have been seriously harmed by the fact that the United States pretended they did not exist. On the other hand, our nonrecognition has made life considerably more difficult for us when it was deemed necessary to negotiate with their governments. Intermediaries then had to be found and subterfuges discovered, such as the fiction that it was not the United States but the United Nations which negotiated with North Korea at Panmunjom. The policy of not recognizing successful new states is childish, petulant, and self-defeating.

The picture is not quite so clear when we examine the effectiveness of not recognizing new governments of old states. If the state is large and self-confident, nonrecognition is simply ineffective. We eventually give up and recognize because our petulance brought no results. But if the state is dependent, nonrecognition may bring the kind of results (in terms of agreeing to respect American property) which we have observed in Latin America.

The question is best examined by distinguishing between the kind of pressure the United States wishes to exert by not recognizing. One type of pressure is the desire to express moral disapproval of the new regime and to push it toward political reform in a democratic direction. This objective is never achieved by nonrecognition. Another objective is the settlement of outstanding financial claims and the obtaining of assurances that such obligations will be honored in the future. This aim is sometimes attained after a period of nonrecognition.

The sixteen years during which the United States did not recognize the Soviet regime illustrate this finding. Between 1917 and 1933, Washington pretended that there was no government in Moscow. The objectives of the United States encompassed both aspects discussed above. The first objective was quietly forgotten by 1933, but in extending full recognition the Roosevelt administration also succeeded in obtaining a compromise settlement of outstanding American financial claims against the former Russian government. It remains a moot point whether this financial gain was worth sixteen years of complicated and embittered indirect diplomatic relations between Moscow and Washington, a period which was ended, in essence, by an American realization that one does not effectively punish a successful foreign government by ignoring its existence.

Much the same lesson can be gleaned from the troubled relations between the United States and the Communist governments of Poland, Hungary, Bulgaria, and Rumania. The aim of nonrecognition was to compel these regimes to observe the human and political rights to which they were bound by virtue of the treaties which ended their belligerency after World War II. The aim was not accomplished—at least not by way of nonrecognition.

Cuba provides the final illustration of this thesis. Actually, this is not a case of nonrecognition, though the lesson is the same. We had recognized the Castro regime and then broke diplomatic relations over the issue of harassment of American embassy personnel and the expropriation of American property. However, the break brought us little benefit. On the assumption that Castro had not yet finally decided to ally himself with the Soviet Union, our act eliminated his ability to choose and drove him toward Moscow. While we set the scene for the collective nonrecognition policy of the OAS, that policy has hardly been an unqualified success. Finally, when circumstances compelled us to negotiate with Cuba (during the missile crisis, the release of prisoners after the Bay of Pigs invasion, and the acceptance of refugees into the U.S.) the same old subterfuges and indirection had to be adopted in order to carry on business which was considered important. Would it not have been simpler never to break off diplomatic relations and express our moral disapproval in some other way? Nonrecognition brought no benefits at all.

This brings us to the policy of conditional recognition and its effectiveness. Let us note first that the policy of conditional recognition is practiced mostly with respect to Latin American countries. While we do not necessarily recognize new African and Asian governments of dubious constitutional legitimacy immediately upon their appearance, we rarely attempt to extract conditions from them. Eventually we recognize them automatically—usually sooner than later.

Typically, the United States has sought to extract three types of assurances before extending recognition in Latin America in recent years whenever the change of government came about by some method other than a "normal" election. The United States, in the case of military juntas, has sometimes insisted that they set a timetable for stepping down and holding elections. Further, insistence on respect for international obligations continues to prevail. Finally, since the advent of the Alliance for Progress, Washington has sometimes been concerned with the continuity of aid and development policies following a change of government, especially when such policies were geared to a national commitment to land reform, tax reform, or urban development. While negotiations governing these conditions go forward, bilateral American aid is sometimes suspended.

How effective are such efforts? It is my impression that we eventually recognize no matter what the negotiations accomplished or failed to achieve. Again, in the case of Argentina and Brazil, the effort to extract assurances is usually futile. Our political investment in Brazil's development is so immense as to preclude any meaningful leverage, such as cutting off all aid. But in the case of Peru, Ecuador, and Central America, conditional recognition sometimes yields the kinds of assurances sought.

It is my contention that such assurances are not very meaningful. They do not assure the legitimacy of the new government with respect to its own internal enemies. They do not spare the United States the accusation of intervention. They do not guarantee against a change of policy of the new government after recognition has been extended. They do not guarantee the effective and speedy implementation of the kinds of domestic policies favored by the United States. Conditional recognition, then, can be "effective" in the case of small countries in the sense of extracting some kind of statement from them; it cannot be effective in the larger sense of making that statement meaningful over an appreciable period of time. Probably no action on the part of the United States can achieve such a long-term state of affairs, since the factors which prompt the American search for special assurances are but symptoms of more fundamental conditions of social, political, and economic instability. But if that is the case, why incur the problems and disadvantages of conditional recognition?

The case against both nonrecognition and conditional recognition has been put superbly by a famous American international lawyer and former member of the Permanent Court of International Justice, John Bassett Moore:

> Our experience with the innovation has clearly demonstrated its ineffectiveness. It has repeatedly been shown that a frown or scowl on the countenance of the United States is not a cure for revolutions. . . .
> But this is not all. Not only does our recent departure keep us in an attitude of intervention in the domestic affairs of other countries, but it has indoctrinated our people in the preposterous and mischievous supposition that the recognition of a government implies approval of its constitution, its economic system, its attitude towards religion, and its general course of conduct. Not only is this supposition contrary to elementary principles of international law, which assure to each independent state the right to regulate its domestic affairs, but it is flagrantly at variance with the facts. It is, for instance, inconceivable that the government of the United States has at any time approved all the governments with which it held diplomatic relations. Even at the lowest ebb of our fortunes, I believe we should have resented such an imputation. As I speak, I hear, in the words of Ossian, "the voice of the days that are gone; they roll before me with their deeds." I hold in review the motley procession: governments liberal and governments illiberal; governments free

and governments unfree; governments honest, and governments corrupt; governments pacific and governments even aggressively warlike; empires, monarchies, and oligarchies; despotisms decked out as democracies, and tyrannies masquerading as republics—all representative of the motley world in which we live and with which we must do business. . . . [13]

His case remains as valid today as it was when these words were written.

V. TOWARD AUTOMATIC RECOGNITION

In view of the ineffectiveness of any other recognition policy—not to mention the inconveniences involved—automatic recognition remains as the most reasonable alternative open to us. It assures that lines of communication with a new state or government remain open. It facilitates the conduct of negotiations without subterfuge and indirection—and sooner or later negotiations become desirable even with one's enemy. It avoids the stigma of passing on the legitimacy of a new entity. *It makes it possible for us to express moral approval or disapproval through other channels and reserve recognition and diplomatic representation for the maintenance of contact.*

By opting for the advantages of a policy of automatic recognition, we should not overlook the fact that such a course is in no sense a cure-all. There are a number of problems to which even a policy of automatic recognition is no solution at all. The fact that we recognize a new state or government unconditionally and reasonably soon after its emergence guarantees us nothing—other than the maintenance of contact and the avoidance of the irritations connected with a period of ignoring the other's existence. The new state or government may not live up to its international obligations. It may encourage subversion abroad and expropriation of foreign-owned property at home. It probably did not attain power by either democratic or constitutional means. Certainly, by automatically recognizing such a regime we forego any thought of bending its behavior in a direction approved by the United States by means of recognition policy.

The point, however, is that any other recognition policy also will bring no assured benefits. Further, it will bring assured failures, embarrassment, and eventual regret. The question, then, is not: Should the United States

[13] John Bassett Moore, *Collected Papers*, Yale University Press, New Haven, 1930, Vol. VI, pp. 360-361; quoted in Briggs, *op. cit.*, pp. 129-130.

seek to influence the conduct of new regimes abroad? Rather, it is: What policies other than recognition policy are useful for bringing about such changes? The larger question does not at the moment concern us. Here our point is merely to illustrate the ineffectiveness of recognition policy in this context.

Even a policy of automatic recognition will not spare the United States the stigma of "intervention." At the moment, the trend of popular thought in underdeveloped countries suggests that a policy of automatic recognition of conservative regimes constitutes "intervention" on the side of "imperialism" and "neocolonialism." A policy of automatic recognition for left-wing revolutionary regimes, of course, is free from this stigma. The facts of the matter are, of course, that right-wing forces overthrow radical regimes as frequently as vice versa. Moreover, many extra-constitutional military regimes (despite the stereotype attaching to them in liberal circles) also opt for social change and reform, as in Indonesia, Peru, Burma, and Egypt. If these regimes survive, the United States sooner or later will find it desirable to deal with them. What good does it do then to make recognition conditional on the meeting of certain criteria of democratic legitimacy or reformist fervor? The clean way out of this dilemma is to recognize *any* new regime automatically and to use other means for expressing American approval or disapproval of its antecedents and policies. However, the adoption of such a policy will not save us from being called names.

At least not in the short run. In the immediate future, the thrust of opinion in Latin America will reserve the legitimacy of automatic recognition for left-wing reformist regimes. Conditional or nonrecognition will be urged for other regimes. However, if the United States manages to practice a consistent policy of automatic recognition for everybody, while using bilateral and multilateral channels for supporting or punishing other regimes, there may grow up a sentiment which grants the essentially *neutral* character of recognition. Recognition will become accepted for what it should be: a decision to admit that the new entity exists and that it is desirable to maintain contact with it. No more and no less. The same argument, of course, holds for the seating of any delegation of a new state or government in international organizations.

It is here that international organizations can be useful in neutralizing the act of recognition, in providing a forum in which the maintenance of contact achieves acceptability even when the parties heartily despise each other. Countries at war with each other still remain members of the United Nations or the OAS. Why, if both are tacitly accepted as equals in the international organization, should not their governments profit from this state of affairs to maintain diplomatic relations, even while they are fighting? But the fact that these events take place in international organizations provides an opportunity for governments to do likewise, without fanfare and ado, in their bilateral relations.

Should there be no conditions at all attendant upon recognition? Should any insurgent group be recognized if it remains alive for a few months? To push the doctrine of automatic recognition to such limits would be to defeat its very purpose—the maintenance of contact to facilitate negotiation. Our purpose is not to multiply recognized centers of authority but to give the globe a modicum of order and predictable conduct. Hence the minimal conditions specified by international law should provide the criteria for automatic recognition: (1) There must be a people, (2) with a specific territory, (3) possessing a government exercising effective control over that territory, and (4) able to engage in international relations.

Peking meets these conditions; so do Hanoi and Pankow. Castro's insurgents did not meet these conditions prior to January 1, 1959; they did meet them thereafter. The royalist rebels in Yemen do not meet these conditions now, who knows whether they will six months hence? In the meantime, the proper policy is the recognition of the government in San'a, though it was a satellite of Nasser. If it fails to maintain effective control, we ought to recognize its successor without asking any additional questions.

To argue that we ought to separate recognition policy from expressions of approval does not suggest that we ought to be equally friendly with all countries. Like every other country, the United States entertains values which it can and should express in its foreign policy. When these values clash with the aims of other countries—as they inevitably will—we must search for ways and means to make our values prevail, though we must recognize that the confrontation of values can end only in a compromise if war is to be avoided. What are these values, as they relate to the issue of recognition and intervention?

They were stated crisply and realistically by Adolf A. Berle in the ever-relevant context of our relations with Latin America. Berle argues that we have the right to insist on three conditions if our relations with any

Latin American regime are to be "friendly": (1) The regime should not pose a military threat to the United States. Cuba did not pose such a threat before the installation of Soviet missiles; it did thereafter. (2) The regime ought to safeguard basic human rights and avoid the techniques of the police state, even if it is not a "model democracy" by European and American standards. (3) The regime must refrain from seeking to export its ideology by revolutionary and subversive means.[14] I would add a fourth condition of approval: demonstrated commitment to the policies of domestic social reform incorporated in the Alliance for Progress. The bundle of four conditions establishes, in operation, the major ideals of the United States while safeguarding its military security.

The methods of achieving these aims, however, do not require any recognition policy other than automatic recognition. If we wish to stigmatize a regime for not meeting some or all of these conditions, we must make known our lack of friendliness and approval by reconsidering our foreign aid policy with respect to that country. Further, we may express our disapproval verbally in Washington, in the United Nations, and in the OAS. If the regime poses an active military threat to the United States, we ought to complain in the United Nations. If the appeal goes unheeded, we may indeed have to take unilateral measures which approach intervention. But we need not link such measures to recognition.

If human rights are violated in Paraguay, Haiti, or the Dominican Republic, the OAS provides us with a means for making known the injustice through its Commission on Human Rights. If the appeal of the Commission falls on deaf ears, we should encourage a policy of collective intervention on the part of the OAS. And if we fail in persuading the other Latin American countries to follow suit, we should abandon the effort. We shall have made our commitment known, a dual commitment to human rights *and* to collective measures rather than unilateral imposition. But we need not therefore break off diplomatic relations with the culprit regime.

Similar opportunities are provided through the instrumentality of the Inter-American Committee of the Alliance for Progress and the Inter-American Economic and Social Council. Again, if other countries decline to follow our lead, we are absolved in a moral sense—because we also refrain from unilateral imposition. If Castro seeks to topple governments in

[14] Adolf A. Berle, *Latin America: Diplomacy and Reality*, Harper & Row, New York, 1962, pp. 23-25.

Panama and Venezuela, the OAS provides the machinery for stopping such adventures, or the United Nations. If other governments do not consider his efforts a threat to them, we ought to respect their views—as long as he does not threaten American security. Again, recognition or nonrecognition will not affect the outcome one way or another.

The United States is a big power. It ought to grow up and recognize that being a big power does not give it the right, the duty, or the imperative to make the world over in its own image. The Dominican Republic did not threaten the American way of life any more than does North Vietnam. Regimes abroad will frequently fail to live up to our values without threatening our life one bit. The United States is neither the mentor of the world's morals nor its policeman. Let us advocate and support our values abroad, but let us not slide into a position of global righteousness in which an acceptance of our values becomes a condition for remaining in the game. Isolationism went too far in seeking protection from the world's vagaries and departures from American norms; global interventionism goes too far in seeking to universalize our creed. A policy of automatic recognition would constitute an acceptance of a moderate middle position.

5

U.S. Strategy and the New Administration

Richard Rosecrance

It is not necessary to belabor the need for ending the war in Vietnam. President Nixon either will succeed in terminating the war or he will not be elected President for a second term in 1972. A conclusion to the bloody war in Southeast Asia is necessary not only because it affects American domestic politics but because it diverts resources from other, even more pressing problems, such as the rebuilding of American urban areas. With the U.S. defense budget spiraling under the stimulus of Vietnam, there cannot be a real solution to the problem of the ghetto; nor can there be any significant alleviation of minority discontent in this country. Since approximately half of the U.S. defense budget now goes for general purpose forces, meaningful savings can only be derived from this quarter, and they will have to be secured.

In terms of longer perspective, however, American strategy will be determined by the requirement of designing a means of getting along simultaneously with Europe and the Soviet Union. In several respects, this is a new requirement. In the days of the Eisenhower administration, it was not necessary to consider Moscow as an equal adversary, nor was there a significant range of common American and Russian interests. Nuclear proliferation had not approached its present potentially explosive threshold. The Soviets seemed more bent on causing than containing local conflicts outside of Europe. And in Europe itself, they provoked two Berlin crises in the space of three years. Further, their nuclear capabilities were still so limited, that despite the temporary furor over the supposed "missile gap" of 1957-1960, the Russians were not in a position to launch a successful first strike on the United States; they had not yet developed secure retaliatory capabilities. In these circumstances, the United States could devote its attention to the strategic and tactical needs of Western European states. Various proposals for nuclear sharing and information exchange developed, culminating in the NATO Nuclear Planning Group. And yet, despite President Kennedy's concern for rebuilding the partnership with Europe, the alliance fell into disrepair. For the last four years of President Johnson's administration Europe was held in abeyance while planners wrestled with Vietnam. And since the solution of the Vietnam conflict was all important to Johnson, he placed an inordinate emphasis upon satisfactory ties with the Russians to procure it. A paradox of Mr. Johnson's term, then, is that he sought to develop closer relations with Russia when those relations were not yet mandatory; he neglected Europe when much might have been done to bring a greater harmony. And one of the pitfalls that President Nixon must avoid is embracing such a diametrically opposed policy. The temptation to put the allies first and ignore or snub Moscow must be resisted as surely as its contrary. For today, Moscow cannot be held at arm's length: Soviet strategic policy, Soviet arms to the Arabs, Soviet rivalry with China for leadership of communism in the less developed countries—these directly impinge on a wide range of American interests and involvements. They must be dealt with in their own terms, not simply as a by-product of U.S. attempts to shore up the European alliance.

In the simplest strategic terms, the original U.S. nuclear guarantee to Europe was based on preventing or greatly reducing the damage that would be done to the U.S. population and industrial structure if war broke out. Since the U.S. and its allies were unwilling or unable to provide the forces to defend Europe in conventional terms despite the urgings of Secretary McNamara for six years, deterrence of a Russian attack came to depend (as it had under Eisenhower) upon Western and American ability to escalate the conflict. It does not appear today that a conventional strategy is any more feasible: Czechoslovakia is likely to hold up further reductions by about one year; it is not likely to prevent them. And, from a purely American point of view, it is the American general purpose forces which contribute both to our trade imbalance and to an overlarge defense budget. Far from increasing these forces, the Nixon administration will have to find means of reducing them if it is to cope with a wide range of new domestic needs and demands. A tactical nuclear strategy might be one possible recourse, but it has appeared that tactical nuclear weapons offer no unilateral advantage and they would wreak enormous devastation within Europe. Even West Germany has been unwilling to embrace a tactical atomic strategy in recent years. The alternatives are some form of strategic escalation. Only an assurance that the United States is both willing and able to assume the strategic initiative in response to a Soviet attack on Europe is likely to prevent further deterioration in the state of Western military relations. And even this will not restore the old political solidarity. Maintenance of even a semblance of former political cohesion will depend upon conceding a much larger range of autonomy to Europe in political-military terms.

But if the United States is to offer even the minimum reassurance to Europe that it will be prepared to give a strategic response to a Soviet attack, it must develop the doctrine or capability for in fact doing so. And that capability or doctrine will have to be consistent with minimizing or at least substantially reducing the damage that would be inflicted in such an event upon the American population. Merely to think in these terms is immediately to see the absolute centrality of the strategic relationship with the U.S.S.R. For if we are to build up our strategic forces to the point where damage to ourselves can be limited in a conflict originating in Europe, we impinge directly upon Soviet capabilities and Soviet security. If we seek a new maximum counterforce strategy which will knock out such a large portion of the Soviet force that the remainder cannot inflict meaningful damage on the U.S., then we have removed the Soviet capacity to deter us. Whatever the theoretical stability of such a state of affairs, it is unlikely that Russian planners would let it persist for any period without rejoinder. We then would have called forth Russian strategic increases similar to those of the period 1966-1969. In the end we might have procured a slightly better capacity to limit damage, but only at the expense of two new rounds of the arms race and new tension between Russia and the United States. And the equilibrium reached would probably be highly unstable. In the past three years we have seen the trebling of the Soviet strategic force to the point where, by the end of this year, the Soviets will have parity or even a slight superiority in fixed-base launchers. It must therefore be acknowledged that the current Soviet leadership has great sensitivity to the size of the American offensive force and probably will be prepared to adjust their force in response to changes in our own. In short, if we seek to reassure Europe by an offensive buildup, we run directly into Soviet resistance. We please or at least try to stop displeasing Europe only at the expense of creating anxiety in the Soviet Union. Even European states, seeking to resume efforts at further *détente* with the Soviets as Prague cools down, may not wish us to embrace a strategy which raises suspicions in Moscow. The dilemma for the next few years, then, is to find a strategic doctrine and force which will reassure Europe without upsetting the strategic equilibrium with Russia.

To put the question in these terms is to see how far we are from re-solving it. At the moment we are testing advanced multiple, independently targeted, re-entry vehicles (MIRV) for use on Minuteman III and Poseidon missiles. These warheads, several in a missile envelope, are accurate and capable of deploying on diverse targets. If newspaper reports are to be be-lieved, they have considerable "hard-target" capability; they might be used against hardened missile sites.[1] Conjoined with a large increase of ABM defenses, MIRV offensive capabilities "could give rise to the ugly possibility of each side's possessing a first-strike capability against the other."[2] It should be noted that the Russians appear also to be working on MIRV systems and have conducted at least one preliminary test.

The problem raised by the current U.S. offensive buildup is that it reassures Europe of our strategic guarantee only by raising uncertainties in Russia. The potential uncertainties are of such a magnitude, moreover, that rapid Soviet efforts toward MIRV capabilities can be confidently pre-dicted. After major deployments of MIRV on both sides, security will come to reside in sea or land-mobile capabilities. And even these capacities would have to be capable of penetrating any ABM that an opponent would put up. Thus, there is either a large degree of strategic uncertainty on both sides which could make strategic pre-emption look more attractive than it

---

[1] See Carl Kaysen, "Agenda for the Nation" (draft paper, July 31, 1968), pp. 20-23.

[2] Kaysen, *op. cit.*, p. 23.

has for the past five years, or there is strategic equilibrium which cancels any assurance the U.S. might want to make to the Europeans. Offensive increases, particularly of MIRV capacities, tend to provoke symmetrical and offsetting responses.

The defect of an offensive increment, of course, is that it demands a margin of advantage over the opponent to be effective. Offensive forces limit damage only if they are superior in numbers or operating characteristics to those of an adversary. In the past this criterion offered no real obstacle to the United States, for American forces possessed an ample offensive superiority over the U.S.S.R. That favorable margin no longer exists, and while U.S. offensive forces will continue to have certain advantages in number or variety over their Russian counterparts, they will no longer possess a sufficient edge to dependably limit damage to the American population. Some other way of satisfying the political requirements of Europe and the strategic requirements of the Soviet Union must be found. The U.S. must resist the temptation merely to multiply its offensive capabilities.

Fortunately, there are other ways of improving one's guarantee to Europe without directly threatening the U.S.S.R. To do this, it is necessary to find means of limiting damage to the United States that also permit the Soviets to reduce damage to their population and industry. In other words, one must find damage-limiting capacities that do not require greatly superior American forces. If such strategies can be discovered, the Soviets should have great interest in them, and they could even form an important part of the discussion at the U.S.-Soviet strategic talks which must soon be resumed. Indeed, the developments of the past few years have seen strategic outcomes which are not entirely in the interest of either major power. The Soviets have greatly increased their ability to damage the American homeland on first or second strike. The U.S. continues to hold a very large fraction of the Soviet population and industrial capacity hostage to its strategic arms. Recent U.S. posture statements have shown the potential impact of an unrestricted missile war with Moscow to be 100 to 120 million American fatalities. The Soviets would suffer just as grievously. The United States has a capability measured at minimum in terms of inflicting damage on the order of 25 to 50 percent of the Soviet population and 50 to 75 percent of its industrial capacity. Since the U.S. calculates in terms of worst case assumptions, moreover, a typical case of hypothetical warfare would inflict an even greater toll on the Soviet Union.

Neither power has perhaps taken due account of the new era of "nuclear plenty" which we are entering. It is difficult to realize that when Secretary John Foster Dulles talked of "massive retaliation," he was referring to a capability to deliver at most a few tens of megatons upon an aggressor. Today, the U.S. possesses the power to launch at least a hundred times as much destructive force, even after absorbing a well-designed Soviet first strike. Equally important, the Soviet ability to devastate the United States has also risen many-fold in the past ten years.

The increasing horrendousness of war should not create dismay among American or Russian planners if foreknowledge of such a result proportionately diminishes the likelihood of attack. If war becomes less probable as it becomes more terrible, the world is no worse off. But it may be difficult for either American or Russian strategists to believe that the world is more stable with 1,000 thermonuclear ICBMs on each side than it was with 500. It is difficult to convince oneself that the strategic balance was shaky with 50 million people dependably held at risk on both sides, and therefore only prospective tolls of 100 or 125 million are sufficient to assure rational deterrence. The buildup of American and Soviet offensive capabilities may make it possible to kill more people, but it does not make war appreciably less likely. It seems more plausible that deterrence "saturates" at several tens of millions of population hostages on both sides, and in the Eisenhower administration even the Air Force chiefs appeared to be satisfied with an ability to cause destruction which was far less than that we now possess.

While we have reduced the "rational" probability of war to a low point therefore, both the Soviets and ourselves have failed in a second objective—that of mitigating the consequences of war. If war should occur, the impact for the United States, the Soviet Union, and particularly Western Europe are virtually beyond calculation. In terms of decision theory, our mutual "expectation" of war is now much worse than it was only four or five years ago. The "expectation" of any event is the "probability" that it will occur multiplied by the "consequences" which ensue if it does occur. One can therefore tolerate a relatively high probability of irritating but essentially innocuous events; even a very low probability of a very catastrophic event, however, may be too high. In the past few years and at least since the attainment of hardened and/or mobile missile forces on both sides of the strategic balance, the probability of strategic war, certainly of war initiated at the behest of a rationally calculating attacker, has been low. But while strategic war has remained improbable, even very improbable, its probability has not been reduced to zero. Accident, miscalculation, inadvertence, catalytic involvement, and escalation might still cause a war which neither the Soviets nor ourselves seek. No matter how horrible war is, therefore, its occurrence cannot simply be ruled out. It is now in the interest of both the United States and the Soviet Union to find means of reducing the consequences of war in a way which does not increase its probability. This should be the main subject of the strategic talks.

From the standpoint of increasing the credibility of the U.S. nuclear guarantee to Europe as well, prospective damage to the United States also should be reduced. In essence this means that the U.S. has to be able to show somewhat greater willingness to escalate in Europe than is presently the case. And if this is true, does that not mean that the Soviet structure of deterrence has weakened? If the Soviets have to anticipate a greater probability of American strategic strikes in response to a Russian conventional attack in Central Europe, does this not indicate that the U.S. is less clearly deterred? Since U.S. strategic response upon the Soviet homeland would only follow a major Soviet attack upon Europe, it would scarcely appear that the independent probability of an unprovoked American strike has risen. Nor would there be any greater U.S. willingness to escalate in other situations. The United States would not resolve on strategic pre-emption as a result of a Middle East confrontation; even in a new crisis it would not permit escalation to strategic war over Southeast Asia with either the Chinese or the Russians unless the American public could be virtually insulated from strategic attack. In Europe itself the Soviets would not have to face any increase in the autonomous threat; they merely would have to recognize a slightly greater restriction upon their freedom of action. What the U.S. would be willing to endure to fulfill its strategic obligations to Europe might be more shattering than what it would accept in other instances. In addition to the ties of tradition, culture, and sentiment, large numbers of American forces would be engaged in a losing struggle with Soviet attacking forces. The probable course of the conventional battle would be likely to raise risks of U.S. strategic escalation. Further, since Europe is the zone of greatest political and military stakes, both for the Soviets and ourselves, even a modest probability of U.S. strategic escalation would be sufficient to deter a Russian advance. From the Russian standpoint of worst-case calculation, it may be true that nothing short of a military balance which indicated a virtual strategic parting of the ways between the United States and Europe would offer a sufficient incentive for Soviet attack. In the final analysis, then, greater damage-limiting capacities in the United States might make the nuclear guarantee to Europe more credible, and to this extent reduce Soviet options; it would not raise the probability either of attack or escalation overall.

At the same time, moreover, the Soviets would be procuring a greater damage-limiting capacity of their own. In symmetrical ways, this could be held logically to reduce American options in Eastern Europe. A reduction of damage impacts on both sides could be regarded as reducing the restraints on strategic escalation in areas of greatest political-military sensitivity. Since the concessions would be bilateral, however, neither power would gain at the expense of the other. And since the unleashing of strategic war could only come in response to very dangerous actions of conventional assault, war would not be more attractive to a rationally calculating adversary. If the restraints on strategic escalation had slightly declined, the restraints on very destabilizing conventional initiatives would have increased. Once again, the probability of rational major aggression would remain low: the major causes of war would still have to be found in accident, miscalculation, inadvertence, and unintended escalation.

There are a number of ways in which greater damage-limiting capabilities could be procured on both sides. Some of these depend on doctrinal shifts, others upon alterations in capability. From an ideal standpoint, the strategic talks might lead not just to a freeze of offensive missile stocks, but to reductions. As long as a reduced number of launchers were not permitted to be augmented by MIRV capacities, the number of warheads available for retaliatory detonation on population targets would decline. This would mean reduced population impacts on both sides. Discussions could center on systems-analytic means of assuring that population hostages dependably held at risk decline by a factor of at least two. The problem with such an alternative is that important strides toward a MIRV capability have already occurred on both sides with the U.S. in the lead. Tests have taken place. The two protagonists would have to be able to believe that sufficient progress toward a MIRV had not been made to permit an implacement of MIRV without further testing. If they could not believe this, nothing short of on-site inspection of launchers and vehicles would suffice to convince a protagonist that MIRVs had not been implaced. Such a requirement would be likely to doom an agreement in advance. It is therefore not likely that MIRVs can be precluded in a strategic arrangement unless agreement can be reached in the very short-term future. Today, the U.S. is engaged in a continued testing program for its MIRVs. If a halt were called in these tests in the first months of the Nixon administration, there would be little apparent reason for the Soviets to question the reality of the U.S. abstention. Nor would U.S. policy-makers have to worry that the Soviets possessed an operational MIRV capability. The longer the two testing programs continue, however, the harder it will be for either side to believe that an operational MIRV capacity is not in hand.

If reduction without MIRV cannot be agreed to, there are a number of other ways in which some degree of damage limitation might be procured for both sides. Acknowledging that MIRV capacities might increase hard-target capability, one should seek to make sure that other elements of the strategic force can perform the minimum assured destruction task. If fixed-base missiles become vulnerable, allowance for a requisite number of sea or land-mobile systems would have to be made. Such a mix would also involve very narrow limitations on ABM on both sides since defensive systems might theoretically be increased to the point where they could cope with a small mobile force. The inclusion of MIRVs could offer damage-limiting capabilities through attacks on fixed land-based forces; the mobile component could then be held to levels which would have the dependable capability of inflicting, say, half the damage that would be attained under current strategic circumstances.

A further possibility would be a prohibition on MIRVs and the buildup of ABM on both sides. No new ICBM launchers could be added, and ABM would seek to take some toll of existing forces. ABM could in this way procure some of the advantages of strategic reductions, though clearly the costs would be larger on both sides. ABM also would give protection against Nth-Country forces, and rule out small or demonstration attacks. Deterrence would continue to function at previous levels, but the population held at risk on both sides would decline.

Damage-limiting capabilities on both sides might also be enhanced through doctrinal change. Secretary McNamara enunciated the first doctrines of strategic restraint in 1962, though he downgraded them in succeeding posture statements. A doctrine of counterforce-city avoidance would stress limitation on strategic strikes, both of attack and retaliation, to force targets or nonpopulous industrial installations. Such a strategy could be useful from two points of view; first, in response to an attack upon

missile installations and bomber bases, it would offer an additional option
to immediate retaliation upon cities. If the U.S. automatically responded to
an attack on American sites by hitting Soviet cities, it would be giving
Moscow warrant and incentive for mounting a further attack, this time directed at U.S. urban areas. In other words a U.S. retaliatory doctrine of
hitting cities only would help to incite attacks on American cities which
otherwise would not certainly take place. Some launchers might possess a
refire capability; not all bombers would have left their bases or been re-
fueled; various radar or ABM installations would remain as attractive
targets. Industrial or technological complexes at some remove from population centers could also be brought under attack. But the most important
facet of restrained counterforce targeting would be the avoidance of cities.
A Soviet doctrine of restrained response could also help ensure that strategic initiatives by the United States in response to an attack on Europe
would also take a city-avoidance form. Both sides would come to recognize
under this strategy that for bargaining purposes it would be crucial to keep
the opponent's population intact as negotiation proceeds. The first power
to lose control and attack his foe's urban areas would have guaranteed his
own demise without gaining original objectives.

It would of course not follow that the development of a city-avoidance
retaliatory strategy would induce limitation upon an opponent. He might
decide, as the Soviets have proclaimed they have done, to employ a mixed
strategy, attacking cities as well as launching sites in a single salvo. But the
development of a restrained retaliatory strategy would mean that an opponent would not have to plan on the basis of a certain and immediate
U.S. response upon cities. Since he would no longer need to do so, he also
would not have to attack American cities on a first strike. The development
of retaliatory options for the United States, therefore, also creates options
for the Soviet Union. Russian planners may not decide to take them up,
but it appears certain that the Soviets would have no incentive to use restraint in their attack if they were convinced that the U.S. would exercise
no restraint in retaliation. Nor would either the U.S. or the Soviet Union
be giving up the capability or the option of hitting cities at a later stage.
Protected, dispersed, mobile forces would remain to deliver a *riposte* upon
cities if called upon to do so. Both powers would know that the other retained such a capability to use on third or later strikes. An aggressor,
therefore, could not hope to gain his objectives and emerge unscathed.
Indeed, the aggressor's only chance of avoiding substantial strikes upon

urban populations would appear to depend upon compromise and restraint in the negotiating sessions designed to bring the war to a close.

Restrained city-avoidance targeting would also have reference to a U.S. strategic initiative in response to a massive attack in Europe. A U.S. strike confined to military and nonpopulous targets could work a substantial attrition on Soviet missile forces. It would not, however, destroy the Soviet's protected ability to retaliate on U.S. cities; nor would it place them in a position where they would either have to retaliate immediately on American cities, thereby provoking an American attack on Soviet urban centers, or face another attack on missile forces which would reduce them below the level adequate for retaliatory purposes. In short, what is proposed here is not a "coercive" strategy which would gain success over the Soviets by reducing their options to two choices, each unsatisfactory. Rather, the Soviets would retain a range of options, none of which demanded immediate execution. Under these circumstances, they could decide to attack U.S. strategic capabilities in retaliation, avoiding immediate attacks on cities, while retaining a protected capability in reserve that might be used against cities at a later stage.

If such strategic doctrines were developed, they would represent a welcome reversion to notions which Mr. McNamara abandoned after 1962. When he spelled out his "counterforce" notions in June and December of that year, his remarks were interpreted as justifying the development of a first-strike capability against the U.S.S.R. While it was true that the United States in a *de facto* sense did retain a considerable strategic edge over the Russians, at least as long as Russian forces were both small in number and vulnerable to attack, McNamara's counterforce doctrines did not apply exclusively to a period in which the United States might possibly hope to make a successful attack on Soviet missile sites and bomber bases. Indeed, if the Soviets were to retain a major retaliatory capability even after the U.S. had launched a strategic strike in response to a Soviet thrust in Europe, it was important that that capability permit the Russians to withhold some protected forces for possible later use against cities. If the Soviets had no ability to withhold, their retaliation would have to take the form of a mixed attack on U.S. sites and population targets, or perhaps an attack on cities alone. In this sense a more varied and flexible Russian capability had certain advantages for the United States. As Secretary McNamara pointed out to Stewart Alsop: "I believe myself that a counterforce strategy is most likely to apply in circumstances in which *both* sides have the capability of surviving a first strike and retaliating selectively." He noted that as long as the United States had the ability to respond with overwhelming force after a Soviet attack, the Soviets would not have the ability to mount any further attacks; they would therefore have to launch their initial attack against both sites and cities. He continued, "This is why a nuclear exchange confined to military targets seems more possible, not less, when *both* sides have a sure second strike capability. Then you might have a more stable 'balance of terror.' "[3] An era of "mutual deterrence" could have mutual benefits.

Such a strategy also might influence Russian doctrine. Since the Soviets saw only first-strike implications in McNamara's counterforce doctrine, it is not surprising that they uniformly rejected them. Citing certain U.S. military specialists, V. D. Sokolovsky noted: "All this taken together places great doubt on the effectiveness of 'counterforce' for, in their opinion, there can be no counting on the complete destruction of the enemy's strategic weapons, especially if the growing number of mobile launchers of strategic rockets and nuclear rocket-carrying submarines is taken into account." Though Soviet criticisms of "counterforce" may have been somewhat tempered in the past year, there is no indication that they have frontally addressed the restrained counterforce formulations that are implicit in notions of "mutual deterrence" or that they fully understand that these notions become more appropriate, not less so, as Soviet forces grow in number, protection, dispersal, and invulnerability. It is therefore possible that a new attempt to elicit a favorable Soviet response to city-avoidance targeting could be more successful. Even if the Soviets decide to develop options to employ such a strategy, however, they may be hesitant to avow it for fear that an indication that they might confine their response to U.S. sites and strategic installations would reduce prewar deterrence. If they believe this, they have reached different conclusions from those calculated by Secretary McNamara when he first broached the theory. Even restrained counterforce targeting would not sanction a rational decision to launch a first strike; the reduction of damage would not be significant enough to warrant a pre-emptive attack; it would scarcely justify escalation in the most fateful tactical battles over the most critical political frontiers.

[3] Stewart Alsop, "Our New Strategy: The Alternatives to Total War," *The Saturday Evening Post*, December 1, 1962.

Indeed, an increase in strategic restraint could not be deleterious to the Soviet Union if it does not plan a major aggression in Europe.

Restrained counterforce, be it noted, produces "damage limiting" not through a *physical* attrition of an enemy's capability, but through an attempt to influence his options and thereby affect his *will*. The doctrine of city avoidance is not a doctrine of the first strike; nor is it a method of "coercing" an antagonist by depriving him of satisfactory options. In one sense, U.S. adoption of such a strategy would increase the range of Soviet choices and make possible strategies which the Russians would otherwise have to abjure. U.S. restraint does not make Soviet restraint certain; but the absence of U.S. restraint makes Soviet restraint impossible.

Such doctrines could scarcely be accompanied by a unilateral buildup in U.S. offensive and defensive capabilities. If they were substantially increased as America turned to counterforce conceptions, the new doctrines would once again be misinterpreted. Once again the Soviets would read "counterforce first strike" for "restrained bargaining strike." Agreement could not be worked out. If MIRV is to be added to our missiles, only a substantial enhancement of mobile forces would be likely to produce a new equilibrium; the latter would presumably mostly take place on the Soviet side. Mutual buildups of offensive forces could be tolerated by a strategy of restraint so long as they are not mutually vulnerable.

While restrained counterforce does not necessarily hold the key to the mutual damage-limitation problem, the technological preconditions for such a strategy have now arrived. It was perhaps too much to expect that Secretary McNamara in 1962 would continue to push a strategic theory which justified a major Soviet buildup, particularly when it was not even clear that he was making a virtue of necessity. Today, that Russian buildup has already taken place, and the question is whether we develop doctrines that concede presumptive strategic equality, or try to regain a decisive superiority. If the efforts of current Soviet decision-makers are any guide, it seems unlikely that they will stand on their current program as we move to a proliferation of accurate warheads.

As we have seen, a greater damage-limiting potential could offer a degree of reassurance to Europeans who wonder about the viability of the U.S. nuclear guarantee. Since the Johnson administration went to great pains, in its efforts to refute the case for ABM, to point out that any damage-limiting that might be produced by strategic defense could be canceled by Russian offensive increases, European politicians are now convinced that the U.S. is and remains crucially vulnerable to nuclear attack. It is not therefore surprising that they are beginning to question the reliability of U.S. strategic response. A successful and mutual damage-limiting program, reducing prospective fatality tolls on both sides (though not below the threshold of unacceptability), would provide an additional reassurance to NATO, needed after the Czech *débâcle*. It would reverse the strategic trend of recent years, in capability and doctrinal terms.

It would not, however, affect basic political tendencies within the alliance. The trend toward separate national action in matters of common concern has now spread beyond France. In fact, one of the American delusions about Gaullism was to assume that it was confined to France. President de Gaulle receives American antipathy for attitudes and to some extent for policies that are becoming more widespread in Europe. Germany has pursued an independent policy toward Eastern Europe and with lesser emphasis toward the Soviet Union. British nationalists lurk under the cloak of the British deterrent. Italy has charted an independent course on the nonproliferation treaty and other matters. Sweden and Switzerland have mooted the question of developing a joint nuclear capability. The old unquestioning reliance upon the United States is gone, and it has not disappeared merely because American policy has seemed to waver. Greater American resolution on behalf of NATO will probably help, but it will by no means remove European strategic discontents.

For some time now Europeans have asked for a much larger share in U.S. strategic decision-making. To some degree this has been granted, and more concessions, such as those having to do with joint strategic contingency planning, are not beyond the realm of possibility. But a true internationalization of the American force, particularly with a nuclear China on the scene, is just not in the cards. The United States will not make its strategic fates dependent upon the vote of a European contingent. If this is true, and most of postwar military history underscores the point, then some other means of satisfying the European sense of grievance, and a just grievance at that, must be found.

To this point, the United States has strongly resisted tendencies toward proliferation in the alliance. It did not help the French in any major way, and it gave the British little help between World War II and the detonation of their hydrogen bomb in 1957. After proliferation had already taken place, however, the United States sought, in both cases, to make joint planning and to some degree targeting arrangements that would prevent the Western deterrent from being used in an uncoordinated and divisive way. As Secretary McNamara stressed: "We are convinced that a general nuclear war target system is indivisible, and if, despite all our efforts, nuclear war should occur, our best hope lies in conducting a centrally controlled campaign against all of the enemy's vital nuclear capabilities, while retaining reserve forces, all centrally controlled."[4] Independent nuclear capacities would enormously complicate this problem, and perhaps make controlled conduct of a strategic war impossible. Presumably America has had some success in devising joint arrangements with the British; the degree of success with France is not fully clear. At any event, if nuclear proliferation proceeds in Europe, it will become more and more difficult to make arrangements with all national nuclear forces. At some point the United States will find itself in the position either of giving "triggers" on its own deterrent to a range of other nuclear states, or else of considering "hot line" contingencies in which it might wish to divorce itself from the strategic actions of European states. Neither possibility is particularly attractive. Eventually the United States will have to derive a strategic policy in the European context which more than mitigates the consequences of a proliferation which it has been unable to halt.

Mr. McNamara's effort in 1962 was perhaps the last attempt to ask fledgling nuclear powers to give it all up as a bad job. From 1962-1964, the United States experimented with multilateral force conceptions, hoping that some measure of joint ownership and control of a special nuclear force would reduce the European appetite for nuclear hardware. The MLF satisfied no one because it really did not give independent control (the U.S. retained a veto), and it did not offer a really potent strategic punch. The British came to see it as a way of paying for part of their own strategic force. The MLF got as far as it did but also held few genuine attractions because it represented a political compromise; even the Germans were cool toward it. They saw it primarily as a means of further involving the U.S. in European security.

Any new attempt to cope with proliferation in the alliance must recognize that the United States cannot hope to set up a new European or multilateral force and at the same time retain a veto on its operation. The force must be independent, just as national nuclear forces are independent.

[4] Speech at Ann Arbor, Mich., June 16, 1962.

But if a purely European force can be constituted at some point in the future, that force could develop relationships of presumptive strategic equality with the United States in nuclear planning and targeting. Europeans have resisted joint planning where an assumed inferiority might be involved. A European strategic force, certainly over time, would not cause worries on that score. Such a force could be used independently. But it would scarcely raise greater dangers to the U.S. than a profusion of smaller forces where the coordination problem would become well-nigh insoluble.

It is inappropriate here to inquire into ways and means. Certainly, strategic forces are the most sensitive national instruments; they are thus the last to be internationalized. It is unthinkable that a European strategic force could come about without a prior European defense organization in less glamorous fields. A European organization of armaments production would be a starter; a greater coordination of armies and tactical air forces could follow. At some point French and British strategic forces could be seen as the nucleus of a genuinely European force, or they could not. One should not approach the ideal of a collective European strategic force with a primary rationale of getting either the British or the French out of the independent nuclear business. In strategic, economic, and technological terms, their cooperation would be invaluable, but it would not necessarily have to involve an inclusion of present national forces.

Such conceptions would give rise to political problems of considerable magnitude. New collective forces would violate the nonproliferation treaty if one or more of the existing European nuclear powers did not resign its own force with the creation of a new one. If both France and Britain refused such an act, German fears of discrimination would be enormously heightened. And discrimination against Germany would doom the proposal from the start. Only a European collectivity could accord Germany nuclear equality without proliferation. An arrangement which prescribed discrimination would not be one Bonn would join. Immanent tendencies in Europe itself, then, would press toward a concept that would neither violate the nonproliferation treaty nor place the Germans at a discount. Most important such tendencies would for the first time accord Europe presumptive strategic equality with the United States. It would therefore help to erase the persistent resentments that have plagued NATO since its inception. It would help to solve the NATO dilemma: how to organize an alliance on the basis of equality among states which are unequal.

Finally, such a force, or tendencies working toward it, would not necessarily prevent a reasonable strategic relationship with the Russians. Far more than most powers, Moscow is aware and fearful of the spread of weapons. It is patent that the United States no longer controls the pace of diffusion in the West, any more than Russia calls the tune in the East. The growth of nationalism on several parts in both Eastern and Western Europe could lead to conflicts which neither Washington nor the Kremlin wants. Resentments of either Russia or America could foster demands for independent capabilities. It may be realistic for the nonce to insist that states individually renounce nuclear ambitions. But for the longer term a policy of simple resistance is not sufficient. Only an alternative to national proliferation offers real help. The Russians may not be happy about European forces, but neither are they pleased with national progress and prospects. A weakening of U.S. influence on the German pivot is not an evolution which Moscow finds altogether heartening. But if Germany cannot be "contained" by the United States, she certainly cannot be submerged by a congeries of European powers. Some collective approach is necessary. A European *démarche* would not be contrary to Soviet interests.

In the final analysis none of these adumbrated policies may hold the key to bridging the gap between Europe and the Soviet Union. But one thing seems clear: we can no longer afford the luxury of having our policy toward one determined as an incident of policy toward the other. Henceforth the two are independent determinants of U.S. strategy.

6

The United States
and Asia

Robert A. Scalapino

What happens in Asia during the coming decade may well determine whether the world as a whole can move away from war, poverty, and backwardness. Its massive population and substantial resources together with the configuration of power rimming the Pacific Basin make Asia as important to our future as Europe. The United States, the Soviet Union, Japan, China, India, Indonesia and Pakistan—to mention only the most powerful or the most populous societies—each have a vital stake in Asia and the Pacific. Moreover, each of these nations comes into contact, often intimate, with the others because of a common presence in the area. Clearly, peace and prosperity in the late twentieth century hinge upon events in this crucial region.

The United States cannot escape the implications of these facts. It should not be necessary to refight the foreign policy battles of the two decades following World War I. The issue of "isolation" versus "international involvement" is totally outmoded. In the first half of the twentieth century, America learned in painful fashion that certain types of international crises would not go away if ignored, and might become progressively more difficult to contain. It also discovered that inaction as much as action represented a major policy decision with consequences that were often far-reaching. The advent of the United States as the foremost power of the late twentieth century, and a nation with vital Asia-Pacific concerns, should only have reinforced those lessons.

The importance of Asia, however, is matched by its complexity. This vast and heterogeneous region does not approach the "regularity" of Europe, divided though that continent may be. Even in its Eastern portions, Asia has political divisions more complicated, more unstable, and less susceptible to viable regional arrangements than those of Europe. Economic development varies enormously. So do the cultures of the area. One could not run a wider gamut than that between the New Guineans and the mountain peoples of Southeast Asia on the one hand, and such people as the Japanese on the other. For a considerable portion of Asia, the nation-building process has only begun, with formidable problems of integration lying ahead. Socioeconomic development represents an equally grave challenge.

Thus, the importance of Asia argues for American policies of concern and commitment. The complexity of Asia argues for policies attuned to that condition, intricate in the degree required, and not resting upon the premise of quick and simple solutions.

The first major task should be to develop a conceptual framework for an Asia-Pacific policy in its broadest dimensions, to determine what is desirable and what is feasible in the most basic terms. Admittedly, this is difficult, given the diversities noted above. It is not surprising that the United States has thus far failed to achieve "an Asian policy," in the sense of a coordinated set of actions and attitudes having validity for the area as a whole. Without some basic framework, however, policies attuned to one nation or one region are likely to be less effective, possibly even counter-productive in terms of overall objectives.

What framework is logical? Perhaps the most critical need in the Asia-Pacific area today is for the creation of a workable international order, a system of interstate relations that can operate to promote peace. To date, the handling of disputes in Asia has been characterized by a high level of violence. Moreover, both the facilities and the will for regularized communications among states have been weak. Indeed, noncontact has been as pronounced as in any part of the world. Intergovernmental ties have often been minimal and fragmentary. The character of Asian foreign relations in many cases has served to strengthen rather than diminish historic enmities, exclusiveness, and xenophobia.

Under certain circumstances, to be sure, one can make out a case for isolationism on the part of an emerging society. When it pervades the area as a whole, however, a dangerous situation exists, given the complex and interrelated problems which most Asian-Pacific states face. Thus, a first goal should be to broaden the channels of communication and contact among these states.

This will not be easy. Ideological as well as cultural differences run deep in this area, with some states and parties currently committed to the use of force to effect change—both within and outside national boundaries. The situation is further complicated by the existence of three "divided states," and the fact that in each of these cases the Communists are currently determined that unity shall be effected on their terms alone and by whatever means are necessary to achieve success. Problems within each state, moreover, including the tensions between religious, economic, ethnic, and regional groups, tend to increase the pressures for violence, across state boundaries as well as within them.

Perhaps an approach to this central problem is available, however, one that has long existed in embryonic form but has recently been neglected. Shortly after World War II, a number of Asian states, including India, China, Indonesia, and Burma, proclaimed their willingness to abide by certain principles of peaceful coexistence. These principles, moreover, were spelled out, at least in basic terms. They included pledges to respect the integrity of states having different social and political systems; to avoid interference in the internal affairs of other states; and to resolve disputes in a peaceful manner.

It is important to remember that these principles were advanced within the Asian community itself, and that the leading Communist state of Asia once proclaimed its willingness to conduct its foreign policies in accordance with them. The rising tension between India and China and numerous other changes in political relationships in the area caused them to fall into abeyance. Is it not desirable now to make these principles common goals for all states in the Asia-Pacific area, with efforts being made immediately to broaden and sharpen their implications, and to find the means—possibly through new international institutions—to supervise and enforce their application in the real political world?

If we are to aim in these directions, it will be necessary at the outset to seek a new set of political definitions. It is clear that the old definitions of "war" and "peace," of "noninterference" and "aggression" no longer suffice in the late twentieth century. In these respects, what does the concept of peaceful coexistence imply? At its root, peaceful coexistence must imply a willingness to acknowledge the right to exist of governments having different ideologies, different political institutions, and different policies. On the positive side, to acknowledge that right further implies a willingness, at a minimum, to accept some form of communications with that government, some means of handling common concerns. On the negative side, it implies a willingness to forego efforts to overthrow that government, whether by such overt means as moving one's own armies against it, or by the wide range of covert means that involve combining with indigenous forces in seeking its destruction.

This is an indication of how principles advanced by Asians more than a decade ago might constitute a fruitful beginning in the quest for a more peaceful order in this troubled part of the world. Those principles underwrite the primacy of the government in existence, and the acceptance of the state as it is. There is no suggestion within them that internal groups seeking to challenge that government are to be accorded support by another government simply because the latter favors the policies of the "outs." On the contrary, the pledge is one of mutual noninterference in the internal affairs of another state.

Against such a background, two broad principles might now be advanced which taken together could constitute the basis for a new approach to international relations in the Asia-Pacific area:

1. Governments in control of a fixed territory, possessing a physical capitol, having established institutions of authority, and possessing *de facto* control over the people within this area shall be accepted as states.

2. All states shall accept in principle the right of other states to pursue political and socioeconomic theories and institutions of their own choosing. They shall reserve the right on behalf of themselves and their citizens to support or criticize those institutions and theories ver-

bally, and to render or withhold assistance of an economic, political, or military nature to the government concerned. However, they shall not undertake actions of two types: (a) Physical assistance in any form to indigenous groups dedicated to the overthrow of the government; (b) physical intervention on behalf of a government when it is engaged in fighting a civil war, to be defined as a war involving only people whose permanent residence is within that government's territory as defined in point 1.

Admittedly, these two points pose certain problems, some of which we shall tackle shortly. The effort to secure a working basis for a new international order will only have commenced with their acceptance in principle, it will not have been completed.

The first point, however, looks toward a new concept of recognition in international relations, one that is at once more flexible and more realistic. Recognition, if the first point is accepted, would come into effect automatically for certain minimal purposes at least, and be completely divorced from questions both of affinity (likes and dislikes) and permanency (the assumption that a *de facto* state will exist for all time, or in precisely the same physical form).

Thus, a government that passes the tests set forth broadly under point 1 above would secure recognition at least for the following purposes: (1) Membership in such international and regional bodies as relate to its needs, concerns, and interests; (2) participation in international conferences on a similar basis.

No one can force a state to belong to the United Nations, for example, but the above proposition would clearly envisage an automatic invitation to all *de facto* states, including the so-called "divided states." It would also support invitations to such states to a diversity of conferences and organizations, *ad hoc* or permanent, relating to the full range of problems that confront mankind.

Beyond that, relations at a bilateral level could be determined by the states involved. Thus, recognition in the above terms would not necessarily require that a full range of state-to-state relations be established in every instance, desirable though this might generally be. In some cases, indeed, there might be no relations between two deeply antagonistic countries. In other situations, only limited bilateral relations might be possible. In any case, however, recognition conceptualized in this general form would not necessarily imply an acceptance of the permanency of any given *de facto* state.

Under these conditions, a new approach to the problem of the "divided states" might be possible. Clearly, this problem is and will remain the most serious obstacle to any workable system of peaceful coexistence in the Asia-Pacific area, and to the applicability of the two broad points set forth earlier. The traditional approach has been for most nations to regard China-Taiwan, South-North Korea, and South-North Vietnam as "legitimately" single states, having only one "legal" government. The recognized government tends generally to be the one which accords most closely with the ideological-political position of the external state involved, with the other government being ignored to the extent possible.

Let it be said quickly that these traditional procedures have been accepted, indeed, frequently demanded by the six governments immediately concerned. And for the Communists, special advantages are involved. Championing unification by force if necessary, they have sought to get the concept of "people's war" accepted as a civil-war technique under all circumstances, thereby causing external aid to the government under attack to be defined as interference in the internal affairs of another state, hence illegal.

These traditional views and approaches, however, do not accord with reality, are not conducive to the settlement of international problems, and greatly increase the risk of wars, small and large. Now is the time to promote fundamentally new doctrines. First, the thesis that these states can be treated as divided but single entities, with military operations between their separate parts defined as "civil wars" conflicts squarely with the facts. In each case, the present *de facto* situation is the product of a complex chain of events, including among other things, incomplete international agreements. None of these "divided states" has ever been unified under any one of the existing governments. In this sense, the term "divided state" itself is highly suspect, despite the desire of many individuals within these states for ultimate unification. (Precisely how many individuals are now committed to such a goal, however, and what priority they are prepared to assign it constitute very legitimate questions.)

Meanwhile, violent incidents between these states have had, and will continue to have, instant repercussions throughout the region as a whole, and in the world. If, for example, the tables were turned and the Republic of Korea suddenly began military actions against the Democratic People's Republic of Korea, does anyone believe that the Soviet Union or China would remain unconcerned? To define conflicts between any of the current *de facto* states of Asia as civil wars is impossible.

What, then, constitutes a realistic and promising approach? First, it should be reiterated that there is no need to judge the issue of ultimate unification at this time. In point of fact, to be sure, the existing states involved in the divided territories are moving away from rather than toward unity in most crucial respects. The divisions between China and Taiwan, South and North Korea, and South and North Vietnam are generally growing wider, not narrower, whether the measurement be economic, social, or political. Nevertheless, there is no need on the part of the international community to determine whether unification is possible or impossible. There *is* a need, however, to determine *how* it can take place. More specifically, it is essential to agree that it shall not take place by allowing one state to force another state into submission by force of arms.

In essence, this means that if peaceful coexistence is to have any meaning in Asia, and in the world, the "divided states" must come under the same basic rules as apply to other states: First, each existing state constitutes a separate entity to the extent it meets the conditions outlined in point 1 above, and deserves recognition in the terms already set forth; second, military action, overt or covert, by one such state against another shall constitute aggression, not civil war, and be treated as such. Unification efforts by peaceful means, on the other hand, shall be regarded as proper and legitimate.

Principles alone, even if broad acceptance were ultimately obtained, cannot be expected to suffice. Some concept of sanctions must be envisaged, together with a system of workable defense should those sanctions fail. Once again, this is a most appropriate time to rethink and reformulate the entire concept of defense against aggression and the creation of incentives for peaceful coexistence.

However unfortunate, there can be no full substitute for a political-military equilibrium in the Asia-Pacific region at this juncture. That is to say, given stated Communist objectives and known Communist means— North Korean and North Vietnamese as well as Chinese—it would be foolish to assume that one could abet the principles and processes outlined above by abandoning non-Communist alliances, including those of a military character. To encourage moderation and discourage extremism requires a policy that combines flexibility and patience with firmness of purpose and a capacity to render the costs of undesirable policies on the part of one's adversaries intolerably high for them, when necessary. Otherwise, one's influence on *their* decision-making processes is marginal at best.

The bridge between the past and the future, however, should be constructed at this point largely with political and economic materials. For example, the principles of peaceful coexistence, even if approved in their essence by Asian-Pacific states, will require constant interpretation and possibly enforcement. Charges of violation will come from diverse sources. The need to act multilaterally may well arise. What institutions can serve to explore charges, survey and publicize the evidence, issue reports, act, or recommend action by others?

Several alternatives deserve to be explored. One possibility is to make use of the United Nations, establishing through it a series of commissions on peaceful coexistence, with each commission attuned in its representation to the key areas of the world. To use the UN effectively for this purpose, however, would probably require that universal membership already have been instituted. Another possibility would be for such a commission (or commissions) to be set up independently, on the initiative of states within the Asia-Pacific region. Perhaps there are certain advantages in experimenting with this problem first on a regional basis—in Asia, where the threat of war is most acute. Moreover, any system which increases the responsibility of the states most immediately involved has much to recommend it.

Whatever the precise formula, some institutional means is needed whereby we can create a new body of international law pertaining to peaceful coexistence—its meaning and requirements. This body of law and its enforcement constitute the most significant political challenge of the late twentieth century. And whatever the institutional device ultimately chosen, it would seem desirable that the particular agency established have these functions exclusively. Charged with this vital problem, it should not be encumbered with diverse other responsibilities.

Handling the issue of peaceful coexistence on a regional basis, however, need not preclude an encouragement to other regional organizations simultaneously. In the economic and social fields, groups like ASPAC, ASEAN and the Asian Development Bank deserve support and strengthening. In addition, new special-purpose organizations might help to extend communications across hitherto unbridged chasms, whether these relate to given economic concerns such as the Mekong River Development, epidemics and communicable diseases, or weather forecasts and controls. In each of these cases, moreover, the constituency of the "region" might well be different.

It is fashionable at the moment to belittle regionalism, just as it was popular a short time ago to endow it with near magical powers. Soon, it might be hoped, we shall cease engaging in the inevitable pendulum swing between wild enthusiasm and total deprecation that tends to operate whenever new concepts are introduced. There are no panaceas. Regionalism at best can be only one of a number of approaches in Asia. Nor should it be regarded as suitable in all matters. Some problems require the concentrated efforts of a single state. Others can only be handled bilaterally. Often, as is well known, geographic propinquity or economic similarity constitute barriers rather than assets to the solution of problems, and other bases of unity must be sought.

Moreover, a realistic appraisal of the Asia-Pacific area at present strongly argues for the establishment of some "neutral" states—Asian equivalents of Austria, Finland, and Switzerland in Europe. The concepts outlined above would enable such states to participate in certain forms of regionalism, should they choose to do so, while not participating in others, for example, those of a strongly political or military character.

If we can assume that the above proposals constitute a desirable framework for a new Asian policy, how do we develop specific policies—military, political, and economic—to accord with that framework? The first task is to see the situation as it is, not as we would have it. The contemporary realities cannot be ignored if meaningful policies are to be fashioned. Let us turn initially to the existing crisis involving the security of states in the Asian area. From the non-Communist perspective, three of the four communist states of Asia currently have a very strong commitment to military power and its use. China not only has the largest conventional military force among Asian states by a considerable measure, but as is well known, it is also engaged in a forced march toward nuclear weapons. North Korea is now the most heavily militarized society in Asia, possibly in the world, measured in terms of its allocation of available resources and energies. And one need scarcely dwell upon the military capacities and commitments of North Vietnam.

As stressed earlier, moreover, each of these states has repeatedly proclaimed its willingness to use force, if necessary, to achieve its objectives. For the present at least, such statements must be given priority over those indicating a willingness to accept peaceful coexistence. Among the Asian Communist states, only Mongolia at this point appears to have modest military capacities and aims, relying as it does for security exclusively on the Soviet protective shield.

Currently, the military power of the three Asian Communist states is being used in a diversity of ways. China, still in the throes of a domestic crisis, employs the great bulk of her army for internal administrative and control purposes, with a smaller portion—probably stretched very thin at the moment—to guard her northern and eastern frontiers against two distinctly different opponents, the Russians and the Nationalists. Chinese external involvement is thus perforce small-scale at the moment, and in the historic Maoist pattern, aimed at assistance to those indigenous groups prepared to challenge "the power holders" via revolution. Support is presently being given to a wide range of dissidents, some of whom are primitive ethnic minorities, not remotely interested in Marxism-Leninism-Maoism.

It is probably a mistake to regard China as either "weak" or "strong" in the abstract. In the most general sense, to be sure, China is "weak," certainly vis-à-vis the Soviet Union or the United States, and likely to remain so for the indefinite future. Some would argue, moreover, that Chinese actions, as opposed to words, will continue to be exceedingly cautious as due to an understanding of that weakness. This could prove to be true, however, without greatly reducing the problem of the small states surrounding China. Whatever the essentially defensive character of Chinese Communist thinking vis-à-vis the two major powers, Chinese leaders have indicated a reasonably high level of confidence in their ability to defend China against superpower threats merely by relying upon their nation's vastness in size and population and its capacity to wear out or absorb any opponent, however strong. If the level of confidence in this respect continues to be strong, it could provide a continuous impetus for intervention in the internal affairs of other states through precisely the type of low-risk, low-cost policies of aid to dissidents of all sorts that has been pursued in the recent past, with no specific timetable for "liberation" necessarily set.

Weakness or strength is in the eye of the beholder, and to the Southeast Asian leaders, China is not weak. Even if the levels of its involvement in that area were not raised appreciably, an uncomfortable amount of violence and disruption could be supported, a fact well understood by all of those in authority.

It should also be clear, however, that intervention in the internal affairs of other states by China does not merely take the form of military arms to Meo tribesmen, support for Naga dissidents, or the sponsorship of a "Thai Patriotic Front" in Peking. It also includes a relatively deep involvement in the politics of the Japanese "left," for example, and a history of involvement also in the affairs of North Korea and North Vietnam. It is precisely because of these facts that it becomes so urgent for all concerned to explore in depth both the requirements of peaceful coexistence and the further means of meeting new forms of expansionism.

Future Chinese foreign policy cannot be predicted with any assurance. Nor is it possible to indicate with certainty the correlation between foreign policy and domestic trends. Should China achieve a higher degree of internal political stability and economic growth in the near future, would this increase or decrease her interest in acquiring hegemony over portions of Asia? Should the internal scene remain troubled, would "left adventurism" of the Sukarno type prove an attractive distraction from pressing domestic problems, or would capacities in this respect be so severely limited as to remove China as a threat to others and pose instead the more classic problem of China as an attractive target for outsiders? One cannot answer these supremely important questions at this point, but it does seem likely that the general framework within which Asian international relations operate can influence, possibly in decisive fashion, the Chinese decisions ultimately made.

Uncertainties about the foreign policies of North Korea and North Vietnam are perhaps less. Whatever their own concern about China, and this is not inconsiderable, both of these small countries have a strong commitment to expand the present sphere of their political control. North Korea intends to "liberate" the south, with a target date of 1970-1971 having been established. North Vietnam's interest extends not only to the absorption of South Vietnam, but to the control of Laos and Cambodia as well. Should that control be achieved, moreover, there would undoubtedly be a strong interest in seeing Thailand gravitate into the greater Vietnamese sphere of influence, albeit through Thai Communists. At that stage, or possibly much earlier, conflicts in the "national interests" of the Chinese and Vietnamese would likely become serious. If events had proceeded to this point, however, that would be of scant comfort to the Laotians, Cambodians, or Thais.

None of these facts can be ignored by the non-Communist states of the Asia-Pacific region, including the United States. At the same time, it is important to project the Communist view of the Asian security problem also, if only for the purpose of trying to determine whether there are any conceivable common grounds on which to rest principles and procedures. In this connection, we must assume that complaints voiced by the Communists, however exaggerated and distorted, represent real concerns on their part. One broad set of complaints, of course, relates to the massive presence of close-in American power in East Asia and to the network of alliances centrally connected with that power. The charge is that the United States and its allies pose an aggressive threat to the security of the Communist states and seek to isolate them from normal intercourse with the external world. A second set of complaints relate to the view already noted, that intervention against "people's wars" constitutes an unwarranted interference in the internal affairs of another state. The Communists seek to uphold the right of revolution against the status quo, and more importantly their right to participate in that revolution indiscriminately, by equating all incidents having any internal element as basically internal affairs.

In these views are signaled the crucial questions to be negotiated in the years that lie ahead. Can a military equilibrium which in the past has necessarily involved a high quotient of American power be altered in content and form as new means of resolving disputes are developed and military technology changes? Can meaningful distinctions be made and enforced between situations truly internal in character and those with external components?

We cannot await the "settlement" of such basic issues, however, prior to beginning those military adjustments that seem warranted in terms of present conditions, and are in conformity with our long-range objectives. If the foregoing analysis of Communist capacities and intentions is correct, the gravest threat to the peace and security of Asia from our standpoint comes in the form of covert aggression, involving a sustained effort to interact with various dissident forces within the target state. Compared to this threat, other dangers such as nuclear war or even the type of overt aggression undertaken against South Korea in 1950 seem remote, providing the United States does not withdraw its broad nuclear umbrella from those allies with whom it has treaty obligations.

This latter qualification is vitally important at this point in time. Now, as in the past, only the United States can deter a big nation such as the Soviet Union or China from aggressive action of a conventional type, should such policies be envisaged. (And where no American guarantee extends, that possibility surely exists, as Czechoslovakia indicates so graphically.) Of equal importance, only the United States can have a significant influence upon the level of risk-taking to which states like North Korea will be prepared to commit themselves. In the final analysis, our deterrent power is one of the primary reasons why overt aggression is the lesser threat in Eastern Asia today.

As long as the United States is willing to play its role, however, the immediate threat will be that of covert aggression, and that involves, in the first instance, the internal viability of the state under real or potential assault. Much that has been written and said about this particular problem up to date is unduly simple. It is an enormously complicated matter, and not one susceptible to any easy formula. For example, the capacity of a state to handle its problems in a reasonably adequate fashion, and to demonstrate economic and political progress does not guarantee its immunity to assault, possibly successful assault, via the combined external-internal forces that can operate against it under the banners of a "people's war."

It should be admitted frankly that any state experimenting with some degree of political or economic "openness," especially a new state, finds itself operating at a signal disadvantage against a highly organized, "closed" system when the two systems are brought into conflict. The notion that this disadvantage can somehow be overcome or contained solely through libertarian or economic reforms is exceedingly naive. How to combine openness with authority; how to develop organizational skills that can offset those of the Communists without succumbing to their system or a near counterpart; how to undertake needed socioeconomic reforms and modernization without destroying all individual rights and becoming rigidly authoritarian—these are the real challenges for the emerging states of our times.

They obviously become more acute problems when such a state is brought under direct Communist attack, with external as well as internal forces involved. Under such circumstances, the degree of openness which the state involved can preserve may well depend upon whether it has external support or not. To put this point specifically, one effect of a general American withdrawal of military protection from non-Communist Asia at present would be that, survive or fall, many of those states would be forced to increase the quotient of authoritarianism in their internal systems, in some cases by a significant amount.

However, it is neither desirable nor necessary at this point for the United States to play the primary role in the full range of defense needs of the non-Communist Asia-Pacific states. With covert aggression the most likely threat, defense begins at home, and it must involve a wide range of techniques. Sound socioeconomic policies, efficient police and intelligence services, legal outlets for political opposition, and modernized military forces are all essential elements in any defense network. And it must be constantly stressed that the primary responsibility rests with the state concerned. The American role should be directed essentially at seeking to prevent or limit external forces from entering the scene.

Indigenous efforts can best be supplemented by bilateral defense agreements and arrangements. These constitute a "second tier" in the security structure of non-Communist Asia, and one still necessary in the light of recent events. Not all of these arrangements need to be highly formal or all-inclusive, and not all can or should involve the United States. For example, cooperation with respect to police and intelligence activities can be vitally important between such states as Thailand and Malaysia. Similarly, Indonesia and Malaysia have good reason to cooperate with respect to issues of security in Borneo.

When it comes to broader regional defense concepts, there is a need for new attitudes and approaches. Conceived in conventional terms, regional defense offers very limited possibilities in Asia at present. Even if it were feasible, it might succeed mainly in heightening the rigidity of the major camps. However, it is not feasible, now or for the foreseeable future. Japan will not play a military role beyond her own territory within the next few years in any case, and thus a regional military agreement encompassing Northeast Asia is not possible. In Southeast Asia, moreover, a number of essential states are not prepared at present to participate in any such arrangement.

It is possible, however, to think of regional defense in more complex terms. In Northeast Asia, for example, Japan does have a vital stake in the security of South Korea, and she is likely to have a growing concern over a nuclear China. Consequently, to her present economic role she may well be prepared even now to add a political one, as a member of a commission on peaceful coexistence, and in other respects as well. In Southeast Asia, a regional defense concept to be meaningful must encompass the idea of allowing, indeed encouraging, the existence of certain nonaligned "buffer" regions like Laos, Cambodia, and South Vietnam, the integrity and security of which would be guaranteed by international agreement and underwritten by means of some suprastate supervisory-enforcement mechanism.

Thus, the general direction of American military policy becomes clear. Our basic position, as suggested above, must be that each state is primarily responsible for its own defense against "people's wars," even when these involve some element of external aggression. Naturally, this does not preclude our giving economic, technical, and military assistance to such states. Moreover, our pledge should be an unremitting effort to get all types of aggression properly defined and made susceptible to various forms of international sanctions. At the same time, we must continue to deter massive, overt aggression in Asia as in Europe. For these purposes, certain bilateral defense agreements must be maintained, notably those with Japan, South Korea, and Taiwan, and possibly, depending upon developments, those with South Vietnam and Thailand. We should be most receptive, however, to the concepts of regional defense noted above, concepts encompassing flexible military-political arrangements, and these should be advanced as rapidly as possible as supplements to or substitutes for current bilateral agreements.

In the meantime, there are many reasons for altering our traditional military posture in Asia now. We should move quickly away from the present strong reliance upon fixed bases in populous areas. These give maximal opportunities for making the United States the forward target of political attack, provide an excuse for procrastination on the part of host governments in constructing their own defense policies, and encourage the tactics of political blackmail, even from certain close allies. Our primary reliance should be upon our mid-Pacific bases and mobile units, including nuclear-powered submarines and airborne troop carriers. It should be the responsibility of those with whom we have defense agreements to maintain bases and facilities immediately suitable to American use in the event of need and request by the country concerned, without the permanent presence of Americans. In no area is it so essential that policies catch up with political realities and technological innovations, including those that are involved in modern guerrilla warfare.

The more dramatic steps on behalf of peace and development, of course, lie in the political and economic realm, essential though sound military policies be. We have already sketched a new political course, revolving around the use of peaceful coexistence and an attempt to move away from policies and attitudes derivative from an era of intensive bipolarism. In the economic sphere also, there is new ground to be broken. Here, truly we stand at a crossroads. On the one hand, the technological breakthroughs of the past ten years, and those promised for the decade that lies immediately ahead, offer more chances for major economic gains than could have been dreamed possible only a few years ago. On the other hand, rigid doctrinaire barriers and a great wall of ignorance remain to be broken down if governments and people are to translate these possibilities into ongoing programs. Moreover, among the so-called "advanced" states of the region, another type of challenge has emerged. The pressures for economic nationalism are almost equal to those on behalf of greater openness.

With respect to the first problem, that of rapid economic development, a series of priorities must be established. Which problems deserve primary attention? Surely population control, agricultural modernization, high-level manpower training, and the development of small and medium industry warrant concentrated efforts. Where does one start? Some states certainly have greater intrinsic importance than others, partly because trends within them will cast a wide influence over the region as a whole. Moreover, some states or regions within states are more prepared at this point to commit themselves to the future, and thereby to demonstrate quickly the benefits of economic development to those not yet ready for innovation or realism. In essence, the United States should support developmental programs in those places and by those means designed to have an early impact, not merely on the sources directly involved but upon the region as a whole, including hopefully those states and people with antiquated economic and social institutions.

Finally, what methods are to be employed? Experience to this point strongly suggests that a full range of governmental and private sources of support should be tapped, that both bilateral and multilateral arrangements are essential, and that the most essential ingredient is always the feasibility of the project and the commitment of those centrally involved to its success. It is perfectly logical to ask tough-minded questions with respect to these latter issues. Until governments have developed workable economic programs and established feasible means of executing them, aid can be of little use. Sometimes, indeed, it can be a major hindrance.

The present pressures within the United States to abandon economic and technical assistance, however, are most regrettable. In many respects, this is the period when such aid in the Asia-Pacific region can have its maximum effect. A first generation of ideological leaders has largely passed from the scene, and the new leadership is more pragmatic, more dedicated to problem-solving, and more technically and administratively oriented. In addition, a sizable amount of high-level manpower has been accumulated, along with extensive experience in planning and management. Thus, it would be tragic if the United States should eliminate the economic component of aid at a time when it can have the greatest meaning.

Nor should the major contributions of private American enterprises be overlooked. Not only does the private sector provide a significant input to developing societies in the form of techniques. It is also training a new class of administrators and skilled technicians. Quite possibly, the combined efforts of American government and private enterprise in the training of a "second generation elite," a generation of managers, technicians, economists, scientists, agronomists, and entrepreneurs, will represent the single most important contribution which we—and other advanced nations—can make to the future of Asia.

It would be most beneficial if a permanent, nongovernmental, international body of officials and scholars could now be set up to draw together the lessons of the past concerning economic development and study the key issues on a continuous basis. These issues would pertain to the "advanced" nations as well as to the "emerging" societies. Under present conditions, many of the mistakes of the past are likely to be repeated by groups and nations not even aware of similar efforts having been made at an earlier point. Ideally, officials and scholars from Communist nations should also participate in such a group—so that developmental methods could be fully compared and debated. If political strictures made it impossible for most Communist states, perhaps Yugoslavia at least would be willing to join. In any case, in no area is it so essential to fully expose and constantly reassess prevailing theories and practices.

Economic development is a never-ending process, with the "advanced" nations now moving into new and uncharted courses. Once again, the risks and the opportunities combine to warrant some new approaches. For many reasons, this is a time to launch a "Pacific community," with its membership initially revolving around the "advanced" Pacific nations—Australia, Canada, Japan, Mexico, New Zealand, and the United States. Such a group could become the nucleus for breaking down the threatening advent of economic nationalism; tackling the urgent problem of cooperation in economic policies toward emerging states; and providing the type of psychological-political imagery so essential if the peoples of the Pacific are to conceive of themselves as a part of a broader, deeply interrelated community.

It now remains to suggest how the programs set forth above might be applied to specific regions and nations. Starting with northeast Asia, a complex situation is immediately discerned. On the one hand, Japan is the most modern nation in Asia and increasingly the most powerful state within the entire area in economic terms. Within a decade or less, the economic role of Japan is likely to surpass that of the United States in every nation of Eastern Asia. Yet on the other hand, Japan is not prepared at present, either psychologically or politically, to play a significant role in the defense of her most immediate region, not to mention such areas as Southeast Asia.

The thesis that Japan can be expected to play the American role in Asia is thus untenable, either now or in the foreseeable future. Unquestionably, a reawakening of Japanese interest in, and concern for Asia has been underway for several years. A reassessment of the Japanese role is taking place. Japanese involvement in the affairs of Asia, political as well as economic, has increased and will continue to do so. Japanese policy, however, is likely to remain basically dependent upon the concept of an American responsibility for the prevention of aggression, including that against Japan proper.

Meanwhile, two thorny issues threaten to make American-Japanese relations more troubled in the future than at any time since World War II. Both require prompt and dramatic measures if we are to establish our vital relationship on a sounder footing. One issue lies in the economic field, and here, the initiative should rest primarily with Japan. Despite the fact that Japan today is third among nations in the world in industrial productivity, she continues to pursue protectionist policies both with respect to trade and foreign investment. There is a growing and justifiable American impatience with such policies. Quite beyond the question of future American-Japanese relations, however, economic nationalism is not in Japan's self-interest. Trading with almost every nation in the world, and with the probability of massive increases in such trade during the coming decade, Japan should be in the forefront of the drive for less restrictive economic practices. Her future hinges upon the prospect that the world can move away from economic nationalism, and she has every reason to lead the way.

A Pacific community undertaken at this point could give strong encouragement to those in Japan who are prepared to break with the past. It could also heighten the sense of responsibility both in Japan and in America for cooperative thinking and planning in the economic field. A decade ago, we took the first step by establishing a U.S.-Japan committee on trade and economic development. It is time now to take a second, larger step into the future.

The second issue, that of Okinawa, provides a supreme test of the wisdom and foresight of the United States. It is very unfortunate that a readjustment of our position on Okinawa has been delayed until it has become a major political liability for us. No current issue illustrates more graphically the fact that the timing of policy is as important as its content.

For nearly a quarter of a century, the million people of Okinawa have been under American rule, living in the midst of a giant base and on a base economy. There can be little doubt that Okinawa has played a major role in the past in helping us to maintain our defense commitments to our Asian allies, especially Korea and Japan, and in signaling to the Communists our determination to meet those commitments. At this point, however, Okinawa has become an issue threatening the entire American-Japanese relationship.

What are the alternatives? Perhaps they are five in number: (1) a continuance of the status quo, meaning full American administration and control; (2) reversion of Okinawa to Japanese administrative control, with the rights retained of keeping all types of weapons, including nuclear weapons, on the island and having free use of the facilities (no requirement of prior Japanese consent, in the event of war); (3) reversion with free use, but without nuclear weapons; (4) reversion on the same terms that apply to bases in Japan proper, namely, no nuclear weapons and prior consent for base use required; (5) reversion and withdrawal of American forces from all Japan-Okinawa bases.

Confronted with these alternatives and given the present mix of political-military conditions, the United States should move in bold fashion away from its present position that the more minimal the concessions, the better. That position, if sustained, is likely to lead to political disaster.

Specifically, the date for reversion should be set in 1969, and that date should be within the 1971-1972 period. At the time of reversion, base use should be established on the same terms as then apply to bases in Japan proper. Moreover, the most serious consideration should be given to restricting American utilization to the bases in Japan proper, giving up the Okinawa bases in exchange for increased Japanese defense commitments, Japanese financial assistance in relocating certain vital American facilities to nonpopulated areas outside Japan, and a Japanese pledge to maintain the Okinawa bases at a readiness level for use in the event of an emergency.

The military utility of Okinawa has steadily declined in recent years, and it will continue to do so. Its use in the Vietnam war was decidedly marginal. It continues to have some meaning with respect to the defense of Korea, but under the conditions outlined above, Korean defense could be underwritten satisfactorily and potential aggressors could realize our determination to meet our treaty obligations to Korea and Japan, an essential requirement of any settlement. The compelling reasons for a dramatic policy shift on Okinawa lie in the most elemental political facts of life. Whatever formal terms are reached, the free use of Okinawa or the employment of nuclear weapons in the event of war are completely impossible politically, once this island becomes a part of Japan. From that point, Okinawa can be meaningful as a base only in situations where the Japanese government *and* people feel their own security directly involved, and only via the uses which they are prepared to accept. Since we cannot delay reversion beyond a few years, to insist upon free use or nuclear weapons is to insist upon fictitious military advantages at huge political cost.

Moreover, we do not want Japan to become accustomed to nuclear weapons on her soil, because we do not want to abet nuclear proliferation in any form. On the other hand, we do want Japan to feel a greater responsibility for her own defense, a responsibility retarded in many respects by our massive presence in Okinawa. We cannot and we should not seek to determine Japanese foreign policies, including defense policies, but we can and should remove certain obstacles contributed by us to her decision-making process. And we must cease paying the heavy political costs involved in current defense arrangements.

It is also clear that in the postreversion period, Japanese-Okinawan relations are going to be extremely delicate and complex. If Americans provide a triangular dimension by remaining on the island, especially as a major force, it is almost certain that the political liabilities for us will be exceedingly high.

There is a real danger that the United States will fail to appreciate the gravity of this situation and the significance of the issues outlined above. Undoubtedly, it will be argued that the cost of the bases alone precludes their abandonment and partial replacement elsewhere. But if one accepts the figure of $800 million as their approximate value, that is only twelve days' expenses for the Vietnam war, scarcely worth jeopardizing the U.S.-Japan alliance, especially if Japan were willing to aid in replacement costs. It may also be argued that the policies advocated above would reduce the credibility of the American commitment, especially to South Korea. As already noted, that need not be the case. Under a settlement that was advantageous to her politically, Japan might be caused to express her own deep concern with the security of the Republic of Korea, thereby signaling the availability of the bases should that security be threatened.

Apart from economic issues and Okinawa, there is a broader problem confronting the United States and Japan in relation to Asian security and development. A myth has been cultivated that must now be challenged. That myth is the thesis that peace and progress in Asia can be made secure if the United States for its part, maintains its defense commitments and the nuclear shield, and Japan for its part, expands its trade and economic aid programs. These functions are both necessary, but they are not sufficient. Indeed, they omit those vital political considerations which are so crucial.

If Japan cannot play a military role in Asia, she can assume certain political responsibilities in addition to economic ones. Already, to be sure, via ASPAC and ASEAN, her political role has increased, and she has begun to be more active in the United Nations also, a body which should some day be reorganized so that Japan and India will be permanent Security Council members. It remains now for Japan to concern herself more meaningfully with the central problem of peace-keeping. It is for this reason that the concept of creating new mechanisms for peaceful coexistence might have special applicability for Japan, providing a means for her fuller participation. Surely no nation has a greater stake than Japan in the peace and security of Asia, and none should have a keener appreciation of the political dimensions of this problem.

The American-Japanese alliance will survive in all probability, because it is based upon a solid set of mutual interests. It will flourish, however, only if the issues that now confront us are resolved on a basis of mutuality and reciprocal responsibilities, a new level of communications, closer cultural as well as economic ties, and the movement toward a broader community.

Let us turn next to Korea, a nation once again under Communist attack. The Republic of Korea in certain respects is a monument to what can be done when commitment is combined with patience. After many bleak years, South Korean progress in the economic field is very encouraging, with an overall growth rate of 8 to 10 percent per annum. Political "growth" has been slower, partly because this society lives under the constant threat of war. A one and one-half party system has been maintained, but tension between the government and the student-intellectual community is substantial (a condition not unknown elsewhere!).

In graphic form, Korea illustrates some of the complexities of modern Asia and the dilemma for Americans. It is not possible for every society to have a Western-style democracy, and to insist upon this as a prerequisite for support is not only hopelessly unrealistic, but represents in itself a form of implicit political imperialism. At the same time, to give support, including the pledge of American lives, to a nation pursuing "illiberal" policies, runs strongly against the grain of our people.

There is no simple answer to this dilemma, but there are two "educational" programs which, if carried on simultaneously, might be beneficial. One should be directed at our own citizens, including a substantial portion of our intellectual elite. It should stress two major points: first, as noted earlier, American withdrawal from Asia would greatly abet the authoritarian forces on all sides; second and more importantly, the distinctions among "nondemocratic" elements or systems cannot be ignored. There is an enormous difference, for example, between one's relative freedom in Seoul and in Pyongyang, and perhaps an even greater difference in the potentialities for political change which the political systems of South and North Korea carry within them. Much the same points could be made with respect to Saigon and Hanoi, Taipei and Peking. Unfortunately, some of our most sophisticated citizens have been unable to grasp the implications of these facts.

On the other hand, it is both appropriate and necessary to point out to our allies in Asia that American public opinion, including that of our political elite, will increasingly challenge heavy American commitments to states where repressive policies are a primary reliance. In the final analysis, the fabric of American relations with our allies *is* dependent upon the image of a government and its relations with its people. Our own government is remiss when it does not signal that point clearly.

At the same time, there is a message to be conveyed also to the "opposition" in such countries. We must challenge the thesis that the United States can or should bear the responsibility for making such changes in their country as they may consider necessary or desirable. We cannot play that role without ultimately being repudiated—by them as well as by others. The myth of American omnipotence, incidentally, has been far more deeply implanted in the minds of certain Asians than in the American mind. It is essential, therefore, to enunciate the limits of American responsibility and power now, and to live within those limits.

This is not to deny the importance—and the legitimacy—of setting up certain conditions for American aid. It is surely desirable to develop "quid pro quo" policies and to enforce them. We have the right and duty to say, "If you do this, we will do that. If you prefer not to do so, we cannot do that, but you are free to operate on your own, or via other sources of support."

There is reason to hope that the problems outlined above will not constitute major issues between the Republic of Korea and the United States. We have been through great ordeals together, and we have learned much about each other. We have a common stake in the peace and prosperity of South Korea, a stake measured in lives as well as resources. This point needs to be underlined to the Korean Communists and their allies. At the same time, the lessons of Korea, in all of their intricacy, deserve to be studied closely, for here are mirrored some of the problems and the potentialities of other "emerging" societies.

Let us turn next to Taiwan and China, areas crucial to our Asian policies as a whole. Perhaps several broad policy alternatives are available, and each deserves careful reexamination. One would be to continue essentially the policy adopted in 1950, a policy based upon the position that the

Chinese government has a single locus of power legally, namely in Taipei, and that it is the only government which we should recognize. That policy, however, has already undergone a number of significant modifications: our refusal to support offensive operations against the mainland; our efforts to aid in the development of a self-sufficient, increasingly indigenous Taiwan; and our willingness to meet with the mainland Chinese government at Warsaw, using as representatives men of ambassadorial status. Moreover, the validity of this policy in terms of the realities of Asia and its capacity to provide a common basis for action among ourselves and our allies are increasingly subject to doubt.

Another policy would be to announce shortly that we acknowledge that there is only one China, leaving open the question of who governs China, but by implication at least, abandoning the thesis that the people on Taiwan have any rights concerning their own future. The strongest argument for such a policy is that it would accord with the present positions of both the Communists and Nationalists, and more importantly, that it might be the *sine qua non* of any improved relations with the People's Republic of China.

There are a number of serious objections to this policy, however, some of which are not immediately obvious. First, it is always hazardous to adopt a policy that is not in conformity with the facts as they are, or as they are likely to be. Mainland China and Taiwan are not one. Moreover, as suggested earlier, they are not growing toward each other. On the contrary, they are growing away from each other at an extraordinary rate, measured in any terms. A younger generation of Chinese—both of mainland and local background—are coming of age in Taiwan in sufficient numbers to dominate that society within a short time. They have far less in common with their mainland counterparts than do young Italians with young Frenchmen, or possibly, young Japanese with young Americans.

The *peaceful* unification of China and Taiwan seems a very remote possibility, now or in the foreseeable future, far too remote to enable policy to be based upon it. Only a major upheaval within China could alter the odds significantly. Meanwhile, we are pledged to oppose any attempt at unification by force, and as long as that pledge is maintained, no attempt is likely to be made.

Meanwhile, a new nation is being constructed on Taiwan, and slowly a psychological adjustment to that fact is being made. Indeed, among the younger generation, that adjustment may be more complete than has commonly been recognized. If we work within the basic principles outlined earlier, we can pursue the logic of this fact. First, we should recognize the existence of two *de facto* states, without having to decide that the present situation, either with respect to the names of those states or their respective jurisdictions, will last for all time. However, we would accept the People's Republic as having control over its people, unless or until that control was clearly in doubt in terms of the criteria set forth earlier, and we would therefore accept at least the minimal consequences of such recognition, namely, the proffering of an invitation to the People's Republic to participate in international conferences of significance to it, to sit in the United Nations, and to participate in other international activities in which it would normally be concerned. At a second level, we would explore the establishment of those bilateral relations of an economic and cultural type that might test the possibilities of full political relations later.

At the same time, we would continue our commitments to and our ties with the Republic of China on Taiwan, and make it clear that for our part there had been no diminution of our commitment to see that state recognized in the international community, part of the network of international organizations, and fully defended against external attack. Military action of any sort by Taiwan against China, however, would meet with our strong opposition.

It is often pointed out that such a policy would garner opposition from both Peking and Taipei. Undoubtedly that is true, but it is not a conclusive objection, especially since there is no evidence that such opposition would be permanent. The fact is that two *de facto* states do exist and for the foreseeable future they will exist, each undergoing evolutionary changes no doubt, but unlikely to grow more closely together. To use the principles of recognition set forth earlier, at least to the extent permitted by each of these states, would be to set the stage for the principles of peaceful coexistence to work.

The case for the unity of China and Taiwan historically is far weaker than for a number of other areas, for example, West and East Germany, or South and North Korea. Even Mao Tse-tung once indicated that Formosa should be independent, and indeed, that was the consistent position of the Chinese Communists prior to World War II. But the important fact is that if the basic position outlined in this essay is adopted, that issue does not need to be settled in order to adjust to the contemporary realities of Asia and the Pacific. Some measures, moreover, can be taken unilaterally, with invitations and seats left open, if necessary, until the desire to accept them is felt.

There remains the question of American policies for Southeast Asia, although these have already been suggested in broad outline. Peace for Vietnam is inseparable in the final analysis from the basic question of peace for the area as a whole. The American position, if it were to be congruent with the themes advanced earlier, would rest upon the following principles:

1. The right of the people of South Vietnam to determine their own future, both with respect to a government for the South and with regard to the issue of unification with the North, should underwrite any Vietnam settlement.
2. Peaceful coexistence among states having different social and political systems will receive its supreme test in this region. Hence, institutions and procedures to this end are urgently required.
3. Those states which choose neutralism, as well as those choosing non-alignment should have multilateral guarantees of respect for their territorial integrity and their full sovereign rights.
4. The withdrawal of American military forces and fixed bases from this region should be undertaken as soon as multilateral agreements and enforcement mechanisms are in effect, with adequate stand-by facilities being maintained by those countries with which we may have continuing defense treaty obligations.

Our major commitment to southeast Asia in recent years, painful and divisive though it has been in terms of the American scene, provides a long-range hope for the security and development of several hundred millions of people. If one compares the Southeast Asia of today with that of 1960-1962, the influence of our actions can be appreciated. The critical decisions, however, lie ahead. If our efforts are not to end in failure, we must exhibit both patience and fortitude in the months and years immediately before us. The basic principles set forth earlier point the general direction in which we should go.

In conclusion, it is essential to raise several issues that concern Asian policies in particular, but also relate to American foreign policy in its broadest dimensions. Our times demand complex policies and a sufficient explanation to our people of those policies. Neither of these requirements is easily attained, given our political culture. Historically, the American people have preferred quick, decisive policies. It should either be "all in" or "all out," either zero or 100 percent, either the isolation of the 1920s—and earlier—or the total commitment of two world wars. The idea of policies that have an incremental character, policies that can be "raised" or "lowered" by small degrees, and that can be held if necessary at the same level for an indefinite period, constitutes a new emotional as well as intellectual experience for Americans.

To date, our policy-makers have adjusted to such requirements reasonably well, but they have not been able to communicate them effectively to the American people. On the whole, this is not the fault of the people. Blame must be shared by our top political leadership and the mass media. Our people can take complexity; they do not need to be fed on the simplicities of yesteryear. Indeed, to raise the level of discourse might benefit the intellectual community as much as the average citizen. All too frequently in recent years, the American intellectual has found it easier to operate at the same simplistic levels as those whom he seeks to attack.

It is extremely difficult, however, to ask our people to think in complex terms, to accept long-range programs that promise no immediate, final "solutions," to live in a reasonably mature fashion with uncertainty when so much that they read, hear, and see is dominated by the sensational and the crisis of the moment. Much has been said about this problem; almost nothing has been done about it. The entire relation between policy and information deserves inquiry in depth, in a nonpolitical atmosphere.

Perhaps this is a suitable time also to reexamine certain "truisms" that are not true, or at least not trustworthy guides to policy. With respect to Asia, several stand out. For example, the thesis that "we should support Asian nationalism" is typical of the type of half-truth that does little to clarify and much to obfuscate policy alternatives and issues. Not all that passes under the label of "nationalism" is good, in Asia or elsewhere. Moreover, individuals and groups of radically different political persuasions and aims have an equal claim to nationalism. If Sukarno is a nationalist, so is Suharto, and as much could be said about almost every other Asian leader on the national scene. Whether the Asian "common man" is a strong nationalist varies with the place and the situation. Simple xenophobia, however, should not be confused with nationalism, nor should one equate mass control automatically with a high level of national consciousness.

In any case, our task is not to support Asian nationalism indiscriminately. It is rather to support those forces that appear to be dedicated to the objectives of peace and the type of development that makes this more possible.

Earlier, we voiced similar reservations about another truism, namely, the thesis that Communist victory is the product of an absence of democracy (Western-style) and socioeconomic reforms. This concept is not false in all cases; certainly, it does not mean that democracy or reform should be opposed. But to formulate the problem in this fashion is to ignore the truly complex elements: the fact that economic development is not necessarily conducive to political stability and that in a contest with Communist forces, organizational skills, elitist commitments, and many other factors are of major, probably decisive importance.

There are other shibboleths which urgently need rethinking, long-cherished beliefs relating to racial attitudes in Asia, the political capacities of the peasant, and the role of the intellectual, among other issues. This task is essential if we are to reach out for new approaches. If done thoroughly and honestly, it is also likely to be very painful to American liberals and conservatives alike.

On balance, our policies in Asia since World War II have been more successful than many critics are prepared to admit. In the light of new developments both in Asia and in the world, however, it is now time to reassess those policies and to chart certain new courses. Our very successes in some instances make this as essential as our failures in other cases. Here, we have suggested the broad direction which a new course in Asia might take and some of the specific policies that could support that course.

7

A China Policy
for the Seventies

Chalmers Johnson

China policy in the twentieth century has been a graveyard for foreign ministers. The Communist victory of 1949, followed by the Korean War, traumatized the United States into positions that, to say the least, have not served American purposes well. Other nations—the Soviet Union, France, Britain, and Japan—have not had much better luck with the Chinese either, in the past or today. Of all the foreign powers, possibly Germany has been best able to do business with the Chinese, first in the form of very cordial relations between Reichswehr advisers and Chiang Kai-shek during the late twenties and early thirties, and again today in the form of trade. Leaving Hong Kong out of account, West Germany is at present China's second trading partner, exceeded only by Japan. Distinguishing Germany from other nations in its approach to the nation that still thinks of itself as the Middle Kingdom—midway between heaven and everything else under the sun—are its relative clarity of purpose and limited objectives. There is a lesson in this.

America's objectives vis-à-vis China are more important than Germany's, but they must also be limited. In short, the purpose of America's China policy should be the prevention of war in Asia—not reversal of the Chinese Communist revolution, nor containment of Communist ideology, nor realization of Chiang's revanchist dreams, nor the economic development of China, nor rescuing the United Nations Charter from some of its more obvious distortions, although some of these things may also be achieved through the maintenance of peace. War prevention is what draws America to Asia, and it is in this regard that one criticism of the conduct of the war in Vietnam is well taken: U.S. policy has not prevented war, although it may have served to prevent a wider one. Vietnam is relevant to this discussion primarily because the situation there must be stabilized before any change in the China tangle becomes politically realistic. However, even if the Vietnam war were to end today in a mutually acceptable agreement, it would still require two or three years to bring about the reorientation of America's China policy that is called for here. Hence, we are speaking of a China policy for the seventies, the foundations of which must be started at once if social change in Asia is to proceed without causing another war such as World War II, or Korea, or Vietnam.

The China problem divides naturally into three dimensions of concern, each of which operates as a variable influencing the others. These are: the military-security dimension, the diplomatic-recognition dimension, and the economic-trade dimension. It is appropriate to begin with the military dimension, since it carries the greatest weight as a variable and, being entirely in American hands, it is the easiest of the three to change, presuming that the State Department and the Pentagon can achieve a unity of intentions.

I

The potential of China to use force to achieve its objectives may be subdivided and assessed along three planes: past behaviors, capabilities, and intentions. None of these three areas of assessment gives an unambiguous picture, but there is evidence of change in the latter two, at least in the short run, indicating that America's policy of military containment requires modification. As for its past behavior, China has gone to war in Korea and India to secure its borders; it has pursued its policy of conquering Taiwan right up to the point where it has risked conflict with the United States; it has supported and is continuing to support programs of internal subversion, even to the point of insurgency, in Vietnam, Burma, India, Laos, Thailand, Malaya, and Indonesia; it has initiated a program of nuclear armament leading to the development of a strategic thermonuclear strike force; it has severely strained its relations with every nation in Asia—even including the Communist states of North Vietnam, North Korea, and Mongolia—except Pakistan; and it continues to call for and endorse so-called "people's wars" against Israel, many nations in Africa, Latin America, and Western Europe, and the United States. Contrary to the views often expounded by intellectual friends and apologists in Japan and the West of the Chinese Communist regime, these past behaviors have not all been dictated by reasons of defense. It is politically naive not to accept the fact that a highly ideological, radical revolutionary regime engenders strong pressures for the ecumenical propagation of its faith and that these pressures pose a security problem for other nations. The threat of the Chinese revolution as a breeder of wars and subversive movements is not a chimera, but to acknowledge the threat does not necessarily mean responding to it in kind.

China's capabilities are limited and have become even more so as a result of the so-called "Great Proletarian Cultural Revolution," which has wracked the country since the autumn of 1965. The Chinese threat to security is limited in both its conventional military capabilities and its strategic nuclear capabilities. With regard to the former, the Cultural Revolution has diminished the military effectiveness of the People's Liberation Army both directly, by making the PLA the key political organization within China charged with social control, and indirectly, by damaging productive capacities and downgrading economic development priorities in favor of Maoist priorities of internal political development. China's relative isolation from international sources of armaments compounds this problem, resulting in an increasingly poorly equipped armed force. Despite the fact that China has virtually unlimited manpower at its disposal, its capacity to turn this resource into an offensive military force has declined since 1965. This is a datum to which American war prevention policies should be responsive.

The nuclear threat is ambiguous. The arguments against taking it seriously are logical and consistent with everything we know about the subject. These include the arguments, all of them accepted here: that China developed the bomb primarily as a consequence of its conflict with the U.S.S.R.; that the Chinese bomb is a "prestige bomb," a piece of national jewelry, not a realistic military means; that China does not have the scientific, industrial, and technological infrastructure to develop a credible weapons system; that if France and Great Britain cannot afford a nuclear establishment, certainly China cannot; that the prestige China gains from the possession of nuclear weapons would be instantly lost if it ever used them, and that this fact is appreciated by Chinese leaders; that China's bomb is its means of escaping the pressures imposed by the superpowers, pressures which impinge on all nonnuclear nations; and that China's bomb is its defensive rejoinder to America's rattling of atomic bombs in Asia.

Nonetheless, the fact remains that no observer charged with estimating Chinese capabilities in this field—American, Japanese, or Russian—predicted the rapidity of the Chinese advance to the thermonuclear test level. The risks of a false analysis or of underestimating the technical shortcuts demonstrably open to an "overtaking" nation such as China are literally the highest in the world. Therefore, a prudent nation must take countermeasures against Chinese nuclear weapons, even though these measures may prove to be unnecessary and carry with them connotations that might adversely affect efforts toward ending China's isolation. Among the democracies, this balancing nation should be the United States. Unless the United States carries out the responsibility of countering the Chinese nuclear threat, the proliferation of nuclear weapons in Japan and India, at the very least, can be expected—with more unforeseen consequences in Japan and India and throughout Asia than merely growing atomic stockpiles.

The need is not for America to abandon its atomic responsibility in Asia but rather for America to carry it out in a manner consistent with the ambiguities of the Chinese position and which does not exacerbate the already heightened nuclear tensions of the region. The best way this can be done is for the United States to avoid basing nuclear missiles and aircraft on the soil of Asian nations, substituting the further development and deployment of missile-launching submarines. In this connection, the decision to build a so-called "thin line" antiballistic missile defense, directed against China, is also a prudent one, for the ABM is defensive and American-based and, given the comparatively minor strategic importance of available Chinese targets, it takes into account China's greater insensitivity to deterrence. Of course the ABM can only be one component of the counterforce; as presently developed, for example, it does not offer protection to nations such as Japan. [1]

The value of military bases in East Asia has moved into the loss column. On November 11, 1968, the people of Okinawa, in the first popular election of an Okinawan chief executive, chose Mr. Chobyo Yara, representative of a coalition of parties demanding the removal of U.S. nuclear bases and the return of the Ryukyus to Japan. On December 1, 1968, the same thing happened in the Okinawan capital city of Naha, when the candidate of the leftist forces, Mr. Ryosho Taira, was elected mayor. These developments mean that the present status of America's single most important bastion in Asia has become untenable, chiefly because Okinawa is an issue not simply with the Okinawans but also with the Japanese, who hold residual sovereignty over Okinawa and for whom the regaining of direct administrative rights there has become a domestic political issue of Japan's independence from the United States.

Japan must be the keystone of any American security policy in East Asia. With a population half that of the United States and the third largest aggregate industrial output in the world, Japan is more important to the United States in terms of economic capacity than any European nation. If its growth rate continues for another decade as it has for the past decade, Japan will outproduce all the Western European nations combined. In order to preserve and maintain the Japanese-American security treaty, which calls for mutual governmental consultations before American forces on Japanese soil can be used in the common defense, the United States must return Okinawa to Japan promptly and negotiate other changes in the treaty requested by Japan. There is no reason why the nonnuclear

---

[1] Considerable controversy surrounds the question of whether or not the antiballistic missile is as yet sufficiently well developed to be put into production and deployed in the United States, let alone in Japan. Regardless of one's assessment of this technical question, the *concept* of the ABM is attractive for East Asia primarily because it constitutes a defensive, deterrent rejoinder tailored specifically to Chinese political and military postures. The older policies of deterrence through counterforce and of limited war—as employed in Korea, for example—were designed with Soviet capabilities and behaviors in mind; they cannot be transferred mechanically to the Chinese case. An offensive deterrent is not as credible vis-à-vis China as a defensive one, and the war in Vietnam already has revealed the limitations of the Korean-type limited-war doctrine. Whether or not the ABM proves to be technically feasible, the special characteristics of Chinese politics and of China's economy must inform strategic concepts implemented in the Far East if disaster is to be avoided.

bases on Okinawa cannot be maintained, primarily for security against any renewed threat to the peace in Korea, although they would have to be included under the provisions of the security treaty. However, there are at present some 145 U.S. military bases or installations in Japan itself, most of them militarily meaningless, and American planners must drastically curtail them, because they are beginning to jeopardize the very existence of the Japanese-American security treaty. Nuclear counterforce against China should increasingly take the forms of submarine-launched missiles, intercontinental missiles based on American soil, and an antiballistic missile defense line.

The government and a large majority of the population of Japan welcome the American defensive effort against China's growing nuclear capability. They are concerned, however, to insure that this nuclear defense appears credibly *defensive* (and not offensive) to the Chinese, and it is in the interests of war prevention in the Far East that the United States join the Japanese in this posture. Of course, Japan must continue to do her part; the United States cannot maintain the security treaty and defend Japan if the Japanese do not want America to do so. In order for the United States to fulfill its responsibilities under the treaty, Japan must be willing to supply a minimum number of air and naval bases on its soil. Nevertheless, through public statements, private exchanges at Warsaw, and the elimination of nuclear bases such as Okinawa, both the United States and Japan should encourage the apparently growing realization in China (which we shall discuss in a moment) that the United States seeks to avoid war with China, not to precipitate it.

China's past behavior is not particularly encouraging, and its military capabilities, though certainly not enhanced by the Cultural Revolution, are sufficiently impressive in the nuclear-weapons field to demand policies of military deterrence. Nevertheless, China's intentions appear to have changed significantly. During 1965, prior to the onset of the Cultural Revolution, Chinese foreign policy defined the primary threat to China to be imperialism, saw the United States as its main agent, and conceived this threat as manifested externally primarily along the China Sea coast and in American bases from Japan to Thailand. During late 1968, it became clear that this set of priorities and evaluations had been altered. As revealed during the Cultural Revolution, the primary threat is now conceived to be so-called "modern revisionism," its agent is the U.S.S.R., and it is manifested both internally and externally, as domestic opposition to Mao and along China's long border with Russia.

China's hostility to the United States remains, but the threat posed by the United States has become more remote and less demanding of scarce resources. One might say that the Chinese Communists regard the United States as abstract, quintessential evil, something like Satan, but they really hate the Russians. It is also true that hostility to the United States performs important social functions in China, providing a focus for fervid revolutionary hatred and an explanation for frustrations and policy setbacks. Nevertheless, hostility to the Soviet Union, as manifested in China's nuclear-weapons program, its condemnation of Russia's occupation of Czechoslovakia, its alliance with Albania, its propaganda, and a thousand other ways, has become the cardinal principle of Chinese foreign policy.

Although the Sino-Soviet dispute and most other elements of Chinese foreign policy are expressed in ideological terms and certainly have an ideological dimension, ideology itself is not a particularly good guide to Chinese Communist foreign-policy behavior. For example, China maintains fairly good relations with two quasi-feudal states to the south, Pakistan and Nepal; yet it has intransigently hostile contacts with two semisocialist states, India and Burma. Similarly, the imperialist enclave of Hong Kong, a British crown colony and possibly the last example on earth of unrestricted capitalism, is tolerated as China's single largest source of foreign exchange earnings. In trade relations generally, China has reoriented its trading activities since 1960, so that what was formerly a pattern of 75 percent trade with Communist nations and 25 percent with the democracies is today 75 percent with Japan and the West and 25 percent with Communist countries.

Nevertheless, ideology is not dead. China still calls for "people's wars," most recently against Israel, but it has silently jettisoned virtually all news of the Vietnamese war from its newspapers since President Johnson stopped the bombing of the North on October 31, 1968. We can expect Chinese subversion and propaganda to continue to pose threats to the internal stability of China's neighbors. The Chinese danger to internal *stability* in such nations as Thailand and India has always been greater than the Chinese danger to their external *security*. Nevertheless, these nations have begun to learn that their own policies constitute either the best antidote or the greatest nutrient for Chinese subversion. Direct antisubversive measures must be backed by responsive, progressive domestic programs and heightened popular participation in politics. Subversion cannot be countered by repression alone or by stationing foreign troops in the threatened country. Certainly, the United States alone cannot check Chinese subversion in any country that is not itself prepared to trust and attempt to win the confidence of its own people nor can it retaliate in kind by organizing anti-Chinese subversive activities. The most that Americans can do in regard to subversion and propaganda is to participate as a member in multilateral economic development and mutual security organizations, such as the Asia Development Bank, and to make credible its determination to answer threats or acts of military intimidation and terrorism by Chinese or Chinese-allied guerrillas.

Despite the fact that Chinese propaganda and incitements to revolution in neighboring countries have not moderated in the slightest, the only recent departures that appear to be dictated primarily by ideological considerations are, first, the injection of veneration for Mao Tse-tung into foreign policy and, second, China's warm support of student revolutionaries around the world. Today China will precipitate a nasty incident whenever it believes that Mao has been insulted or even inappropriately praised; it has engaged in such antics with the British, Italians, Russians, and Japanese, to name only a few cases. As for the student movement, it has become a major issue in the Sino-Soviet dispute ever since the French *petite révolution* of 1968. China applauds student violence in Europe, Japan, Mexico, and the United States, whereas the Soviet Union condemns it as anarchism and its practitioners as false revolutionaries.

These trends in China's foreign-policy intentions offer opportunities for the United States at least to begin to end China's isolation. Leaving out of account the problem of Taiwan, to which we shall turn below, the outstanding issues between China and the United States are America's military bases and China's ideological hostility to what it regards as the successor to German and Japanese fascist imperialism. The latter issue, as we have suggested, is not likely to be an obstacle to an increase in Sino-American contacts, so long as the realistic situation does not appear menacing to China. America's military bases therefore should be restricted and brought under existing defensive treaty restraints. China already has reason to believe, in light of the fact that the Vietnam war did not take the form of an American "roll-back" against Communist governments, that the United States position in Asia is primarily defensive—including, of course, the defense of

Taiwan, real estate that the Chinese Communists believe belongs to them. This incipient credibility in the American position should be nurtured and developed.

The military threat of China in conventional terms has declined, calling for a commensurate reduction of American land-based, conventional forces in the Far East. China's nuclear threat is ambiguous but too dangerous to trust to a so-called "liberal" interpretation. It can, nevertheless, be deterred and the undesirable consequences of deterrence reduced by an accelerated exploitation of non-land-based nuclear defensive technology in the Far East. These changes in American policy can and should be (indeed, must be, in the case of Okinawa) undertaken at once. They are in response to conditions that are very rapidly coming into being, and they are prerequisite to the more difficult diplomatic initiatives necessary to achieve a stable, long-range alteration of the Sino-American deadlock and to allow any accommodation between the Chinese revolution and the world.

II

There is a Hong Kong wisecrack to the effect that Chiang Kai-shek has decided not to die before Mao Tse-tung and Mao Tse-tung has decided not to die before Chiang Kai-shek. If the matter were truly in the hands of these elderly gentlemen, it would pose an insoluble dilemma for the United States. For, whatever policies their successors may pursue, it is unlikely that they could ever match these two Chinese leaders in sheer stubbornness. Until Chiang and Mao do die, however, the United States must take into account their two positions on the status of Taiwan, which constitutes the single most important and intractable obstacle to any alteration in the American policy of not recognizing the Peking government.

Foreign-policy commentators not familiar with socioeconomic trends in Asia often confuse the concrete situation on Taiwan with the lingering pretensions of the Chiang Kai-shek regime to reconquer the mainland, about which there exists a good deal of international ennui in east Asia and around the world. Taiwan itself is a large island with a population of approximately 13 million. Its size makes it potentially a middle-ranking member of the United Nations, larger than virtually all of the new nations of Africa. More important, Taiwan has been evolving in a different direction from the Chinese mainland for more than half a century, first as a

Japanese colony between 1895 and 1945, and then as a part of the global non-Communist economic system since approximately the end of the Korean war. Today Taiwan is on the verge of becoming the second industrialized area of the Far East (Japan being the first), and any proposal for its reintegration with the mainland—under either Communist or Nationalist auspices—would involve a catastrophic lowering of the level of living of its population.

The economic achievements on Taiwan have been the result of effective leadership by the Kuomintang, investments of Japanese and overseas Chinese capital, and grants of American aid. In one sense, the best thing that ever happened to the latter-day Kuomintang was the lesson it learned in 1949 from its defeat by the Communists. The party on Taiwan purged itself of corrupt members, carried out an effective land reform, and overcame many of the deficiencies that had rendered it ineffective and unpopular during the late 1940s. Certain political lessons, however, it has never learned. In international politics the Kuomintang remains its own worst enemy, destroying virtually every source of international goodwill it might have enjoyed.

Taiwan has the potential of being admired as a Far Eastern Israel. It is a small nation, surrounded by hostile and threatening powers, yet its industrious people are prepared to defend themselves and have worked hard to achieve the material prosperity that is the goal of all the underdeveloped countries. However, by keeping alive the Chinese civil war and continuously threatening the mainland regime, the Kuomintang has not only played directly into the hands of Chinese Communist foreign policy; it has also made it very difficult for the nations prepared to give Taiwan economic and military assistance (primarily the United States and Japan) to do so. Communist China has never been under the slightest realistic pressure to relinquish or modify its claims to Taiwan, because the Taiwanese government has always proclaimed itself to be the true and rightful government of all China.

It is possible that during the 1950s the Kuomintang and the approximately 1.5 million mainland refugees who also fled to Taiwan needed the myth of exile in order to justify their claims to ruling Taiwan and bolster their own morale. This is an arguable proposition, although many Americans believe there were clearly better alternatives to a refugee dictatorship over the indigenous Taiwanese population (compare the more admirable relationships between European and Middle Eastern Jews in Israel), and that the Kuomintang leadership has been notably lacking in either political vision or creativity in building a Chinese nation on Taiwan. Even if one accepts the proposition that dictatorship and a refugee political monopoly were necessary for the first decade after 1949, these political institutions are clearly excessive today and tend to undermine the very real economic achievements of the KMT and its allies. Fortunately, this internal problem is moving toward a natural solution as mainlanders are slowly dying off and Taiwanese are moving into positions of political and military leadership.

The KMT's external posture—its claim to being the legal government of all of China and its maintenance of a shadow government for every province on the mainland—is not likely to change of its own accord without a great deal of pressure from the United States and its allies. Even under this sort of pressure, the Taiwanese regime may continue to base its legitimacy on revanchism and the mystique that it alone maintains the continuity of Chinese culture so long as Chiang Kai-shek is alive. Nevertheless, it is precisely the abandonment of revanchist claims by Taiwan that emerging conditions in Asia require, regardless of any inconvenience this may or may not cause the Kuomintang.

There are two overriding reasons why the Kuomintang should be urged to adopt a defensive posture. First, the willingness of the Chinese Communists to reach an accommodation with non-Communist nations must be seriously tested; and second, Japanese popular attitudes are clearly pushing the pro-American government of Japan toward a one-China, one-Taiwan position.

Communist China's often-proclaimed policy of conquering Taiwan has never been tested for its flexibility. So long as the Taiwan government continues to deny that it has lost its claim to ruling the mainland (just as it long denied that Communist China was independent of the U.S.S.R.), it is inconceivable for Communist regime to take any but the most intransigent position. However, the actions of the Chinese Communists in the Taiwan Straits have never matched their words, and Taiwan, meanwhile, has been evolving further and further away from the Communists politically and economically. To be sure, the population of Taiwan is Chinese, like the populations of Singapore and Hong Kong, and China has a somewhat dubious legal claim to Taiwan based on the policy pronouncements and summit decisions of the Big Three allies during World War II (dubious because the wishes of the population on the island have never been considered and because in 1947 the Taiwanese people resisted violently the imposition of mainland rule). The realistic trend of Taiwanese national identity and development, however, has drawn it into the emerging arc of growth and cooperation stretching from Tokyo to Singapore. It is this evolution away from the mainland that is given *de facto* recognition by Japan and Germany, both of whom trade with Taiwan as well as the mainland, and which the Chinese Communists have tacitly acknowledged by accepting such trading partners.

If the Taiwan regime were clearly pursuing a defensive foreign policy, Communist China might conceivably modify its hostility. Taiwan's allies could make it attractive to Peking to scale down its claims to the island by reciprocating its moderation with trade, capital investments, and recognition. The testing of the Chinese Communists on this matter becomes more urgent every day, as the need to bring China into nuclear disarmament treaties continues to grow. The popular pressure in Tokyo, Washington, and European capitals to make an accommodation with Peking at *any* price (even Taiwan's independence) could soon become irresistible. Even if the Chinese Communists will not moderate their claims, the concerned nations can bring influence to bear on Peking only if Taiwan has accepted the verdict of the last twenty years.

The position of Japan on the China problem is very delicate. There is no question that if the United States acted unilaterally today to recognize the Peking regime, the pro-American government in Tokyo would fall tomorrow. This is because Japan has followed America's lead in the field of China policy, recognizing Taipei and not Peking, but it has done so more because of the high value it places on American friendship than because of any widespread agreement with the American position. Japan believes in and pursues the "two-China" policy: It trades extensively with both Taiwan and the mainland and believes that force should not be used to reunite the two territories under either Chinese regime. Therefore, although the present Japanese government has been willing publicly to tie itself to America's position on China, it would be only too happy to see a change in this position—provided *it* were not made to look foolish in the process. For this reason the Japanese government would have to be carefully prepared for any forthcoming change in United States China policy, and very possibly—for reasons of domestic Japanese politics—Japan would have to be allowed to take the initiative in recognizing Peking.

Some commentators in the United States and Japan believe that on balance the only realistic solution to the Taiwan problem is the passage of time, and they counsel against any change in the status quo. There are, of course, risks in attempting to alter a situation that is at least *stable,* if highly undesirable. The risks of complacency and supporting the status quo are also growing, however. Chinese nuclear weapons are already generating tremendous pressure for proliferation in India and Japan, and arms control and disarmament agreements could all collapse unless China is brought within their provisions. The United States therefore should take advantage of the opportunity offered by the changing politics of the Communist nations, neither relinquishing its commitment to defend Taiwan from aggression nor being deterred from seeking contacts with Peking by the pretensions of the Taipei government. After scaling down its military bases on China's borders, the United States should: first, dissociate itself clearly from Taiwan's "mainland counterattack" propaganda; second, strive for a renunciation of force in the Taiwan Straits by *both* sides; third, offer diplomatic recognition to both Taipei and Peking in conjunction with or slightly following a similar initiative by Japan; and fourth, support and defend the sovereign independence of Taiwan so long as that accords with the wishes of the Taiwanese people.

The Taiwan problem also has a United Nations dimension, although it is not, as is so often assumed, a question of admitting Communist China to the UN. According to the UN Charter, China is and always has been a permanent member of the United Nations and the Security Council. The issue is *which* Chinese government represents China. An alteration of America's China policy along the lines called for here would require American acquiescence in the admission of a Republic of Taiwan to United Nations membership and its seating in the General Assembly, the relinquishment by the Kuomintang government of its seat in the Security Council, and the seating of a Communist Chinese delegation in both the General Assembly and the Security Council. Enthusiasts for the United Nations should anticipate that any such series of moves would decrease further the already attenuated effectiveness of the Security Council and provide Peking with new propaganda platforms in both forums. On the other hand, such a change would be in line with the universalist orientations of the United Nations, would involve China in United Nations debates (the consequences of which are as unpredictable for China as for the

United Nations), and would open up United Nations channels of communication and aid to China to those nations who wish to use them.

By far the best solution to the problem of Chinese representation in the United Nations is one that avoids dealing with it as a "China problem" at all. In accordance with the principle of universalism maintained by the UN, the United States and its allies should support a successor-states formula for determining whether or not a sovereign, independent government exists for a people and a territory. By putting the problem in terms of *de facto* successor governments, the United States could obtain the admission of two Vietnams, two Koreas, two Germanys, as well as two Chinas—which is in line with a universalistic orientation—and the China problem itself could be couched in the more realistic terms of a *de facto* outcome of political struggle rather than in terms of the rightful victor of the Chinese civil war. Adoption of the successor-states formula should also be linked to a thorough and long-overdue reorganization of the United Nations itself, bringing nations such as Japan or India into permanent representation on the Security Council. It is not at all clear that the present members of the UN would support either the succession principle or reorganization, but its advocacy by the United States would remove the onus of America's blocking universalism and would support United States interests in East Asia and the United Nations.

The United Nations aspect of the China problem is not as important as it once appeared to be. The reason for advocating the explicit adoption of the one-China, one-Taiwan policy by the United States is not that China constitutes one (and it is only one) of many distortions in the UN Charter; rather the reason is that the current United States policy tends to perpetuate and reinforce the ideological and revolutionary belligerency of the Chinese Communist regime while at the same time it relieves the Communist regime of any responsibility for alleviating the warlike situation. So long as it tolerates Nationalist revanchism, the United States remains a party to the claims arising out of the Chinese civil war, and it thereby obscures its genuine support for the separate existence of and achievements on Taiwan.

III

All of America's allies maintain the embargo on trade in strategic goods with Communist China but not one of them joins the United States in its total trade blockade. One might argue that the distinction between strategic and nonstrategic commodities, once one leaves the black-and-white area of guns versus butter, is more verbal than real, but this is an argument against the Americans maintaining such a policy since all the other democracies, including some who contribute forces to Vietnam like Australia, trade with the mainland regime. Although the embargo of items clearly related to weapons development should continue, it is time to abandon the total trade blockade, as one facet of an integrated policy of change in America's relations with China.

There are good reasons why the United Nations should end the total trade embargo even if it changes nothing else in its China policy. For one thing, the policy is a failure: America's allies are China's leading trading partners. For another, the policy is very difficult to administer and holds the United States up to ridicule. The fact that a Hong Kong wig-maker cannot sell a wig to an American woman unless he also supplies her with a certificate testifying that the hair came from a Hong Kong head rather than a Communist head has caused amusement throughout the Far East. More to the point, if American tourists and importers could buy goods of Communist Chinese origin in Hong Kong, their purchasing power would heighten the colony's economic value to China and thereby make it more secure politically. The direct sale of goods to Chinese residents of Hong Kong is China's greatest source of foreign exchange earnings, and anything the United States can do indirectly to secure the future of the four million inhabitants of Hong Kong will help to prevent a potentially disastrous refugee situation should China decide to end the colony's present status.

In order to avoid damaging non-Communist businesses in Hong Kong, it would be wise, at least at the outset, to restrict Sino-American trading activities to Hong Kong (rather than allowing the Communists to shift them to the Canton Trade Fair, for example) and to provide Hong Kong with favorable quotas for exports to the United States during a transitional period. So long as China's primary source of foreign-currency earnings is sales of foodstuffs and other commodities in a Chinese cultural milieu, it is to the advantage of both China and the United States to maintain the prosperity (hence purchasing power) of the population of Hong Kong. One further consideration in opening up economic relations is that the United States can make this change unilaterally and can time it to coincide with other initiatives in a new China policy.

Trade with China, in the absence of military and political changes such as those advocated earlier, will not of itself make much difference in Sino-American contacts. The China market is not very large—the Chinese have relatively little cash or attractive commodities to exchange for American exports—and no nation is going to get rich doing business with China. Moreover, no trading country, such as Japan, wants to tie up a very large share of its exports in so politically volatile a market as China at the present time. From the Chinese point of view, there is no need to trade with the United States so long as China can buy what it needs in Germany or Japan; therefore it probably will not reciprocate an offer to trade unless a change in trade relations is made a part of change in other relations as well.

Thus, the real focus of a changed trade policy will be the opportunity it offers a post-Maoist Communist leadership to participate in and profit from the expanding East Asian economy based on Japan. The Communists are not likely to take this bait eagerly or without stringent controls of their own, but even under Mao Tse-tung they have found it ideologically not impossible to eat Canadian and Australian wheat or to import Japanese fertilizers. By entering the East Asian economic system more fully, China will be able to speed its economic development, one of the authentic goals of the Chinese revolution, a goal which predates and is likely to survive Mao Tse-tung.

The long-range prospects for the economic development of China are good. Explorations by the Communists have revealed greater resources of petroleum, hydroelectric power, coal, iron, and light metals than any observer, Chinese or foreign, believed to exist twenty years ago. In addition, the capacity of the Chinese people for social organization, hard work, and frugality suggests that the human prerequisites for development, including capital accumulation, exist at the present time in China. Even birth control, undertaken through the more disciplined methods of late marriage and delayed childbirth rather than through contraception alone, appears to have made headway despite Marxist prejudices. It is only in the short run, and largely because of the political leadership of an aged, possibly senile and megalomaniacal revolutionist, that China's economic development and the level of living of the Chinese people appear bleak.

This short-run situation is changing at the present moment and is likely to be totally transformed in the relatively near future. Mao Tse-tung and his generation must soon pass from the scene. Mao's efforts in the Cultural Revolution to predetermine the qualities of his successors have, if anything, brought to power in positions of regional and local leadership men who are more pragmatic and more nationalistic (i.e., the 2.5 million men of the Peoples Liberation Army) than his defeated enemies in the Communist Party bureaucracy. Thus, it is entirely in conformity with events to predict that the emerging generation of Chinese leaders will be—in Communist parlance—"revisionist," but with the added meaning that they will redirect their energies toward the two main goals of the century-old Chinese revolution of which the Chinese Communist movement is only a segment—namely, great-power status and economic development for China.

A realliance between China and Russia seems utterly improbable. The binding force of Marxist-Leninist ideology has become as weak as water, both because of Mao's thorough de-Europeanizing of it for the benefit of Chinese communicants and because of Russia's sharp turn toward imperialism. The Chinese have good reason to remain hostile to the Soviet Union for decades to come. Not only did Russia support China in a niggardly and authoritarian way, but it also tried, during the 1960s, to cripple China economically and to isolate it from all other Communist nations. The conquest of Czechoslovakia and the proclamation of the "Brezhnev doctrine" (whereby Russia stakes out an imperial claim to direct the policies of all so-called "socialist" nations) have only thrown up further and more difficult obstacles to any Sino-Soviet rapprochement. Even Mao Tse-tung seems to appreciate that there are worse things on earth than doing business with "capitalist" nations; he has recently elevated "Soviet revisionism" to the same level as "American imperialism," calling them common enemies of the Chinese and "all progressive peoples of the world."

American foreign policy in Asia, worked out in conjunction with our Japanese partners, should become responsive to and aligned with these overall economic and political trends. The United States must, through its treaty commitments and actions to implement them, convey to the Chinese leaders what they will not be allowed to do: plunge East Asia into another war because of the ideological pressures and pretensions of the Asian Communist revolutions. At the same time, the United States must adjust these necessities of containment so that they support and encourage what the Chinese have every right to do: develop their own country, feel secure, and participate in the international life of the world as an equal.

8

The United States
and Southeast Asia

Daniel S. Lev

The war in Vietnam has forced the United States to begin a reevaluation of its international purposes. Particularly is this so with respect to areas of the world where the engagement of American power has been brief but strenuous. Southeast Asia may not be a basically more vexing problem than the Middle East, but it has involved the United States more painfully, and the rethinking of American goals in Asia is and will be nearly as painful.

This period of review and change, if it comes to that, will also be painful for Asia, especially perhaps for Southeast Asia, whose foreign policies are necessarily dependent upon the alternatives of action chosen by the great powers concerned with the region.

The attitudes of Southeast Asians occasionally have been used as weapons by one side or the other in the American debate over the war in Vietnam. Those who favor the war, or the policy views behind it, have no difficulty in finding Southeast Asian reinforcement. Most, though not all, governments in the area have in fact made their support of the American position plain. Opponents of the war can also find a good deal of hostility to American policies, frequently within the very governments which publicly applaud those policies. But both the support for and the opposition to the United States in Southeast Asia are more complicated and subtle than has usually been portrayed in current arguments. Nor are these views related only to Vietnam, which has done most to bring Southeast Asia to American attention.

The war has in odd ways both weakened and strengthened the American position in Southeast Asia. Whichever decision the United States makes—to leave Vietnam or to stay—there will be critical consequences for the Southeast Asian states, which American power will have helped to bring about. The problems created for all the countries concerned not only by the war but by the entire history of great-power involvement in Southeast Asia make it imperative now to consider just what Southeast Asia and the United States want and expect from one another.

This is no easy task, for as the United States is divided on this question, so are most of the states of Southeast Asia. What I want to do in this brief paper, however, is touch on some of the sources of tension in American relations with Southeast Asia and the possibilities of a different kind of American involvement in the area.

THE COLD WAR AND INTERVENTION

Except for the Philippines, American concern with Southeast Asia has been very recent. Before World War II there was limited contact among the Southeast Asian colonies and little if any need for the United States to seriously define its national interests in the region. Attention focused rather on China and Japan. Only during the decades just before the war did Japanese interest in Southeast Asian resources begin to cause anxiety in Washington, and with the final defeat and occupation of Japan this issue disappeared. What remained were some sentiments about self-determination for the Southeast Asian colonies, which President Roosevelt had forcefully expressed during the war with respect to Indochina. But these hardly constituted a policy. At this time there were few Southeast Asian specialists in Washington, only a handful of people recruited during the war from the academic world (where there had been very few in the first place). They were in no position to counter the weight of State Department staff concerned with Europe. Although Washington did soften

British demands for indemnities from Thailand, which had sided with Japan during the war but had not fought, American sympathy for national independence movements elsewhere in Southeast Asia was at first subordinated to a greater interest in European recovery.

Our subsequent and precipitate involvement in Southeast Asia during the late 1940s was basically informed by the cold war. More than anything else a fear of Communist expansion stimulated the American government to begin developing expertise in Southeast Asian affairs. (In a more general sense, the same sudden awareness of a great world struggle in which the United States was a major protagonist led to an expansion of academic resources on Southeast Asia in American universities, one result of which has been to make the debate over Vietnam more interesting and better informed than it might have been.) This fear was greatly exacerbated by the rise to power of the Communist Party in China and, shortly thereafter, the Korean war. In Southeast Asia, except for the Philippines, the United States had few economic interests to defend. At the same time there were insufficient social or cultural attachments to temper American political perceptions in the area. Consequently the images that American policymakers and the informed public developed of Southeast Asia tended to be distorted and dichotomous, related primarily to images of the cold war. Only a great deal more knowledge than Americans then possessed, short of a quite different political world view, would have produced a different outcome.

In this context of anxiety, the quality of relationships between Washington and the capitals of Southeast Asia was interpreted in narrow terms. For American eyes, relations tended to be good in direct proportion to the depth of local commitments to resist communism, and bad in direct proportion to the size of local Communist parties or the degree of local unwillingness to take sides—especially during the 1950s—in the world conflict. Southeast Asian leaders soon came to take it for granted that the United States and the Soviet Union were primarily interested in one another, and if American assistance was required for other goals the likelihood of getting it was increased by somehow relating it to anti-Communist purposes. There were instances, however, when the primary goals of Washington and a Southeast Asian government coincided. In the Philippines, American assistance to President Magsaysay's effort to overcome the Hukbalahap rebellion was a case of effective and successful cooperation, perhaps because the assistance was not always in evidence and Magsaysay's government had a firm grip on policy. Elsewhere, as in South Vietnam, such cooperation has been less successful. In both cases the conditions that determined success or failure in dealing with domestic rebellion were clearly domestic, and over these conditions the United States had and has little influence.

In other countries of Southeast Asia, the position of the United States was often damaged by attempts to influence domestic conditions or to impose goals not congruent with those of the governments in power. Burma and Indonesia are illustrations of this point.

In Burma, which became independent in 1948 and was immediately beset by numerous rebellions, a serious conflict with the United States arose over American and Formosan support of several thousand Chinese (KMT) troops that fled China in 1950 and ensconced themselves in northern Burma. From the perspectives of Taipeh and Washington, the KMT troops were a useful threat on China's flank. Burma, understandably, did not see it this way: Not only were the Chinese troops a serious domestic nuisance, but more seriously, they gave China good reasons for invading Burma. Having failed to move Washington to force the withdrawal of the troops, Rangoon finally terminated an aid agreement with the United States in 1953 and later brought the matter before the United Nations. Only then did Washington pressure Taiwan into removing some, though not all, of the Chinese soldiers. Economic assistance to Burma was resumed in 1957, but cut off again by Burma following the coup of 1962. Nevertheless, Burma undoubtedly remains interested in whatever protection and assistance the United States may offer in keeping Burmese borders safe from China.

United States relations with Indonesia have been more complicated than with Burma, partly because of the greater importance of Indonesia in Southeast Asia and because of the greater complexity of Indonesian politics. There have been more opportunities for an American involvement in Indonesian political conflicts—with frequently more encouragement from Indonesian groups.

A divergency in American and Indonesian interpretations of world politics was apparent almost from the beginning of their relations. Americans, for example, have long felt that the United States was instrumental in pushing the Dutch out of Indonesia, and for basically altruistic reasons. Indonesians, on the other hand, take the view that they won their own revolution by force of arms. As they see it, the United States in fact did not bring much pressure to bear on Holland during the early years of the revolution, which began in 1945, but on the contrary refused to deny aid to the Netherlands when such a move would have helped most to prevent a colonial war. Washington did intervene in 1948 to offer good offices, but many Indonesians interpret this move as less friendly and anticolonialist than essentially anti-Communist. At the time Communist activity was becoming more evident in Indonesia, and the growing tension between the Soviet Union and the United States seemed to Indonesian leaders to be the main impetus to American interest in their revolution. On balance the evidence favors the Indonesian view, though not entirely, but that is less important here than the differences of perception.

As if to prove the point that American interests in Indonesia were motivated primarily by American interpretations of the larger world struggle, in 1952 the government fell in Djakarta partly because the American ambassador had convinced the foreign minister to sign a section (511a) of the Mutual Security Act which, on the face of it, committed Indonesia to the United States side of the cold war.[1] Herbert Feith has pointed out the ideological significance of the idea of Indonesia's independent foreign policy. The attempt by Ambassador Cochran to ignore such views, or to undercut them, aroused considerable resentment. Again, in 1957 and 1958, while Indonesia was suffering a serious crisis of regional dissidence, Washington decided to encourage the rebels. American opposition to the government in Djakarta had begun in early 1957, when President Sukarno had pronounced the view that Indonesia needed a more authoritarian "Guided Democracy," and that the Communist Party was too strong to be left out of the government. Not long afterwards Secretary of State Dulles spoke deprecatingly of Guided Democracy, and some assistance began to flow to the rebels. By late 1957 and 1958, military equipment was being dropped in Sumatra and Sulawesi, and in mid-1958 a bomber piloted by an American was shot down near the island of Ambon. The rebellion, which actually broke out in February, 1958, turned out to be too weak for the central government's army, though it continued until

---

[1] The most objectionable item in section 511a was the obligation, that if military as well as economic aid were to be given, to "Make a full contribution, consistent with [the receiving state's] political and economic capacity, its population, natural resources, facilities and general economic situation, to the development and maintenance of its own defenses and to the defensive strength of the free world." See Herbert Feith, *The Decline of Constitutional Democracy in Indonesia*, Cornell University Press, Ithaca, 1962, pp. 198 ff.

1961. Within a few months after the rebellion started, Washington began to repair relations with Djakarta, but skepticism as to American purposes, which the intervention aroused on all sides in Indonesian politics, remained. This did not mean that anti-Communist forces were any less interested in cooperating with the United States when possible, but the American involvement in a domestic issue made it less influential for other purposes than it might have been.

Laos is another case in which the United States decided to intervene against a government thought to be too weak to stand up to Communists. This situation was complicated by the proximity of Laos to Vietnam, which brought other concerns into play, but basically the pattern was the same. Premier Souvanna Phouma was driven out of power by an American-supported army which, it was believed, would form a stronger bulwark against the Communist Pathet Lao. As it turned out, this proved not necessarily to be true. Souvanna Phouma was later returned to office, following the Geneva Conference in 1962. By this time, however, the level of American involvement in Laos, a very small and poorly integrated state, was proportionately greater than in any other state in the area except Vietnam.

Finally, Vietnam itself is the most obvious and best known case of American intervention predicated on a concern with communism overriding all others. The history of this conflict is well known enough by now to pass over a discussion of its development. It is worth pointing out again, however, that the Vietnam war has brought about what may be the beginning of a turning point in American foreign policy thinking. The debate which it has inspired, for all its bitterness and vitriol, has opened up for consideration matters previously taken for granted.

Among the more important of these, so far as Southeast Asia is concerned, are the images that Americans have held of Southeast Asian political problems and the power of the United States to influence them. What is striking about the cases of intervention mentioned above is that they all flow from the assumption that most countries in Southeast Asia cannot be trusted to handle by themselves problems considered critically important by the United States, even when they themselves believe the problems to be crucial to their own survival. Otherwise, Southeast Asia has been essentially peripheral to American interests, however they have been defined. Indeed, as China has become the focus of attention in Asia, Southeast Asia has become literally peripheral. Whether the Communist threat is pictured as monolithic or vaguely pluralistic, Southeast Asia tends to be seen as passive prey. Even some of the more sophisticated observers of the area tend to perceive the various Communist parties as somehow fully bound up with one another in a common enterprise transcending national interests. Communists themselves frequently like to think this is true, but there is by now enough evidence to indicate that nationalism rather than communism is the dominant theme of twentieth-century international politics. The inability to perceive this, given the former state of our knowledge about Southeast Asia and communism, promoted both the American engagement in Vietnam and the way in which the war would be fought. The Viet-Minh could not be recognized as a nationalist force—though it was during World War II—and one likely to oppose an overextension of Chinese influence, because communism was understood *a priori* to preclude nationalism, a semantic oddity which does however reflect a distinct set of perceptions.

The case is made even more restrictive by a world view—shared by Americans with Russians, Chinese, and perhaps other powerful nations in history—that divides mankind neatly into (usually) two parts: "free and Communist" or simply "ours and theirs." Such dichotomies, which for all that has been said about them remain with us still, deny significance to the relatively unpowerful and probably make it all the more difficult to bring about any kind of international stability. "Nonalignment," "neutralism," "third-world forces," "new emerging forces," and the like are all partial attempts to find some rubric that offers significance to a part of the world that is in short supply of it.

How deeply ingrained these views have been in American policies is evident in the conflicts mentioned above. Burma's interests were not considered when aid was sent to General Li Mi's troops, and this apparently was not thought an important matter until the Burmese government made a strong international case. And as John Cady has said of Laos: "Tribal friction in the mountains, tensions between hill folk and valley Lao, pro-Thai and anti-Thai feelings, and the personal rivalry and veniality of persons in high position, all operated to becloud and confuse what the United States attempted to oversimplify as a case of national freedom versus Communist aggression."[2] Similarly in Indonesia, the utter complexity of political and social cleavages which contributed to the rise of the regional rebellion of 1958—an event comprehensible only in terms of a

[2] John Cady, *Thailand, Burma, Laos, and Cambodia,* Prentice-Hall, Englewood Cliffs, N.J., 1966, p. 139.

specifically Indonesian history—was all reduced to an exceedingly simple issue. Washington was drawn in by a view which perceived only one element in the conflict. That element was blown up out of all proportion— and perhaps gave the Communist Party a boost as a result of the foreign intervention issue.

American interpretations of the Indonesian coup of 1965, which led to the destruction of the Communist Party and the fall of Sukarno, are additional evidence of a distorted conception of Southeast Asian politics and of American influence. It is often claimed that the Indonesian army and allied groups could not have crushed the Communist Party were it not for the presence of American forces in Vietnam. Presumably Chinese troops were thus prevented from rushing to Indonesia to save the day for the Communists. Quite apart from the problem of how Chinese forces were to get to Indonesia, in view of inadequate transport, there is as yet no evidence at all that Indonesian military commanders gave any thought to China during the first few weeks following the coup. The point is, however, that the *a priori* argument of American centrality requires no further reasoning or a demand for evidence, in the same way that the threat of communism is often assumed to be the major issue of Southeast Asian politics.

The difficulty with these sorts of conceptions is that they frequently lead to policies which are either intrinsically untenable or contradictory to other United States goals. In the one case, an inflated notion of American power, one that does not distinguish precisely the various uses to which it can and cannot be put successfully, leads to an overinvolvement of American personnel in programs where they are likely to be dysfunctional. Counterinsurgency efforts in which Americans take the lead are an example. The result may be that the essential political basis of such efforts is neglected, because outsiders cannot easily deal with domestic political conditions. Or the insurgency may actually grow in part as a reaction against the foreigners.

In the other case, that of contradictory goals, the emphasis in American policies upon eliminating the Communist threat tends at times to place a high premium on forces of stability to the disproportionate detriment of forces of change. In an open letter to President Nixon, F. Sionil Jose, editor of the intellectually influential Philippine political and literary review, *Solidarity*, argued that it might be best for the United States to leave the Philippines altogether, for then the power of peasant discontent might be able to force the governing elite to correct inequities of social and economic life in the Philippines. Jose argued that since the United States intervenes in the affairs of other nations anyway, why not intervene on the side of change? He is convinced that American policies have helped to maintain the present Philippine elite in power and, moreover, made it possible for the government to avoid change. This view too probably reflects an inflated conception of American power, at least as it applies to the Philippine political system. But Jose may be correct when he states: "It is this American obsession with order, with anti-communism that blinds them [to] the real causes of dissidence and desire for change." [3] There is no intrinsic reason why the United States should be concerned with social and economic change in other countries, except insofar as such change may affect American interests, as it may indeed. But the fact is that American leaders are concerned to promote change, and a great deal of assistance has been given to the Southeast Asian countries as well as others with that in mind. Nor is it always directly related to the struggle against communism. But where the Communist issue exists, in any number of real or imaginary forms, Jose is probably right in assuming that order takes precedence over change, at least in the minds of policy-makers. [4]

Though Jose's is a minority view in Southeast Asia in all likelihood, it is significant to the extent that it represents a common tendency among intellectuals in the area. Moreover, the antagonism aroused by the cases of American intervention often is subordinated by Southeast Asian governments to a greater interest in maintaining good relations with the United States and obtaining assistance from it. This is a function of American power. It is a constantly troubling question, however, both to America and to the states of Southeast Asia, how that power will be used.

CULTURE AND COLOR

Yet another kind of problem has affected our relations with Southeast Asian countries, though it is not clear in what measure, and probably will

---

[3] *Solidarity*, November, 1968.

[4] This does not always mean, however, that change can be prevented. Frequently an unintended consequence of American aid aimed at achieving greater stability is precisely the creation of more volatile political conditions. The extreme case of this is one in which an elite becomes so dependent upon foreign financial inputs that it neglects its ties to mass followings.

continue to unless we begin to contend with it. It is the matter of American cultural and racial predilections, which cannot receive adequate attention here but does deserve mention, for it is not discussed enough. Six years ago Norman Podhoretz published an article in *Commentary* entitled "My Negro Problem—And Ours." He startled many of his readers by admitting frankly to the fears and images of black men with which he and most whites have grown up. One implicit reason for writing the article as he did was that unless such images are let out of the bag they cannot be understood; hidden from view they are kept alive in their most insidious form. The same thing needs to be done—and some writers have begun to do it—for American images of the world and the various peoples in it with whom America must deal and who must themselves somehow deal with the remarkable power of the United States.

It is not unfair to say that Americans often have a hard time taking the nations of Southeast Asia seriously. The Chinese to an extent have been exempt from this, for although they have been regarded somewhat ambivalently in American folklore, their numbers (and perhaps their culture) have always lent them an aura of latent power. In recent years this latency seems to have fulfilled itself in the Communist state, and Americans have gone to an extreme perhaps in taking China's power more seriously than its development actually warrants. But power at least lends some dignity, and if the Chinese remain "Oriental" and all that implies to the American imagination—which for various reasons, mainly related to economic development, has a hard time classifying the Japanese anymore—they cannot be denied a significant place in the world. The countries of Southeast Asia, on the other hand, suffer the double disadvantage of being relatively small (except for Indonesia), as well as economically underdeveloped, and being former colonies (except for Thailand). Much of what Americans knew of these countries, until quite recently, came from colonial sources. Along with this knowledge came the common myths which help to support colonial systems, myths which are not on the whole favorable to those who were dominated. The sense of superiority lent to those who ruled is still buttressed by an equally evident sense of inferiority which colonial peoples carried over from their earlier political condition. Now the United States is commonly regarded as the epitome of all those attributes of the "West" which made the age of imperialism possible: technical superiority, organization, and possession of all the essential keys to advanced knowledge. The psychological relationship between Americans and Southeast Asians promoted by these conditions is not only delicate but likely to lead to misunderstanding. While Southeast Asians tend to overrate the magic of technology and the ease with which it may be acquired, Americans tend to dismiss older cultural traditions as either irrelevant or hopelessly inadequate to "modernization." Translated into political terms, these latter views have sometimes encouraged a disregard of Southeast Asian assessments of the demands and interests of their own political systems.

The color theme in American (and other) foreign relations has been explored recently by Harold Isaacs in an article for *Foreign Affairs* (January, 1969). It can no longer be ignored as being of minor importance. For Southeast Asians it is made clearer by the existence of such a pact as ANZUS, whose underlying rationale is hard to understand except in terms of an alliance of white nations. However badly the white world is divided within itself, Southeast Asian leaders sometimes fear, partly because of their own color biases, that whites are more likely to side with whites than nonwhites. Chinese vituperation against Soviet-American "cooperation" becomes comprehensible in this perspective, as Isaacs points out, though the importance of this recognition is considerably reduced in Southeast Asia by a much greater fear of China than of any white nation.

A century ago the sensitive king of Thailand, Rama IV, made the following remark to his ambassador in Paris concerning the competition of France and England in mainland Southeast Asia and its meaning for Thailand: ". . . the British and the French can entertain no other feeling for each other than mutual esteem as fellow human beings, whereas the likes of us who are wild and savage, can only be regarded by them as animals. We have no means of knowing whether or in what way they have contrived beforehand to divide our country among themselves. . . ."[5] This comment had primarily a cultural dimension in the context of Thai values, though elsewhere in Southeast Asia, possibly because of the colonial experience, similar views would be invested with racial meanings as well. In any case, such attitudes show no evidence of disappearing in Southeast Asia.

It may be that the growing sophistication of Americans about the world and the knowledge now being accumulated about Southeast Asia by American scholars, journalists, diplomats, businessmen, soldiers, and so on is actually beginning to influence our comprehension of the area. One can

[5] A.L. Moffat, *Mongkut, the King of Siam*, Cornell University Press, Ithaca, 1961, p. 119.

see this in some American newspapers and journals and in the debate over Vietnam. But matters of race and culture run too deeply to change quickly; therefore they will likely condition relations between the United States and Southeast Asia for some time to come. If there is a solution to this problem, it remains obscure; it is helpful at least to be aware of it.

CHINA AND SOUTHEAST ASIA

China is the key to the present character of American involvement in Southeast Asia, and it is hard to imagine any resolution of tensions there that does not incorporate a new interpretation of China's position and interests. The competition between the Soviet Union and the United States in Southeast Asia has long since undergone a mellowing process, determined at least in part by the antagonism of both great powers toward China.

The presence of China is of course an obvious fact of life in Asia. The wish of much of Southeast Asia and the United States that this were not so, and the attempt to make it mean as little as possible, has been a root cause of conflict in the area. At least two major conditions are necessary in order to keep China's influence in Southeast Asia to a minimum: The first is China's own weakness; in the past Chinese influence in the South rose and fell according to the state of Chinese politics. The second condition is the willingness of some great power—the European colonial metropoles, Japan during World War II, and now the United States—to maintain a vigilant presence determined at any cost to bring a greater influence to bear on Southeast Asia. Over the first condition the United States does not, under normal circumstances, have a great deal of control. With respect to the second, the Vietnam war poses the question whether America has the necessary wealth and internal consensus to endure the problems that a vigilant presence in Asia may now create.

The alternatives considered, both in the United States and in Southeast Asia, frequently have been distorted by prevailing conceptions of the Communist and Chinese threats. In the most extreme views, a diminution of American force in the area would lead either to Communist victories in every Southeast Asian state or to a military subjugation of the area by China. There is considerable reason to doubt both possibilities.

But there is no doubt that a reduction of American military power in Southeast Asia would inevitably mean an increase in Chinese influence.

This is as much a fact for Southeast Asia as the presence of the United States is for South America, that of the Soviet Union for Eastern Europe, and—to make the picture even clearer—as the presence of Germany is for Holland, Egypt for the Sudan, Thailand for Cambodia, and Indonesia for Malaysia. This reality in Southeast Asia has in a sense been distorted by the imposition of a quite different reality, that of the superiority of American to Chinese power. But the first reality is only dormant and will revive unless the United States chooses to remain forever. The assumption that if only America stays in the area long enough, China will change for the "moderate" better, seems to be basically irrelevant. Quite apart from the point that the United States may not in fact be able to remain that long in adequate force, there is little reason to suppose that Chinese views will change so much as to make what happens in Southeast Asia less important to Chinese interests.

Recently there have been indications that Southeast Asian leaders are becoming concerned with the reality of China, only partly with a view towards the possible withdrawal of the United States from Vietnam and from Southeast Asia generally. In the Philippines, for example, there is growing interest in opening up relations with Communist countries, including China itself. In Indonesia, even after the 1965 coup and the extreme tension between Djakarta and Peking which followed, there was a distinct reluctance actually to break off relations, a reluctance evidently shared by Peking. And in Cambodia, Norodom Sihanouk has long made it clear that, whatever else he may think about China, it would be worth the trouble to avoid conflict with it. Thailand, however, has drifted into a relationship with the United States which has rather reduced its flexibility. There are Thai intellectuals who, though they might otherwise agree with American policy in Vietnam and greatly fear the spread of communism, are afraid that Bangkok has dangerously limited its own freedom of diplomatic movement. They pose this problem in terms of Thailand's having departed from the traditional policies of noninvolvement and balance that kept this state independent. The essence of those traditional policies was precisely the recognition of superior powers and the adjustment to them with a maximum number of options. Whenever China was strong it necessarily figured in Thai policy as it does now, but in a way that has reduced Thai options.

What this all means essentially is that eventually Southeast Asian states must come to terms with China, and the longer this is put off the more dangerous it is for those states. Indeed, hostilities have already been built up which are likely to affect relations between several Southeast Asian states, particularly Thailand, for some time.

Coming to terms with China means fundamentally that China's interests must be considered carefully. Among other things, these interests involve the treatment of overseas Chinese in Southeast Asia, a problem which will undoubtedly create considerable tension. The possibility should not be ignored that China may try to promote an expansion of Communist parties or insurgent activities in some of the Southeast Asian countries, if for no other reason than the additional leverage it will lend to Peking's diplomacy. But it has to be emphasized once more that the success of domestic rebellion depends primarily on domestic political and social conditions, which have sometimes been ignored in recent years because of an excessive reliance upon foreign military assistance. In any event, the need to deal more directly with China will cause a great deal of tension and some hardships for Southeast Asia, particularly the mainland states, cannot be denied or treated lightly. Whether such difficulties will be greater than those current in the area is, at least, in question.

The foremost of China's demands on Southeast Asia, however, will likely be that the territory to its south not be used to harbor potential threats against China, for this is now the cause of China's anxiety about the area. Some argue that America's motives in Asia should not be suspect, that the presence of American bases in Thailand, Vietnam, Taiwan, Korea, Okinawa, Guam, and the Philippines, plus a half-million troops in Vietnam ought not to cause China concern. But China's fear of American power is legitimate and reasonable. China has no more reason to trust America than America has to trust China; and China is in the worse position because the United States is far better prepared to execute its threats.

Conceivably, Chinese fear of the United States and the history of America's involvement in Southeast Asia may offer the states of Southeast Asia considerable freedom of movement even when American armies are not in the immediate vicinity. If another reason were needed to keep Chinese armies out of the Southeast Asian mainland, it would be the possibility that the United States might react again. Apart from that, however, the mobility of United States military forces and the fact that these forces have been used in Southeast Asia might make political stability in Southeast Asia important to China as well. The argument that once America leaves Vietnam it will not easily return to Southeast Asia may bear some weight in Chinese thinking, as it does in American thinking, but the ability of the United States to become involved again at least has to be considered by Peking.

Short-run anxieties about international aggression, among the Southeast Asian states themselves as well as from China, perhaps can be calmed somewhat by means of multilateral guarantees. To have any effect these would have to involve the United States, the Soviet Union, China, and possibly Japan, as well as the Southeast Asian states. But whether this approach would work is in doubt, and the precise content of such guarantees is not easy to work out: One obvious stumbling block is internal unrest and insurgency, which international guarantees cannot and should not attempt to prevent. Within Southeast Asia itself there may well be considerable conflict between the mainland states that will be difficult to contain, unless these states can themselves work out a system of multilateral and bilateral agreements. Thus should Vietnam eventually be unified, Laos may well become a major bone of contention between Vietnam and Thailand. Conceivably overt conflict could be avoided through international protection of Laos, but this might become embroiled with ongoing internal Laotion conflict, which is not likely to stop.

As for Chinese military aggression in mainland Southeast Asia, there is, again, some reason to suppose that Peking itself will want to avoid getting bogged down in nationalist wars. In this case international guarantees are probably less important than bilateral accords between Peking and the capitals of Southeast Asia which begin to define with some precision their mutual interests. The same is true of other parts of China's rim, where the United States will be most concerned with Japan, Taiwan, and Korea.

The United States will no doubt play a critical part in this lengthy process. Indeed, in an important sense the chances for relative peace in Asia must depend upon the willingness of the United States to give China her due as a great Asian power. While America has been able to recognize the influence of the Soviet Union in Eastern Europe—shown by the absence of any attempt to interfere with the invasion of Czechoslovakia—it has been unwilling to recognize a much lesser influence of China over Southeast Asia. The situations are not fully analogous, but the incongruities favor a relaxation of the American posture towards China, if for no other reason than that American interests have been more clearly defined in Europe than in Asia.

THE UNITED STATES AND SOUTHEAST ASIA: "POST-WITHDRAWAL"

What does it really mean to say that the United States will "withdraw" from Southeast Asia once its military forces are removed from Vietnam, if they are? It is often argued, in Southeast Asia and in the United States, that if America leaves Vietnam to be unified under Communist rule, it is not likely to ever again get involved in Southeast Asian affairs. Those favoring military withdrawal have indeed sometimes been labeled "neo-isolationists," one of the more misleading epithets produced by the Vietnam debate. One is tempted to suggest that those who see military withdrawal as necessarily leading to total withdrawal basically cannot understand an American presence which is not a military presence. But military involvement should, it seems to me, be avoided in the future, unless some very concrete interest can be identified in terms unburdened by ideological fantasies.

This is not to say, however, that the United States will be uninvolved in Southeast Asia, for it is very hard to conceive of the United States being totally uninvolved nearly anywhere in the world. In Southeast Asia America has no critically important economic or cultural ties, though the ties that do exist are not likely to be ignored. And a certain amount of concern generated over the past twenty years among various groups in the United States will not disappear. The influence of American hopes for economic development in the new states should not be ignored in this connection. Moreover, the close relationship between the United States and Japan will contribute to America's ongoing involvement in Southeast Asia, where Japanese economic interests will undoubtedly continue to grow.

But what kind of influence and commitment would the United States have in Southeast Asia without a military involvement? This question has caused anxiety everywhere in the area, possibly including North Vietnam. China is again the main worry, and Norodom Sihanouk probably speaks for most in hoping that without war the United States can remain sufficiently engaged to maintain a balance of power in the region. Some Southeast Asian leaders have publicly supported the war in Vietnam precisely because they fear that without it the United States would have no reason to stay in Southeast Asia. Nor is the China issue solely at the root of this anxiety. It is hoped that the United States will in some other ways influence the international relations of the area. In Singapore, for example, the United States is seen as serving as a kind of substitute for Great Britain, which will soon withdraw its forces from the area; American influence, in this view, could be instrumental in softening relations between Singapore and Malaysia and helping to maintain Singapore's independence from Malaysia and Indonesia. Cambodia too would benefit from restraint which the United States could impose upon Thailand. In the past hopes of this kind have been unfulfilled because of American concentration on broader issues which, in fact, at times has had a contrary effect. Yet such conflicts within Southeast Asia frequently take precedence, in the minds of Southeast Asians, over the problems of primary concern to Washington.

To a considerable extent, the kind of influence the United States has in Southeast Asia is up to the United States, and it is possible that without the burdens of war the varieties of influence may even grow. Less anxiety about communism, for example, would make the United States less vulnerable to pressure on that score than in the past. But this problem aside, it should be clear that even without military force the United States has enormous purchase in Southeast Asia. It is not only a question of the economic assistance which these countries need and which America has within its capacity to give. It is also the psychological force of trends and examples set in the United States which tend to be emulated elsewhere. Both kinds of influence represent a kind of power that creates resentment. But the great powers do exercise control over the smaller and especially the economically underdeveloped states, and this is unavoidable.

What is avoidable, if the resentment is to be reduced and international stability given a slightly better chance, is the conscious interference of great powers in basically unfamiliar political conditions. This point is raised here because of the tendency, encouraged in the United States partly by cold-war conceptions, to attempt to strengthen the new states by remaking them (very often) in one's own image. Southeast Asia has had its share of this experience. Lack of success has had little effect on the ambition, and many recent writings on political development, so far as they are policy oriented, indicate lines of policy that should in fact be avoided. The notion that the United States can contribute greatly to the "political development" of other societies is on the face of it rather presumptuous. Not only does the idea assume an ability to manipulate societies over which we do not have full control, it also assumes that the United States is disinterested enough to do a fair job. These points have been stated a bit extremely here, and I do not mean to argue that the United States should not be concerned with development or that it should not have concepts of development in mind when assistance is given. Economic and technical aid is obviously needed and wanted in Southeast Asia, but under conditions that do not appear to threaten existing political interests and conventions.

There are those who insist, like Mr. Jose in his letter to President Nixon, that the United States should assist the forces of change rather than the conservative forces of existing political and economic orders. There is something very attractive in this argument to those in America who are committed to helping the new states to achieve better conditions of life. But it hardly takes cognizance of the difficulties for American policy-makers of deciding what constitutes desirable change and of relating such decisions to American interests elsewhere. For Southeast Asian states themselves the safest kind of American (or other) involvement may be one that is as much as possible neutral with respect to existing or future political systems. That is, the United States should make no special effort to keep groups in power when such support enables them to escape change. But in avoiding the dangers of overinvolvement it should not become actively engaged in promoting change against the wishes of existing governments. Much foreign aid is likely to have social and political consequences anyway, and one might hope for the best. None of this makes it impossible to encourage change, for the levers are held by the donor state; and one might also hope that neutral sources of outside pressure, the United Nations for example, would become more active with American support. Clearly these are hard lines to follow, and at times no doubt impossible, but they have the advantage of a caution that respects both American and Southeast Asian capabilities and interests.

But a big question is begged here. If there are in fact few significant interests to justify a massive commitment of American energies to Southeast Asia, why should aid be given at all? One can rationalize it, as Edwin Reischauer and others have, on the grounds that it is in American interests to help achieve prosperity and stability everywhere in the world, to avoid tensions which might lead to great wars, to develop good relations with countries which may in the future be more powerful than they now are, and to fulfill our own moral obligations to people who are economically deprived. We do not really know how influential these incentives are in the making of American foreign policy. On existing evidence the case may be argued either way, but this on balance is at least a hopeful sign.

9

Evolution of
American Policy
in the Middle East

George Lenczowski

Relations between the United States and the Middle East-North African area have existed for about 150 years. The first 100 years of this period (approximately 1820 to 1920) saw sporadic contacts, mostly restricted to private American groups and individuals, and only occasionally involving the United States government. Early American "pioneers" in the Middle East consisted primarily of missionaries. The Boston-based American Board of Commissioners for Foreign Missions sent over the years a number of its representatives to the Ottoman and Persian empires with an eye to spreading Christianity.[1] Before long, this objective was tacitly abandoned inasmuch as apostasy from Islam was a punishable offense in the host countries and there was a genuine resistance of Moslems—followers of an

[1] For early American contacts with the Ottoman Empire, see David H. Finnie, *Pioneers East: The Early American Experience in the Middle East*, Harvard University Press, Cambridge, Mass., 1967.

advanced monotheistic faith—to conversion. Consequently, American missions shifted their focus from religious to educational, humanitarian, and medical work. In due course, under the sponsorship of various protestant groups, there arose a network of American schools, some of which achieved a college status. Foremost among them was the Syrian Protestant College (subsequently renamed the American University of Beirut), founded in 1866. Other institutions offering secondary and/or advanced education were Robert College in Istanbul, Aleppo College in northern Syria, and the American University at Cairo. All of them began under Protestant religious auspices but in due course underwent a process of secularization. Later, the first Catholic institution of higher learning, the Hikma College, was established by American Jesuits in Baghdad.

Side by side with this educational effort went the humanitarian activities. Most notable were the achievements of the American Near East Relief, an organization which came to the aid of dispossessed Armenians and Greeks during and after World War I. Subsequently renamed the Near East Foundation, it enlarged the scope of its operations, focusing on agricultural training and extension work.

During this period, which may be appropriately called the "era of innocence," official American involvement was kept at a minimum. An early concern was the protection of American merchant shipping in the Mediterranean against the piracy by the North African Barbary states. This necessitated the presence of an American naval squadron in the Western Mediterranean (based on Minorca) in the 1820s. Likewise, to protect American traders in the Ottoman Empire, a treaty was sought and signed with the Sublime Porte in 1830. American relations with Persia were relatively uneventful through the nineteenth century. During the Persian revolution of 1906-1909, some Americans were embroiled in the turmoil in the northern city of Tabriz, causing some strains in the diplomatic relations between the two countries. [2] America, however, projected a good image of herself as a country politically disinterested, adhering to high humanitarian principles, willing to help the oppressed minorities, and able to provide some much-needed skills. In the latter sector, two events deserve mention: construction of naval shipyards and many ships in Istanbul by American naval

---

[2] This period is reviewed by Abraham Yeselson in *United States-Persian Diplomatic Relations, 1883-1921*, Rutgers University Press, New Brunswick, N.J., 1956.

architects and mechanics during the period 1831-1841, and the engagement by the Persian government of Dr. Morgan Shuster as Financial Administrator in 1911.[3] Even in those early preindustrial stages, the United States was exporting some much-appreciated know-how to the Middle East.

THE ERA OF IDEALISM

World War I brought about the first major American involvement in the politics of the Middle East. Point Twelve of Woodrow Wilson's Fourteen Points (January 8, 1918)—an official program for peace accepted by the Allies—spoke of the Ottoman Empire. Its Turkish portions were to remain fully independent and sovereign. As for "the other nationalities which are now under Turkish rule," i.e., Arab, Armenian, and possibly Kurdish, they "should be assured an undoubted security of life and an absolutely unmolested opportunity of development."[4] Thus, as a matter of broad policy, the principle of national self-determination was to apply to the lands of the Ottoman Empire: (1) to be applied without reservations to Turkey proper; (2) to be subject to some delaying or modifying formula, possibly in the form of foreign tutelage, to the Arab and other non-Turkish areas. What this formula should be was not specified in the Fourteen Points; at that time, the President preferred to leave specifications until some later date. However, in terms of basic principles, Wilson's Fourteen Points clearly contradicted the wartime secret agreements concluded among Britain, France, Russia, Italy, Greece, and the Zionists, which aimed at the partition of the Ottoman Empire among them. Furthermore, the principle of "open covenants openly arrived at" enunciated in Point One was obviously incompatible with the secrecy of those deals. No wonder therefore that at the beginning of the Paris Peace Conference Wilson refused to discuss the claims arising from the secret agreements as opposed to his Fourteen Points. The latter, he claimed, by being accepted as a basis for peace by the Allies, automatically invalidated any earlier agreements.

[3] His experiences are recounted in Morgan W. Shuster, *The Strangling of Persia*, Century, New York, 1912.

[4] Text of Fourteen Points in H. W. V. Temperley (ed.), *A History of the Peace Conference in Paris*, Henry Frowde and Hodder and Stoughton, London, 1924, vol. I, p. 433.

Wilson's stand caused much unhappiness among the British and French delegations as well as the Zionist representatives in Paris. The President's proposal to send an international commission to ascertain the wishes of the native populations fell on deaf ears; whereupon Wilson decided to proceed on his own by dispatching two purely American missions to the Middle East. One, headed by Henry C. King and Charles Crane, was sent to Palestine, Lebanon, and Syria; the other, led by General James G. Harbord, went to Turkey and Armenia. It recommended the establishment of a mandate over Turkey and Transcaucasia to be exercised by a single power. This recommendation was rejected, as well as the proposals formulated by some other quarters (including the Armenians) that the mandate should be exercised by the United States. Instead, the subsequent Treaty of Sèvres (August 10, 1920) concluded between the Allies and Turkey, recognized independent Armenia and provided for President Wilson's arbitration regarding her boundary with Turkey. Wilson's arbitral award of 1920 assigned sizable areas of eastern Turkey to Armenia. It seemed to be based more on Armenian historical claims than on the principle of self-determination, inasmuch as the areas in question were overwhelmingly Turkish in population and had been so even before the forced deportations of the Armenians during the war.

As for the King and Crane commission, it learned that the Arabs of the Fertile Crescent (whom it was interviewing) definitely favored independence and rejected any scheme that would sanction Zionist immigration in Palestine or Hindu immigration in Iraq. Should immediate independence be denied, representatives of Syria (including Lebanon and Palestine) wished to see the United States as a mandatory power on behalf of the League of Nations. Their second choice was Britain. Representatives of Iraq (Mesopotamia) mentioned independence as their only objective and protested against the very principle of mandates as embodied in Article 22 of the League of Nations Covenant. Wilson's return from Paris to the United States, the press of other important business claiming his attention, and his subsequent illness caused the King-Crane report to be disregarded and shelved.[5] Without Wilson's dominant presence, the peace conferees effectively buried Point Twelve of his Fourteen Points: Turkey emerged as a truncated little state subject to formally recognized spheres

[5] For a comprehensive account, see Harry N. Howard, *The King-Crane Commission*, Khayat's, Beirut, 1963.

of influence of the Big Powers in Anatolia, while the Arab areas were subjected to the British and French mandates. Furthermore, against the Arabs' explicit wishes, the Balfour Declaration of November 2, 1917, promising the establishment of a Jewish National Home, was formally incorporated into the document establishing the British mandate over Palestine.

THE ERA OF ISOLATION

Failure to ratify the League of Nations Covenant marked the first major step in the policy of isolation followed by the United States in the interwar period. The official American posture toward the Balfour Declaration was positive and friendly but did not go beyond the generalities of good will. Implementation of the declaration was gladly left to Britain as a mandatory power responsible for Palestine. While already in the early 1920s Arab resistance to Zionist settlement was evident—as shown by sporadic outbursts of violence, particularly in connection with access to the Wailing Wall in Jerusalem—the matter did not have the urgency which the subsequent Nazi persecutions of Jews gave it in the mid-1930s. Consequently, though aware of the Arab-Zionist controversy, both official Washington and American public opinion were not prepared to accept an active role in the solution of the problem. The Middle East as a whole was viewed as basically a British preserve, with a lesser French participation, and as such not subject to American political intervention.

In one field, however, the hands-off policy did not apply. American oil companies were interested in seeking concessions and expanding their operations in the Middle East. They were critical of the Anglo-French exclusivity practiced in their mandated territories and based on the decisions reached at the San Remo conference of 1920. These practices were contrary both to the provisions of mandates as sanctioned by the League of Nations and to the "open-door" principle which the United States tried to apply to international economic relations. For these reasons the U.S. government gave its full support to the American oil companies in their endeavors to break the Anglo-French monopoly.[6] Joint efforts of the com-

---

[6] For the role of the State Department in support of American claims, see George Lenczowski, *Oil and State in the Middle East,* Cornell University Press, Ithaca, N.Y., 1960, pp. 15ff. For a broader look at basic policies of this period, see Benjamin Gerig, *The Open Door and the Mandates System,* Allen and Unwin, London, 1930.

panies and the State Department eventually resulted in the admission of American oil companies into the Iraq Petroleum Company, a joint enterprise henceforth to be owned by the British, French, Dutch, and American interests. The American share was to represent 23.75 percent of the stock. In return for admission, however, the American participants (Standard Oil of New Jersey and Socony Vacuum Oil Company) had to sign the restrictive Red Line Agreement, which forbade them to seek separate concessions in the area corresponding to the Asian parts of the old Ottoman Empire. This was a heavy price paid by a dynamic American industry for admission to the "club"; twenty years later it became a major bone of contention between the American interests and their European partners. Obviously, however, the restrictive clauses of the agreement were binding only upon its signatories. Other American companies were free to seek concessions in the area without impediments. Thus, the Standard Oil Company of California in 1933, successfully outbid British competitors and secured a major concession in Saudi Arabia. This new American presence in the Arab East did not become immediately obvious. By the time exploration and drilling had yielded the first positive results, World War II broke out. Operations in Arabia came to a standstill largely due to wartime allocations of the necessary material to other priorities. Operations were not to be resumed until 1945-1946.

THE ERA OF STRATEGIC AWAKENING—WORLD WAR II

World War II brought the United States into a closer contact than ever before, and on a more massive scale, with the Middle East. American involvement was largely strategic but also, to some extent, political and economic. Campaigns fought in Egypt and Libya by the British and their allies against the Italo-German armies under General Erwin Rommel would not have succeeded ultimately without substantial help from America, mostly in the form of tanks. When the Allied pincers closed in on the Axis forces in North Africa in 1942-1943, its western arm was composed mostly of American troops operating from Morocco and Algeria, two Arab countries at that time politically remote from the Middle East but which, fifteen years later were destined to become seriously enmeshed in Arab politics. Delivering arms to the British as well as fighting in North Africa necessitated naval operations in the Red Sea and the Mediterranean, thus bringing this area into the scope of American global strategy. A few years later, General Eisenhower expressed the view that, in strategic terms, the Middle East carried more weight than any other area in the world.

Forwarding arms and supplies to the hard-pressed Russian allies through the Iranian "corridor" was another undertaking which brought 30,000 noncombatant American troops to Iran and the Persian Gulf. Although their task was primarily logistic and technical and Iran had long been considered to lie outside the American sphere of interests, its special position as a gateway between Russia and the vast areas bordering the Indian Ocean aroused more than a passing political interest in Washington. At the Teheran Conference in 1943, President Roosevelt signed a declaration signifying American interest in the preservation of Iran's independence and pledged aid to its development.

Roosevelt's presence in Teheran was not an isolated event. It was a link in the chain of inter-allied conferences which included also meetings in Cairo, Casablanca, and Yalta, all located within the broader Mediterranean basin. On one of these trips, the President arranged for a series of meetings with Arab heads of state (King Ibn Saud, President Shukri al-Quwatli of Syria, and King Farouk of Egypt), held on board an American warship in the great Bitter Lake in Egypt (February, 1945).[7] With his customary flair for colorful expression, Roosevelt commented after the meeting with Ibn Saud that five minutes of the conversation with the Arab ruler had taught him more about the Palestinian problem than an "exchange of two or three dozen letters."[8] How sincere the President was in uttering these words is a moot question. While there is no doubt that a talk of this sort increased his awareness of the Arab-Jewish controversy, one might wonder how deep was his understanding of the basic incompatibility of Zionist and Arab claims. Roosevelt always professed sympathy for the Zionist aspirations. However, one of his last public acts was to write King Ibn Saud to assure him that the United States would not undertake any decision regarding Palestine without full consultation with Arabs and Zionists alike.[9]

---

[7] For a first-hand account of the most strategic of these meetings, see William A. Eddy, *F.D.R. Meets Ibn Saud*, American Friends of the Middle East, New York, 1954.

[8] Robert E. Sherwood, *Roosevelt and Hopkins: An Intimate History*, Harper, New York, 1948, pp. 871-872.

[9] *Department of State Bulletin*, October 21, 1945, p. 623.

AFTER WORLD WAR II: THE ERA
OF INEVITABLE INVOLVEMENT

Oil, Russia, and Palestine may be regarded as the three main factors that brought about intimate involvement of the United States in the Middle East in the postwar period. Barring major changes in the nature of world economics, oil promised to be a fairly constant factor, even though subject to some fluctuations. Basic data about this factor could be summed up as follows: (1) The Middle East (with its Arab North African extension) possessed about 76 percent of the proven free-world oil reserves. (2) About 75 percent of Europe's fuel requirements and about 80 percent of Japan's needs were supplied by Middle Eastern oil. (3) Oil was steadily displacing coal as a source of energy on world markets while providing a base for numerous petrochemical industries; advances in hydroelectric and atomic technology did not diminish the role of oil and were not likely to do so in the foreseeable future. (4) Supplies of oil from the Middle East-North Africa were conditioned not only by normal commercial considerations but also by internal politics and international relations in the area, which was passing through a vulnerable phase of liberation from Western control and of mounting opposition to the Western-sponsored solutions to the Palestine problem. (5) The American share in the ownership of Middle Eastern oil concessions followed an upward curve, with the U.S. oil firms reaching parity and eventually outpacing their British counterparts; by the early 1960s the American stake in the principal oil concessions of the area was as follows (round figures):

Saudi Arabia	100 percent
Trans-Arabian Pipeline	100 percent
Bahrein	100 percent
Saudi-Kuwaiti Neutral Zone	100 percent
Kuwait	50 percent
Iran	40 percent
Iraq	25 percent
Qatar and the Persian Gulf	25 percent
Libya	dominant holdings in the most prolific concession areas

(6) Within ten years after the end of the war, revenue from oil concessions overshadowed all other revenues of the oil-producing countries of the

Middle East; by 1967, these revenues in the Middle East, with Iran and Algeria at its eastern and western extremities, reached an imposing total figure of $2.9 billion. (7) Middle Eastern and North African oil investments have been the single biggest earner of hard currency, accounting for over $1.1 billion in 1966 and thus playing a major role in the U.S. balance of payments. [10]

The heavy dependence of the major industrial nations of the free world on Middle Eastern oil supplies for their peacetime economies and the strategic needs of America's NATO allies have contributed to making oil one of the main determinant factors of United States policy toward the Middle East and Arab Africa. Though not exclusively geared to it, this policy has as an aim to maintain a steady flow of oil by avoiding disruption of operations in the producing countries and by assuring the availability of facilities (pipelines, the Suez Canal) in the transit countries. Inasmuch as revenues from oil are the most important source of income to the host countries and, as such, permit them to launch ambitious development programs, the United States has a dual interest in seeing that these revenues continue without crises and interruptions: first, because development of these countries has been one of the broader goals of American foreign policy; second, because the existence of this independent revenue has eased the burden of extending U.S. financial aid to the underdeveloped areas.

THE SOVIET FACTOR

Soviet expansionist aspirations toward the Middle East, explicitly stated in the Nazi-Soviet documents discovered at the end of the war, together with the Soviet pressures applied in 1945-1946 to Iran, Turkey, and Greece, have been one of the two main reasons (the other being the extension of Soviet power in Central-Eastern Europe) for the formulation of the policy of containment and, more broadly, for the advent of the cold war.

American response to the challenge of Soviet threats, military pressure, and subversion in the northern tier of the Middle East was expressed in a series of unilateral, bilateral, and multilateral moves aimed at: (1) extension of American security guarantees to the threatened countries,

---

[10] For these and other economic data, see George Lenczowski (ed.), *United States Interests in the Middle East*, American Enterprise Institute for Public Policy Research, Washington, D. C., 1968, pp. 39-76.

(2) granting economic and military assistance, (3) commitment, in some cases, of American troops, (4) securing bases, and (5) strengthening the defense potential of the recipient countries.

In chronological sequence, the first of these moves was diplomatic support given Iran in 1946, accompanied by warning to Russia by President Truman that Soviet procrastination in removing troops from Iran would result in American military intervention in that country.[11] Almost simultaneously, the Communist guerrilla war in Greece and Soviet territorial demands upon Turkey, coupled with the abdication of Britain's defense responsibilities in that region, brought to a head the need for defining United States posture in the crisis. The Truman Doctrine of March 12, 1947, was the outcome.[12] It pledged American economic and military advisory assistance to Greece and Turkey to safeguard their independence and territorial integrity against Communist subversion and aggression. Although the President's statement addressed itself explicitly to Greece and Turkey only, implicitly it was extended to Iran as well. Thus the northern tier was placed within the American security zone. There is no doubt that the doctrine achieved its main goal: Russia, forewarned of American resistance, refrained from committing aggression against Turkey and did not risk reinvading Iran after withdrawing her troops in May 1946. By the same token, American aid and advice to the Greek government resulted in due time in the curbing of the guerrilla movement and the restoration of order in the whole territory of Greece.

Encouraged by the success of its containment policy in the northern tier, the United States turned its attention to the Arab core of the Middle East with an eye to organizing a regional defense organization. In 1950-1951, a proposal to form a Middle East Defense Organization (MEDO) or a Middle East Command, to be based on Egypt, was promoted by both the United States and Britain. Its timing was poor because it coincided with the aggravation in Anglo-Egyptian relations, to be followed by the Free Officers' revolution of 1952. Both the royalist and the new revolutionary governments in Cairo rejected the proposal as incompatible with Egypt's view of its independence and as a disguised way for imperialism to reenter the area it was ostensibly leaving. One of the first acts of Secretary of State

---

[11] Harry S. Truman, *Memoirs*, Doubleday, New York, 1956, vol. II, *Years of Trial and Hope*, pp. 94-95; also Mr. Truman's subsequent statements, *New York Times*, April 25, 1952 and August 25, 1957.

[12] Text in J. C. Hurewitz, *Diplomacy in the Near and Middle East: A Documentary Record: 1914-1956*, Van Nostrand, Princeton, N.J., 1956, vol. II, p. 273.

Dulles upon the advent of the Republican administration in January, 1953 was to make a trip to the Middle East to gain first-hand impressions of current moods and attitudes. Upon his return, the Secretary reported that the Arab East was not ready for any military or political engagements with the West and that it would be preferable to acknowledge this realistically.[13] Dulles was undoubtedly right: The Arab world had no sense of Soviet danger, having never been subjected to Russian imperialism; its only experience had been with Western imperialism, the last traces of which it was seeking to remove; and it was deeply suspicious of "foreign pacts" as a device to perpetuate Western control and draw it into the cold war.

Having acknowledged the futility of attempts to line up Egypt and other Arab states in closer military links with the West, Washington's attention shifted back to the northern tier in the hope of firming up its defense potential via a regional organization. The fruit of these endeavors was the Baghdad Pact of 1955, concluded by Turkey, Iran, Iraq, Pakistan, and Great Britain.[14] Fearing possible nonratification by the Senate (partly because Israel was not included) and anxious to avoid an outburst of Egyptian hostility, Secretary Dulles decided to keep the United States from becoming a formal signatory of the Pact. However, the United States joined as an active participant in the Pact's working committees on anti-subversion, military liaison, and economic cooperation, thus becoming *de facto* if not *de jure* a member of the Pact. Iraq, in geographical proximity to Russia and plagued by the recurrent Kurdish problem, was the only Arab member of the alliance. Its adherence to the Pact made it a target of Arab nationalist hostility, with Cairo leading the chorus of condemnation. It accentuated Iraq's isolation from the rest of the Arab world and must be regarded as one of the causes of the military coup which overthrew the monarchy in July 1958. Following the coup, the new regime of General Kassem denounced the Pact, which was subsequently reorganized as the Central Treaty Organization (CENTO) with headquarters in Ankara.[15]

If the Baghdad Pact was seen as a barrier to Soviet advances in the Middle East, it withstood the test of time only partially. It did play a posi-

---

[13] Text in J. C. Hurewitz, *op. cit.*, pp. 337-342.

[14] Text in *ibid.*, p. 390.

[15] Although the United States did not formally accede to CENTO, it entered into alliance relationships with the three remaining Asian members of the organization in 1959 by signing bilateral defense agreements with Iran (March 4), Turkey (March 5), and Pakistan (March 5).

tive role in strengthening the defensive posture of the northern tier; however, it did not prevent the Soviets from skipping over this barrier in their new offensive—inaugurated in the very year of 1955—to woo and influence the Arab world.

While Soviet advances in the Arab countries represented a patient and continuous policy of penetration, they were accentuated by certain spectacular exploits. In 1955, by purchasing arms from Russia and Czechoslovakia, Egypt defied, in a major symbolic move, the Western monopoly on arms deliveries to the Middle East. This, combined with continuing attacks on the Baghdad Pact, caused serious deterioration in Cairo's relations with Washington and served as an indirect cause for the withdrawal of the Aswan Dam aid offer by Secretary Dulles in 1956. In due time the place vacated by the United States was filled by Russia who thus linked her name with one of the most publicized development ventures in Afro-Asia. In the meantime, President Nasser responded to the withdrawal of the American offer by seizing and nationalizing the Suez Canal. In the ensuing crisis (autumn 1956), in which Israel's invasion of Sinai was combined with Anglo-French landings in the Canal zone, the Soviet Union gave all-out diplomatic and propaganda support to Egypt, trying to project an image of a power friendly to Arab national aspirations and opposed to Israeli expansionism and Western imperialism in the area. In well-publicized notes sent to Israel, Britain, and France, Moscow hinted darkly at the possible use of terrible and devastating weapons against these countries, while Soviet propaganda alluded to the likelihood of the arrival of Soviet "volunteers" to fight imperialist-Zionist aggression in the Middle East.

Under the circumstances, segments of Arab public opinion, together with certain Arab governments (particularly those of Egypt, Syria, and Jordan—the latter in the winter of 1956-1957), proved receptive to Soviet advances. There was a marked intensification of Soviet political activity in the area, expressed by new aid-and-trade agreements, cultural penetration, and good-will visits. In response to this challenge, President Eisenhower on January 5, 1957 sent a major policy message to Congress, in which he proposed to extend American military and economic aid to any country in the Middle East threatened by "international Communism" that requested such aid.[16] Pronounced ten years after the Truman Doctrine, the Ei-

---

[16] Text in U.S. Senate Foreign Relations Committee, 89th Congress, A Select Chronology and Background Documents Relating to the Middle East, Washington, D.C., 1967, pp. 76-82.

senhower Doctrine had a similar objective of containing Soviet penetration. It differed from Truman's statement in that (1) its main focus was on the Arab world (though formally addressed to the area as a whole) and (2) it pledged the use of military force. Paradoxically, the only time it was applied in the military sense was in Lebanon in the summer of 1958 to oppose not Soviet aggression but an outburst of revolutionary Pan-Arabism. The latter seemed to have reached its high point after the conclusion in February, 1958 of a union between Egypt and Syria. Its by-products were, on the one hand, the intervention of the United Arab Republic in the civil war in Lebanon and, on the other, the revolution in Iraq of July 14, 1958. The existing status quo in the Arab East, thus far acceptable (though far from perfect) in the eyes of official Washington, seemed on the verge of crumbling, and swift action was deemed necessary to prevent total surrender of the region to new forces both hostile to the West and friendly to Russia. Thus the Eisenhower Doctrine was implemented not through strict adherence to its letter but through interpretation of its spirit. This interpretation, though it appeared somewhat farfetched, did not contradict the main intent of the doctrine.[17]

The doctrine was well received in the capitals of the Arab World that had moderate governments and pro-American orientation, primarily those of Saudi Arabia, Lebanon, prerevolutionary Iraq, Libya, Tunisia, and Morocco. Jordan's response was schizophrenic: Its pro-Western king inwardly was pleased with the doctrine's objectives, but its left-of-center cabinet was suspicious and resentful. By contrast, reactions in revolutionary Egypt, in "progressive" Syria, and in the Pan-Arab press in the region as a whole were definitely hostile. The doctrine was likened to the Baghdad Pact as an instrument of American imperialism (a term appearing with increasing frequency in the Arab political vocabulary). Its basic premises, namely those of the "power vacuum" in the Middle East caused by the shrinking of British influence and the need to oppose Soviet penetration, were rejected as malevolent and unilateral American scheming and gross interference with the sovereignty of the Arab states. The United States, ran the argument from Cairo and Damascus, was trying to protect the Middle East against the imaginary danger of Soviet aggression, while

[17] For a discussion of the doctrine, see John C. Campbell, *Defense of the Middle East: Problems of American Policy*, Harper, New York, 1958, pp. 120ff; Ralph Magnus, "Political-Strategic Interests," in G. Lenczowski (ed.), *United States Interests in the Middle East, op. cit.*; and Fahim I. Qubain, *Crisis in Lebanon*, The Middle East Institute, Washington, D.C., 1961.

in reality the real aggressors were the Western powers and Israel as demonstrated in the recent Anglo-French-Israeli invasion of Egypt. In the heat of these arguments strong American disapproval of the tripartite aggression against Egypt and Washington's insistence on early evacuation of Israeli forces from the conquered territory were conveniently forgotten. Nationalist Arab propaganda against the doctrine was seconded by similarly hostile criticisms from Moscow. Russia was clearly scoring successes in identifying herself with Arab revolutionary nationalism in spite of the fact that Communist parties were outlawed in Egypt and other Arab states. The clue to this success had to be sought in the principal cause of Arab-Western dissension—Palestine.

THE PALESTINE FACTOR

The year 1942 was in two important ways a turning point in the history of Zionism. The Biltmore program adopted by the World Zionist conference abandoned the earlier gradualist approach characteristic of the Balfour Declaration and the subsequent mandate period by calling instead for the creation of a Jewish state in the entire territory of Palestine. Secondly, 1942 saw the transfer of power in the World Zionist movement from the British to American Zionists. As a result, the American government, justly anticipated as an emerging superpower of the postwar world, became the principal focus of Zionist endeavors.

While the previously mentioned policies of Franklin Roosevelt in the last years of his administration could be called ambivalent and erratic with regard to Palestine, the Truman era, by contrast, was one of strong pro-Zionist posture. In 1946 the President called upon Britain to admit 100,000 displaced Jewish persons to Palestine. In 1947 the American delegation to the United Nations not only cast its vote for the Zionist-espoused partition of Palestine but also was instrumental in lining up votes of minor Latin American republics to assure the necessary two-thirds majority. On May 14, 1948, President Truman extended recognition to Israel within minutes of its proclamation as an independent state, and on May 25, 1950 he concluded a Tripartite Declaration sanctioning the new territorial status quo and regulating the flow of arms to the area by the United States, Britain, and France.[18] In the ensuing five years United States aid to Israel ex-

[18] Text in Hurewitz, *op. cit.*, p. 308.

ceeded, in terms of dollars, the amounts granted or loaned to all the Arab states. The years of the Truman administration corresponded to the first postwar period in the history of the Arab states when parliamentary or authoritarian regimes of moderate or conservative tinge were still dominant. These regimes, though strongly dissatisfied with the outcome of events in Palestine in 1947-1948, were not willing to burn their bridges with the West despite the latter's friendly predisposition to Israel. Consequently, the threat of Soviet penetration in the Arab world did not yet arise as an immediate problem. While Mr. Truman became acutely aware of the Soviet problem soon after assuming the Presidency, he saw it primarily as a direct threat to the northern tier and was not prepared to cope with it in terms of a long-range policy in the Arab world. His attitude toward the Arabs was, to say the least, one of aloofness and lack of understanding. Thus, on one occasion, he spoke of the creation of Israel as conforming to the principle of national self-determination yet disregarded the right of the Palestinian Arabs to self-determination at a time when the whole of Afro-Asia was entering the decisive phase of its struggle for liberation from foreign control. [19]

The seeds of discontent in the Arab world sown in the Truman era bore fruit in the Eisenhower era. The assumption of power by President Eisenhower and Colonel Nasser in their respective countries was almost simultaneous. It was the Eisenhower-Dulles team which had to face the first outbursts of revolutionary Arab nationalism and to live with it through the entire length of its term. And it was during the Eisenhower era that the dichotomy between the revolutionary and conservative Arab camps became the dominant feature of Arab politics. While frustration with the defeats at the hands of Israel in 1948 and 1956 was a major catalyst in mobilizing Arab revolutionary energies, the main thrust of the revolutionary movements between 1957 and 1967 was not toward a revival of conflict with Israel but toward a political and, in some cases, military struggle against the conservative and largely pro-Western Arab monarchies, particularly those of Saudi Arabia, Jordan, Iraq, and Libya. This being the case, an uneasy status quo was established between Israel and its

[19] "I was fully aware of the Arabs' hostility to Jewish settlement in Palestine, but, like many Americans, I was troubled by the plight of the Jewish people in Europe. The Balfour Declaration, promising the Jews the opportunity to re-establish a homeland in Palestine, had always seemed to me to go hand-in-hand with the noble policies of Woodrow Wilson, especially the principle of self-determination." Harry S. Truman, *op. cit.*, p. 133.

Arab neighbors. It was not perfect from either party's point of view: Israel was denied formal recognition and access to the Suez Canal and was subject to continuous economic boycott; the Arabs had to accept Israel's access to the Red Sea through the Strait of Tiran and Israel's refusal to repatriate the Arab refugees. However, both sides could live with it and, in fact, increase their prosperity. This status quo, furthermore, had the blessing of the United Nations symbolized by the presence of the UN Emergency Force (UNEF) guarding the eastern approaches of Egypt along the Israeli border and the coast of Sinai.

Eisenhower's administration was much more alert to the Arab problems than Truman's. But, despite many evidences of good will toward the Arab world, it followed policies which resulted in serious clashes with Arab nationalism, such as the promotion of the Baghdad Pact, cancellation of the Aswan Dam offer, and the proclamation of the Eisenhower Doctrine. In addition, its alignment with the conservative forces of the Arab world was a matter of public record. Consequently, when John F. Kennedy assumed the Presidency, he inherited a condition of considerable tension and irritation in American-Arab relations. His first moves were to relieve this tension by resuming a "dialogue" with Arab leaderships regardless of their hue. In contrast to the Eisenhower policies, the Kennedy administration tried to erase the impression of identification with Middle Eastern conservatism. The President seemed more inclined to accept the advice of those who saw in Nasser and Arab nationalism a progressive force likely to prevail in the future over their opponents in the Arab world. [20] Certain appointments in the State Department and the Foreign Service reflected this new trend. Surplus food assistance to the UAR was continued. Similarly, the official declaration of support to Saudi Arabia on October 25, 1962 (which at that time was threatened by Cairo on account of their conflict over Yemen) was couched in such terms as to link the support with the progress of Saudi reform about to be inaugurated by the premier, Prince Faisal.

However, full identification with progressive (and revolutionary) forces in the Arab world was not possible because the preservation of important United States economic and strategic interests hinged on the good will of certain conservative Arab regimes. These regimes were consistently

[20] For such an attitude, see Richard H. Nolte, "United States Policy and the Middle East," in Georgiana G. Stevens, *The United States and the Middle East*, Prentice-Hall, Englewood Cliffs, N.J., 1964.

exposed to threats from militant Arab nationalism radiating from Cairo, Damascus, and Algiers. Protecting these basically friendly governments against Egyptian aggression (as evidenced by UAR bombings of Saudi border towns) or subversion (sabotage of oil installations in Libya) often claimed more attention from Washington policy-makers than the Arab-Israeli relations in the early and mid-1960s.[21]

Though somewhat subdued in comparison with spectacular flare-ups of inter-Arab feuds, Arab-Israeli relations nevertheless were not free of recurrent tensions during both the Kennedy and the Johnson administrations. Three such tensions, in each case erupting into a crisis, can be singled out:

1. The Jordan Waters

Israel had long pressed for the proper utilization and sharing of the Jordan River waters to supplement and replenish its own depleted reserves. Repeated attempts by Eisenhower's special envoy, Eric Johnston, to secure an Arab-Israeli agreement on this matter ended in failure because of Arab opposition. Despairing of an international solution, Israel in 1963 began unilaterally diverting waters from Lake Tiberias to its own territory. The Arabs, at Nasser's initiative, responded by holding a summit meeting in January 1964 in Cairo and following it up with two other summit meetings in Alexandria and Casablanca (1964-1965). These conferences resulted in: (a) a decision to divert the headwaters of the Jordan River system, located in Lebanon and Syria, into Jordanian territory; (b) a decision to set up the Palestine Liberation Organization, with a military arm called the Palestine Liberation Army, to be financed jointly by the Arab League states. Subsequent endeavors to begin diversion of the headwaters, however, met with armed Israeli intervention in the form of bombings of the Lebanese and Syrian crews engaged in preliminary earthworks. As a result, work on the project was virtually suspended, with a corresponding increase in political tension. In the meantime, the slogan of liberation of Palestine from Zionist control was gaining in popularity and was adopted by various commando groups operating from Syrian and Jordanian territories with greatest encouragement from the radical Baath Party government of Syria.

---

[21] Illuminating comments on this subject may be found in John S. Badeau, *The American Approach to the Arab World*, Harper & Row, New York, 1968, pp. 132-151.

2. Arab Guerrilla Warfare and Israeli Reprisals

While infiltration of Arabs, individually or in small groups, into Israel with attendant acts of terrorism was a permanent feature of Arab-Israeli relations, these incursions gained in intensity in the mid-1960s, partly because of increased tension occasioned by the Jordan waters crisis and partly because of the marked radicalization of the Syrian regime, itself an indirect result of Israel's challenge to the Arab world. The Syrian-Israeli demilitarized zones near Lake Tiberias provided an especially fertile ground for mutual irritation. Peace in this region was frequently disrupted by clashes between the Syrian and Israeli armed forces. Lack of precision in the wording of the 1949 armistice agreement gave rise to Israeli insistence on the right to engage in farming activities in these zones. Syria challenged this interpretation and was prone to fire on any Israeli vehicles or groups penetrating the contested area. To the basically insecure Syrian Baathist regime, this continuous irritation provided a welcome opportunity to divert popular attention to foreign dangers and to pose, at Arab summit meetings, as the most intransigent and patriotic regime on the Palestine question. For its part, Israel had long followed a policy of reacting to Arab infiltrations not by a dense policing of the border but by occasional well-organized, massive reprisal raids against Jordanian border towns. The paradox of this policy was that in delivering blows to Jordan, Israel was punishing the party which was the most moderate, inasmuch as the policies of King Hussein's government were basically geared to preserving some *modus vivendi* between the two countries. Responding to stepped-up Arab commando activities, Israel's reprisal raids after 1965 gradually increased in scope and intensity.

3. Exclusion of the UN Emergency Force from Israel

In the wake of the Sinai war and the Suez crisis of 1956, the UN Emergency Force was established to promote peaceful border conditions between Egypt and Israel. The important fact generally disregarded by news media and commentators was Israel's refusal from the very outset to permit the presence of UNEF on its territory. Consequently, the force was stationed only on the Egyptian side of the border, as well as on the Egyptian coastline bordering the Gulf of Aqaba, by sovereign consent of Egypt's government. Legally, this consent could be withdrawn, but for ten years (1957-1967) President Nasser not only preferred not to avail himself of this option but, generally, avoided publicity regarding this essentially unequal and embarrassing arrangement. The polycentric character of Arab revolutionary politics, increasingly more evident in the mid-1960s, led to an inevitable exposure of Nasser's position on this issue by the rival nationalist regime in Damascus. Syrian Baathists began accusing him of insincerity with regard to the liberation of Palestine, of hiding himself snugly behind UNEF's protective shield, and, implicitly, of cowardice. Nasser's conservative adversaries in Jordan and Saudi Arabia joined the chorus, obviously relishing an opportunity to embarrass him.

THE WAR OF 1967 AND ITS CONSEQUENCES

The three above-mentioned tensions provided the background for the eruption of the Arab-Israeli crisis of May 1967. According to Nasser, Russia informed him of an alleged impending Israeli aggression on Syria, which prompted him to demand the removal of UNEF from UAR territory so as to be able to come to Syria's aid without exposing the UN forces to possible Arab-Israeli crossfire. Removal of UNEF meant the UAR's automatically regaining access to the Gulf of Aqaba. Again, saving face demanded the reimposition of the blockade in the Strait of Tiran, an act which Nasser publicly announced and which provoked strong Israeli protests. After the ensuing debate in the UN Security Council proved disappointing to Israel, Israeli forces invaded Sinai and the Gaza Strip on June 5. The six-day war ended in an overwhelming Israeli victory over Egypt and its Jordanian and Syrian allies, as well as the occupation of territories about three times the size of Israel and containing about a million Arabs.

From the point of view of American foreign policy, the June war brought about major shifts in the position of the Big Powers in the Middle East, generally unfavorable to the United States. The general Arab reaction was one of resentment and hostility to the United States, best symbolized by ready acceptance of the allegation made by Nasser and King Hussein that the invading Israeli forces were shielded by a massive protective umbrella of American and British military aircraft. Even Nasser's conservative opponents in the Arab world found it hard to resist this allegation. As a result, a number of official actions were taken against the American interests in the area:

1. Five Arab states broke off diplomatic relations with Washington (the UAR, Syria, Iraq, Algeria, and Sudan);
2. A temporary embargo on oil exports to the United States, Britain, and West Germany was instituted by the Arab oil-producing countries;
3. A total trade boycott was applied by certain Arab states, coupled with a boycott of American tanker shipping;
4. The UAR, Syria, and Iraq denied overflight rights to airplanes of American registry;
5. A number of American schools (including the American University at Cairo and the Jesuit Hikma College in Baghdad) were sequestrated by Arab governments;
6. American libraries and cultural centers were ordered closed in the states which severed diplomatic relations with Washington;
7. Certain American-owned oil-distributing companies were nationalized in Algeria;
8. The possibility of withdrawing the cash deposits of Arab governments from American banks was seriously considered.

These actions largely resulted from the widespread conviction held by the Arab governments and public alike that America was partial to Israel. Official declarations by State Department spokesmen that the United States was neutral in the conflict "in thought, word, and deed" tended to be brushed aside as insincere and hypocritical. This Arab disbelief was based on a number of considerations. Perhaps the most important of these was a lack of any open American rebuke of Israel for using force in disregard of earlier warnings addressed to Israel and the Arabs to practice restraint. By the same token, Arabs pointed to the contrast between the early American insistence (prior to the outbreak of the war) on respect for the territorial integrity of *all* the states in the area and the absence of such emphasis after Israel had occupied much of Arab territory. Similarly, Arabs viewed with skepticism an apparently docile American acceptance of Israeli explanations of error in the bombing of the communications ship *U.S.S. Liberty* in the Mediterranean. This was linked with a lingering suspicion that the ship was employed not only to gather intelligence but also to transmit intercepted Arab signals to the Israeli military authorities. Added to this were two concrete instances of American behavior during the UN debates that followed the war: (1) abstention from voting when the General Assembly condemned Israel, by 99 votes to none against, for annexing the Arab part of Jerusalem;[22] (2) abstention from a subsequent vote on the proposal to launch a United Nations investigation into the treatment of Arab populations in the Israel-occupied areas, particularly cases of massive expulsions, expropriations, and intimidations. Subsequent deliveries of arms and airplanes by the United States—crowned by President Johnson's pledge to sell fifty Phantom jet fighters to Israel while agreeing to sell token quantities of less powerful arms to Jordan and Saudi Arabia—further confirmed the impression that, despite Israel's already existing military superiority, the United States was bent on not merely maintaining but even increasing it.

Some of these criticisms the U.S. government could answer with varying degrees of persuasiveness. The reply to the most important point—the sending of additional U.S. arms to Israel—was that in the months following the June war the Soviet Union had reequipped the UAR, Syria, and Iraq so thoroughly as not only to replace destroyed weapons and vehicles but even to surpass former levels in number and quality. This, it was argued in Washington, was likely to produce such a marked imbalance in armaments in favor of the Arabs as to warrant supplying Israel with additional weapons and aircraft to permit it to defend itself by its own means without necessitating American intervention in case of renewed hostilities. However, the explanation regarding American voting on the Jerusalem resolution in the United Nations was weak and not overly convincing to the Arabs. The U.S. delegation abstained from the vote largely on the issue of a technicality: The vote was to condemn Israel for annexation, whereas Israel formally had not annexed the Arab part of Jerusalem but merely "unified" it administratively with the Jewish part. Furthermore, it was explained in Washington, the United States did not need to change anything in its long-standing policy of not recognizing *de jure* either the Israeli or the Jordanian jurisdiction in the city as contrary to the original Palestine partition resolution which designated Jerusalem as an international enclave.[23]

AMERICAN POLICY DILEMMAS

Basically, official American response to the June war focused on two main points: first, to avoid military confrontation with the Soviet Union; second,

[22] Text in *New York Times*, July 15, 1967.
[23] Text in Hurewitz, *op. cit.*, pp. 292-295.

to bring about a speedy settlement which would lay sounder foundations for peace than the previous Arab-Israeli armistice agreements. The first point formed the subject of the Glassboro meeting between President Johnson and Premier Kosygin in June 1967. While the two parties held far from identical views on the merits of the Arab-Israeli crisis, both expressed their resolve to avoid direct military intervention and confrontation. As for the peace settlement, on June 19, 1967, President Johnson made public his position under the following five points: (1) recognition of the right to national life; (2) justice for the Arab refugees; (3) assurance of innocent maritime passage in international waterways; (4) limitation of the arms race; (5) respect for political independence and territorial integrity. [24] In a purely formal sense, the President's statement could be taken as a reaffirmation of neutrality in the conflict. However, on closer scrutiny it might be viewed as weighted in favor of Israel, inasmuch as it failed to spell out the American position on the continuing Israeli occupation of Arab lands. It should be pointed out that, in a similar situation eleven years earlier, President Eisenhower insisted on and obtained unconditional withdrawal by Israel from occupied territories. This time the implicit assumption seemed to be that Israel could not be blamed for holding onto the conquered areas so long as it did not have adequate reassurances and guarantees. President Johnson's speech, therefore, could be viewed more as a pronouncement of basic principles than as a concrete program for peace, with the sole exception of point 3, in which nondiscriminatory access to the Arab-controlled waterways was made explicit.

The following five months did not yield any tangible progress toward a solution of the Arab-Israeli controversy. The Soviet Union seemed to derive psychological benefits from the stalemate: The longer the Israeli occupation lasted, the deeper grew Arab frustration with the United States, which continued to be regarded as the only power capable of persuading Israel to withdraw. Other benefits accrued to Russia: increasing penetration by Soviet experts of the military and civil state apparatus in Egypt, Syria, and Iraq; increased economic links and Arab dependence on Soviet technology; as well as access to certain Arab ports by the greatly increased Soviet Mediterranean Fleet, whose strength—estimated at nearly fifty ships—began to match that of the American Sixth Fleet. However, the closure of the Suez Canal adversely affected Soviet maritime traffic with

---

[24] Text in *Department of State Bulletin*, July 10, 1967, pp. 33-34.

areas east of Suez, including North Vietnam. This was generally regarded as one of the reasons Russia favored some sort of peaceful settlement—the other being Soviet reluctance to see her Arab clients plunge prematurely into another round of war in which they either might be defeated or make explicit demands for Soviet assistance and thus place before Russia the choice of refusing or risking confrontation with America.

It is not unlikely that such considerations led the Soviets to vote for the resolution which the UN Security Council adopted unanimously on November 22, 1967. The resolution called for: (1) withdrawal of Israeli forces from the occupied territories; (2) end of belligerency and respect for the right of every nation to live in peace within secure and recognized boundaries; (3) free navigation in international waterways; (4) a just settlement of the refugee problem; (5) guarantees of territorial integrity and political independence including the creation of demilitarized zones; and (6) delegation by the Secretary General of his representative to assure the implementation of the foregoing program in consultation with the interested parties. [25]

Although the resolution partly overlapped President Johnson's five principles of June 19, 1967, it marked a certain shift in the American position. While the rights of Israel were safeguarded by references to the end of belligerency and the right to live within recognized boundaries (thereby implying Arab recognition of such boundaries, hence also of Israeli existence), by voting for the resolution the United States went formally on record as favoring Israeli withdrawal from occupied areas.

On May 10, 1968, the UAR and Jordan accepted the UN resolution. Israel did not give unconditional acceptance; instead, it continued to insist on direct negotiations with the Arab states before discussing substantive implementation of the resolution. This explains why the efforts exerted by the UN special representative, Ambassador Gunnar Jarring of Sweden, met with very little success through most of 1968.

In the meantime, the position of the Johnson administration was becoming increasingly more difficult. Faced with elections at home and attendant competitive appeals of rival candidates to the Zionist groups on the one hand, and with the steadily growing Soviet presence and anti-American trends in the area on the other, the administration was torn between two conflicting policies. This dilemma found its dramatic expression

[25] Text in UN doc. S/RES/242(1967) (S/8247), of November 22, 1967.

on September 8, 1968, when presidential candidate Nixon in an address to the B'nai B'rith Anti-Defamation League took what appeared as a strong stand in favor of "a policy that would give Israel a technological military margin to more than offset her hostile neighbors' numerical superiority." "If maintaining that margin," continued Mr. Nixon, "should require that the United States should supply Israel with supersonic Phantom F-4 jets— we should supply those Phantom jets." [26] Although on closer scrutiny Mr. Nixon's statement was not unconditional, its main thrust was clearly weighted in favor of Israel.

Two days later, on September 10, President Johnson's speech to the same group conveyed friendliness to Israel with restraint, the latter presumably dictated by his official status as contrasted with the greater freedom of political candidates. While reiterating the gist of his five principles of June 19, 1967, the President made two significant additions: (1) He warned that the future peace settlement must not reflect the "right by conquest"; and (2) he implicitly rebuked Israel for giving priority to the method (direct talks with the Arabs) over the substance of negotiations. He urged both parties to seek any available channel, including that of UN Ambassador Jarring, to concentrate on the substance of a peaceful solution. [27]

Johnson's statement was significant in that it tended to crystallize American policy on two vital points: first, the need to differentiate between the essential and the nonessential in the Israeli situation, the essential being the right to survive within recognized boundaries free of the threat of annihilation, the inessential being the control of extended conquered territories inhabited by the hostile and inassimilable population; second, the necessity to seek a settlement by any means and not to delay it by insistence on direct Arab-Israeli negotiations.

While thus the position of the United States reached a greater degree of clarity, there still remained the problem of how to persuade the parties (i.e., Israel, UAR, Jordan, and possibly Syria) to begin implementing the UN resolution. In concrete terms, Israel would have to concede more than the Arabs because in return for Arab declarations, i.e., words (of nonbelligerency, recognition of boundaries, and readiness to admit Israeli shipping into the Suez Canal and the Strait of Tiran), it would have to give up its physical control of sizable territories and populations which it could use as

[26] *New York Times*, September 9, 1968.

[27] Text in *Weekly Compilation of Presidential Documents*, September 16, 1968, pp. 1340-1343.

a "mortgage" and a lever of pressure. Persuading Israel (and the Arabs) could be attempted singlehandedly by the United States or as a joint effort of the big powers, including the Soviet Union. The UN Secretary-General, U Thant, in January 1969 urged the Big Powers jointly to exert such an effort within the framework of the United Nations.

Mr. Thant's and similar Soviet and French proposals coincided with the first weeks of the Nixon administration. In his policy-making, the newly elected President gave the Middle East crisis top priority, virtually on a par with the simultaneous Vietnam peace talks in Paris. His interest in the Arab-Israeli controversy already was manifest when, early in December 1968, he dispatched William Scranton, former governor of Pennsylvania, as his personal representative on a fact-finding mission to the Middle East. At the end of his trip, Mr. Scranton declared that in his view the United States should launch a new, "even-handed" policy toward the Arabs and Israel. This declaration, received with much uneasiness in Tel Aviv, seemed to indicate that the new administration was being urged to desist from the previous policies of too close an identification with Israel. Although the President-elect's office declared subsequently that the envoy was expressing merely his own ideas, it was not without significance that the need for an "even-handed" treatment of Arabs and Israelis was publicly reiterated by Mr. Scranton after his conference with Mr. Nixon and that his statement was not repudiated.

Inasmuch as the four major powers had previously reached unanimity on the November 22, 1967 UN resolution, it was not illogical to expect that any new move to secure their mutual cooperation to implement it would further accentuate America's neutral approach to the crisis. Early in February 1969, President Nixon indicated his willingness to respond positively to the Franco-Soviet proposals. Fearing a dictated solution by the Big Powers which would compel it to evacuate the occupied areas without the benefit of a formal peace treaty with the Arabs, Israel expressed serious reservations about the proposed procedure. In response, an assurance was given by the U.S. government that no imposed settlement was contemplated. While this might sound reassuring in a broad sense, the meaning of "imposition" is flexible and may vary from military coercion to more subtle and less tangible forms which in the long run could prove even more effective.

To conclude this paper, let us reiterate that each of the three factors bringing the Middle East to the attention of American policy-makers, i.e., oil, Russian penetration, and the Arab-Israeli problem, has necessitated the formulation of policies geared to meet America's economic and security requirements in each of these sectors. Though specialized in a purely technical sense, these policies have been and are bound to be interdependent. Thus the initial successes in securing oil concessions through the open-door policy or containing Soviet expansionism by political-military cooperation with the northern tier of states cannot be considered as conclusive and treated in isolation from the broader regional scene. Unless the United States were to opt for an old-fashioned imperial policy of securing its objectives by physical force alone, it is obliged to take into account the attitudes of the peoples and governments in the entire region of the Middle East. In this connection, the Arab-Israeli dispute, especially since 1967, has been the major conditioning factor of the success or failure in other sectors, apart from its own intrinsic merits. Since 1945 United States policy on the latter issue has been oscillating between the realities of domestic politics— as seen and interpreted by successive administrations—and attempts to define more broadly the national interest in terms of America's global interests and responsibilities.

Contributors

Ernst B. Haas is a professor of political science at the University of California, Berkeley. Among his publications are *The Uniting of Europe* (1958, 1968), *Dynamics of International Relations* (with Allen S. Whiting, 1956), *Beyond the Nation-State* (1964), *Collective Security and the Future International System* (1968), and *Tangle of Hopes* (1969), as well as shorter monographs and articles dealing with regional integration in Western Europe and Latin America, the international protection of human rights, and the functional approach to the study of world institutions and processes. Formerly Associate Director of the Institute of International Studies at Berkeley, Professor Haas is the principal investigator in the Institute's project "Studies in International Integration."

Chalmers Johnson is a Professor of political science and Chairman of the Center for Chinese Studies, University of California, Berkeley. He is the author of *Peasant Nationalism and Communist Power* (1962), *An Instance of Treason* (1964), and *Revolutionary Change* (1966).

George Lenczowski is a professor of political science at the University of California, Berkeley. Specializing in international relations and comparative politics, he has focused much of his research on the problems of big power rivalry in the Middle East. He has authored *Contracts in Private International Law, Russia and the West in Iran, The Middle East in World Affairs*, and *Oil and State in the Middle East*, and has recently edited *United States Interests in the Middle East*. He is currently serving as Director, Middle East Project, American Enterprise Institute for Public Policy Research.

Daniel S. Lev is an assistant professor of political science at the University of California, Berkeley. He is author of *The Transition to Guided Democracy in Indonesia*, published by the Cornell Modern Indonesia Project, and various articles on Indonesian political and legal change.

Leslie Lipson is a professor of political science at the University of California, Berkeley. He is author of *The American Governor, The Politics of*

Equality, The Great Issues of Politics, and *The Democratic Civilization.* He is Chairman of the Committee on Atlantic Studies, and has served for the United Nations, as consultant to various agencies of the United States government, and as Director of Studies of the Atlantic Institute, Paris.

Richard Rosecrance is a professor of political science at the University of California, Berkeley, and author of *Action and Reaction in World Politics, Defense of the Realm: British Strategy in the Nuclear Epoch,* and editor of *The Dispersion of Nuclear Weapons.* During 1967-1968 he was a member of the Policy Planning Council, Department of State. He previously served as Director of the Security Studies Project at UCLA.

Robert A. Scalapino is professor of political science at the University of California, Berkeley, and editor of *Asian Survey.* He is currently writing a book on North Korean politics and is conducting research on the comparative political elites of North Korea, North Vietnam and mainland China for the Communist Elites Project. Major publications include *The Japanese Communist Movement, 1920-1966; The Communist Revolution in Asia* (ed.); *North Korea Today* (ed.); *Parties and Politics in Contemporary Japan* (with Junnosuke Masumi); *The Chinese Anarchist Movement* (with George T. Yu); *United States Foreign Policy—Asia* (Study for the Senate Foreign Relations Committee); *Reflections on American Relations with Japan;* and *Democracy and the Party Movement in Pre-War Japan.*

Paul Seabury is a professor of political science at the University of California, Berkeley. He is the author of various works on foreign policy and international politics, including *The Wilhelmstrasse: A Study of German Diplomacy* (1954); *Power, Freedom and Diplomacy* (1963); *The Balance of Power* (1965); and *The Rise and Decline of the Cold War* (1967). A former Chairman of the National Executive Committee of Americans for Democratic Action, he is currently Chairman of the faculty of the College of Letters and Science at Berkeley, and Vice Chairman of the National Board of Foreign Scholarships.

Max Singer is President of Hudson Institute and one of the principal founders of that organization. In addition to his management responsibilities, he is continuing to do research on the spread of nuclear weapons, U.S. policy toward underdeveloped areas, European force arrangements, and the possible roles of tactical nuclear weapons. A member of the bar in New York State and in the District of Columbia, Mr. Singer has written several articles on arms control, which have appeared both in Hudson Institute reports and in other publications.

Aaron Wildavsky is a professor of political science and Chairman of the Department, University of California, Berkeley. He is author of *Presidential Elections* (with Nelson Polsby); *The Politics of the Budgetary Process; Leadership in a Small Town; Dixon-Yates: A Study in Power Politics;* and *Studies in Australian Politics: The 1926 Referendum.*

5/20   MIDNT.

MAR 10 1974 -7 00 PM

MAR 11 1974 -10 00 PM